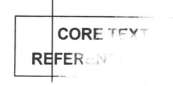
Penny Tassoni's Practical EYFS Handbook

www.heinemann.co.uk

✓ Free online support
✓ Useful weblinks
✓ 24 hour online ordering

01865 888080

Heinemann is an imprint of Pearson Education Limited, a company incorporated in England and Wales, having its registered office at Edinburgh Gate, Harlow, Essex, CM20 2JE. Registered company number: 872828

www.heinemann.co.uk

Heinemann is a registered trademark of Pearson Education Limited

Text © Penny Tassoni 2008

First published 2008

12 11
11

British Library Cataloguing in Publication Data
A catalogue record for this book is available from the British Library

ISBN 978 0 435 89991 2

Edited by Caroline Low of Virgo Editorial
Designed by Hicks Design
Typeset by Tek-Art
Original illustrations © Pearson Education Ltd, 2008
Cover design by Hicks Design
Picture research by Virginia Stroud-Lewis
Cover photo/illustration © Masterfile/Michele/Salmieri
Printed in China (CTPS/11)

Websites
The websites used in this book were correct and up to date at the time of publication. It is essential for tutors to preview each website before using it in class so as to ensure that the URL is still accurate, relevant and appropriate. We suggest that tutors bookmark useful websites and consider enabling students to access them through the school/college intranet.

Contents

Foreword

The seeds of change for early years were sown in 1994 when, speaking at the Conservative party conference, the prime minister pledged nursery places for all 4 year olds whose parents wanted them. This sparked a period of massive change, with some very positive developments which included: increased placements for children under five years, marked financial support which resulted in impressive new buildings and good quality resources, a programme of training to improve the quality of the workforce, enlightening research to inform policy, and a comprehensive and revised system of inspection for all registered provision. The government's growing interest in the early years phase was marked in the Children Act 2004 and the implementation paper 'Every Child Matters'. For the first time the government revealed a long-term vision for children and families. Guidance steered practitioners towards good practice and recently this has been enshrined in a mandatory Framework for England, the Early Years Foundation Stage (EYFS).

The Framework has had a big build up and has been disseminated across England through some very effective training. However it is ambitious in scope, multi-layered and heavy on content. In a busy climate many practitioners, particularly those relatively new to the work, have not had time to accommodate all the messages in the Framework, to make links to past frameworks or to recognise how their practice fits in. Penny Tassoni's comprehensive book is published at a critical time and will meet genuine professional needs.

The book gently guides the reader into the EYFS framework. It scrupulously explains the different materials and introduces the rubric. However there is much more for the reader. The four principles are examined and brought to life. All aspects of the six areas of learning are unpicked in relation to the needs of different age bands of children and usefully elaborate on the Development Matters section in the Framework. The final section, Implementing the Early Years Foundation Stage, is refreshing as Penny moves away slightly from the Framework and provides some sound practical advice on pivotal topics such as play and planning.

This book is invaluable for many different audiences. Less experienced practitioners will warm to the direct conversational style while trainers can use it to lift out a strand of practice and hold it up to the light. The format is varied and helps to keep the reader's interest. There are clear headings for content, boxed sections with points to consider and examples of evidence of good practice to produce for senior managers and those monitoring and inspecting provision. Diagrams summarise main messages in the text.

The book is not designed to be read from cover to cover. Penny wisely suggests that it should be used alongside the EYFS to see how the two fit together. It is a practical handbook which encourages the reader to pick up a strand of practice and examine it in some detail.

No Framework by itself can change practice. However, this book brings its requirements and guidance to life and will surely help all those who work with young children to recognise and provide for their needs.

Marion Dowling, Early Years specialist and trainer

Acknowledgements

Author Acknowledgements

I would like to thank the many early years practitioners and advisers that I have met over the past few years. Our discussions have influenced this book. In this respect, I would like particularly to thank Helen Smith, Gill Heseltine, Rita Curtin, Judy Harrison, Katriona Ismail, Penny Cartwright and Leman Cetin who have all contributed material or ideas. I need also to thank Ayse and Nilufer who have kept my practice up to date, as well as their mother, Amanda Ferguson, who has allowed me to try out activities and carry out observations.

Thanks must also go to the Heinemann production team including Virginia Carter, who has guided me through this project, Caroline Low of Virgo Editorial and also Shirley Bartley for her faith in me. Finally, I would like to thank my home team: Anne-Marie and Marie-Lise and Jean-Michel.

Photo and Text Acknowledgements

We would like to thank the staff, parents and children at Lutterworth Day Nursery for their invaluable help and co-operation during the photoshoot.

Every effort has been made to contact copyright holders of material reproduced in this book. Any omissions will be rectified in subsequent printings if notice is given to the publishers.

The author and publisher would like to thank the following for permission to reproduce photographs:

Monika Adamczyk/iStockphoto, page 36; Daniel Allan/Getty Images, p 176; Alamy/Peter Bonek, p 224; Alamy/Bubbles Photolibrary, pp 16, 68; Alamy/Stephen Chiang, p 188; Alamy/Alistair Heap, p 218; Alamy/Janine Wiedel Photolibrary, p 21; Alamy/Peter Usbeck, p 174; Vaidas Bucys/Shutterstock, p 152; Corbis/amana/amana images, p 112; Corbis/Laura Dwight, p 208; Corbis/Gaetano, p 118; Corbis/Ronnie Kaufman, p 25; Corbis/LWA – Dann Tardif, p 45; dellison/Shutterstock, p 200; Sonya Etchinson/Shutterstock, p 45; Xavier Gallego/iStockphoto, p 34; Gelpi/Shutterstock, p 100; Getty Images/Photographer's Choice/Andrea Olsheskie, p 182; Getty Images/Kei Uesugi, p 138; Hallgerd/fotolia.com, p 168; Hallgerd/Shutterstock, p 196; iStockphoto/Cheryl Casey, p 210; iStockphoto/Rhienna Cutler, p 190; iStockphoto/Stephen Ludgate, p 186; iStockphoto/Glenda Powers, pp 194–5; Sergey Kolodkin/Shutterstock, pp 156–7; Rich Legg/iStockphoto, p 42; matka_Wariata/Shutterstock, p 120; Vanessa Morosini/iStockphoto, pp 98–9; Losevsky Pavel/Shutterstock, p 33; Pearson Education Ltd/Jules Selmes, pp 8, 28, 45, 62, 64, 66, 70, 72, 74, 76, 78, 82, 84, 86, 88, 90, 92, 94, 96, 102, 104, 106, 108, 110, 114, 116, 122, 126, 128, 130, 132, 134, 136–7, 140, 142, 144, 146, 148, 150, 154, 158, 160, 162, 164, 170, 178, 180, 184, 192, 198, 212, 220, 222, 226, 228, 230, 232, 234, 236, 238; Photolibrary.com, p 124; Glenda M. Powers/Shutterstock, p 39; Shutterstock/Jamie Duplass, p 214–15; Shutterstock/Larisa Lofitskaya, p 204; Shutterstock/Monkey Business Images, p 202; Shutterstock/Christopher Parypa, p 216; Igor Stepovik/Shutterstock, p 166; Superstock/age footstock, p 80; Penny Tassoni, p 172; WoodyStock/Alamy, p 206; 2734725246/Shutterstock, pp 60–1

Crown copyright material is reproduced with the permission of the Controller of HMSO.

About the Author

Penny Tassoni is an education consultant, author and trainer who specialises in the whole spectrum of learning and play. Penny has written 25 books, including the best selling *Planning Play and the Early Years* (2005, Heinemann). She also writes for several magazines, including features for parents. Penny is a well-known speaker, both in the UK and internationally. In addition to training, Penny also works as a reviser for CACHE, the awarding body for childcare and education qualifications.

Introduction

Starting out with the Early Years Foundation Stage

Few people enjoy change, so the arrival of the Early Years Foundation Stage (EYFS) may well have caused you some dismay, particularly if you were feeling that you were only just getting the hang of the previous frameworks and Care standards in England. The good news for those of you already following good practice is that you have nothing to fear here. Some of the terms and statements may seem difficult, the EYFS pack's layout might seem wordy, but at its core the EYFS is about quality care and education. This section is designed to help you unpick the pack, so to speak. Read it while flicking through the pack so that you can start the journey of familiarisation. You might also like to try out the quiz at the end of this section on page 5. (If you are working as part of team, you could do the quiz at a staff meeting!)

Note: The Early Years Foundation Stage is statutory only in England, so if you are looking at this book and are working in Scotland, Wales or Northern Ireland, I hope that you will enjoy the chapter on Themes and the large section on activities, but you will need to read them in conjunction with your country's framework.

Looking through the pack

The Department of Children, Schools and Families (DCSF) did not send this pack out automatically to settings so you may need to obtain your own copy. This is very easy to do. You can order online at http://publications.teachernet. gov.uk/ or by phone on 0845 602 2260 or 0845 600 9506. At the time of going to press, the reference for the pack is DCSF-00261-2008. The advantage to ordering online is that you can have a look at the other free resources and order them at the same time. You will need to register before you can order.

In the DCSF pack you will find two key documents which you must take time to read.

- Statutory Framework for the Early Years Foundation Stage
- Practice Guidance for the Early Years Foundation Stage

As well as these two documents, you will also find a CD-ROM, a pack of *Principles into Practice* cards and a poster.

Statutory Framework for the Early Years Foundation Stage

This is a key document because it sets out the legal requirements for the Early Years Foundation Stage. This is the only statutory guidance and it is therefore essential reading. The EYFS is mentioned often in the context of education and early learning goals, etc., but that is just one part of it and this Statutory Framework sets out the other important component, which is the Welfare Requirements.

The Statutory Framework is divided into three sections.

- Section 1 – Introduction
- Section 2 – The Learning and Development Requirements
- Section 3 – The Welfare Requirements

Section 1 – Introduction

This is an overview which explains the aims and purpose of the EYFS and how it became a legal requirement under the Childcare Act 2006.

Section 2 – The Learning and Development Requirements

The educational programme along with the early learning goals is given here. They are a statutory requirement for all Ofsted-registered settings that provide for children from birth to five years. When looking at the early learning goals, remember that these are expectations for children when they are at the end of the academic year in which they are five years old. This is likely to be at the end of the Reception year.

On page 17 of the Statutory Framework, assessment arrangements are set out. While practitioners working with all ages of children must assess children in order to comply with the legal requirements, the final assessment – known as the Early Years Foundation Stage Profile – is likely to be the responsibility of a Reception class. If you are working in a Reception class, it is worth noting that most of the judgements that you make must be based on children's self-initiated play.

Section 3 – The Welfare Requirements

The Welfare Requirements set out on pages 19–40 of the Statutory Framework have to be read through

carefully. They replace the previous Care standards, so you should not refer to these any more. Whereas the old Care standards changed according to the setting, the Welfare Requirements are universal and have to be met by all Ofsted-registered settings including schools. The Welfare Requirements are divided into three sections, as shown below.

As well as reading through the Welfare Requirements, you must also look at Appendix 2 on pages 49–51. This provides the specific legal requirements for ratios of adults to children.

Principles and Themes of the EYFS

There are four Principles that underpin the EYFS. Each Principle has been converted into a Theme and then broken down again into four Commitments. Each of the Themes is colour-coded and has accompanying *Principle into Practice* cards.

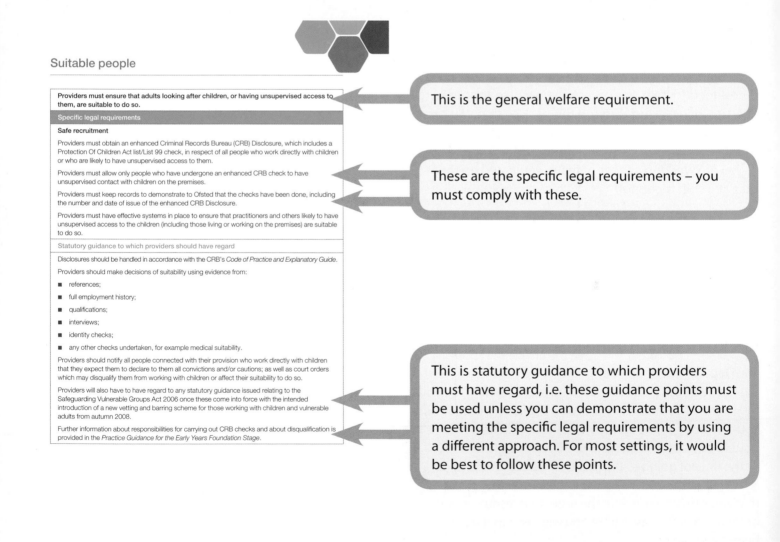

Each of the Welfare Requirements is divided into three sections (© Crown copyright 2007)

You will see the colours of the Principles and the Themes displayed prominently on the materials within the EYFS. Your practice is meant to reflect these Themes, so it is worth taking a look at the *Principles into Practice* cards. Themes are described further in this book on pages 6–29.

Practice Guidance for the Early Years Foundation Stage

This is non-statutory guidance which means that you do not, in theory, need to look at it at all. That would of course be a little foolish, because it does break down further each of the areas of Learning and Development, and provides plenty of suggestions as to activities and resources that you might use to deliver the education programme.

The Practice Guidance is in three sections followed by the weight of the document – Appendix 2: Areas of Learning and Development.

- Section 1 – Implementing the EYFS
- Section 2 – Learning and Development
- Section 3 – Welfare Requirements
- Appendix 1 – Criteria for effective paediatric first aid training
- Appendix 2 – Areas of Learning and Development

Section 1 – Implementing the EYFS

This is an introduction to the Practice Guidance. Six key issues are pulled out as being important to the success of delivering the EYFS, as follows:

- meeting the diverse needs of children
- partnership working
- flexible provision
- play
- quality improvement
- transition, continuity and coherence.

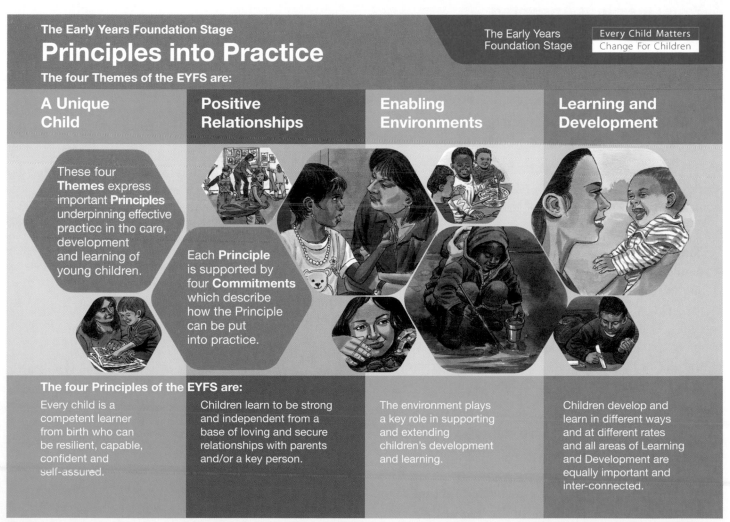

The Early Years Foundation Stage
Principles into Practice
The four Themes of the EYFS are:

The Early Years Foundation Stage

Every Child Matters
Change For Children

A Unique Child	Positive Relationships	Enabling Environments	Learning and Development
These four **Themes** express important **Principles** underpinning effective practice in the care, development and learning of young children.	Each **Principle** is supported by four **Commitments** which describe how the Principle can be put into practice.		

The four Principles of the EYFS are:

Every child is a competent learner from birth who can be resilient, capable, confident and self-assured.	Children learn to be strong and independent from a base of loving and secure relationships with parents and/or a key person.	The environment plays a key role in supporting and extending children's development and learning.	Children develop and learn in different ways and at different rates and all areas of Learning and Development are equally important and inter-connected.

The first Principles into Practice card for the EYFS materials clearly outlines the four Themes and their related Principles (© Crown copyright 2007)

Section 2 – Learning and Development

This section explains the headings used in Appendix 2 (the bulk of the Practice Guidance), which describe the areas of Learning and Development.

Section 3 – Welfare Requirements

It is important not to rely on this section when thinking about the Welfare Requirements, although you do look at Appendix 1 in order to comply with the criteria for effective paediatric first aid training (see page 31 of the Statutory Framework). Some of what is written here is a repeat of the Welfare Requirements in the Statutory Framework, but some parts add more detail in terms of what you can do to meet the requirements.

Using the CD-ROM

With the pack there is a CD-ROM. When you insert it into your computer, you will probably find that it tries to link up with an Internet connection. If you do not have Internet access, do not worry. You can get at many of the resources without connecting to the Internet. You may also find that your computer gives you a warning sign about 'Active Content'. You will not need to worry about this if you are not connected to the Internet, but if you are connected to the Internet you must make sure that you have some security protection before proceeding.

As with any new resource, you may find that it will take you a few minutes to work your way around the CD-ROM, but in my view it is fairly accessible, even if you are not a computer buff.

Things to look out for on the CD-ROM

- Video clips – there are many video clips which look at aspects of practice
- Links to websites
- Sample planning sheets

Your Questions Answered

What should I do with the old Care standards?

Put them in the bin! They were the previous welfare requirements that Ofsted would look at when registering a setting and inspecting it. The Statutory Framework should in theory simplify things, as all settings have to work to the same set of requirements.

What is the difference between a specific legal requirement and statutory guidance?

A specific legal requirement means that you must comply with the requirements as otherwise you would be in breach of law. Statutory guidance is slightly different as in theory you do not have to follow what is written, but you would have to prove that you are still able to comply with the law. To avoid difficulties, it is usually best just to follow the statutory guidance. Do not fall into the trap of imagining that statutory guidance is simply 'good practice' that is optional!

Should I plan using the Principles into Practice cards?

The cards are non-statutory material so it is not necessary to plan using them directly, unless you find it helpful. It is, however, important that you understand the basis of the Themes as they underpin the EYFS. We unpick what these Themes and Principles are about on pages 6–29 of this book.

Should I keep the old Foundation Stage folder?

You do not have to, but you may find it useful as it has plenty of ideas for planning and resources for the 3–5 years age range. It is important, though, that from September 2008 your planning reflects the EYFS, so treat the folder as a resource only.

I am a childminder. Do I have to follow the EYFS?

Yes, you must. All childminders should be registered with Ofsted and this in turn means that you are required to comply with all aspects of the EYFS including the educational programme.

We are a crèche in a shopping mall. Sometimes we have children and will never see them again. We don't always know what age of children will be coming either. How do we implement the EYFS?

As you are an Ofsted-registered provision, the EYFS is mandatory. This means that you must comply with the Welfare Requirements and the Learning and Development Requirements. While Ofsted will recognise that children's attendance will be of short duration and infrequent, you should still show in your planning and provision that you are providing opportunities to deliver the areas of Learning and Development. You may find it helpful, therefore, to look at the way in which I have mapped some of the common types of play and activities to the areas of Learning and Development (see Appendix pages 258–64).

Do I have to display the poster?

No, not unless you want to. (You could always turn it over and pin it to the wall so that children can use it for drawing on.)

How important is the CD-ROM in the pack?

Some of the materials on the CD-ROM repeat what you will find in the Statutory Framework and the Practice Guidance, and this can be a little frustrating. On the other hand, the CD-ROM when connected to the Internet will allow you to navigate onto other websites and materials. There are also some good video clips of practice, which can be shown to other members of staff or parents. To get a quick overview of the resources on the CD-ROM, click on the 'Resource index' tab that is found at the top right of each screen. This will lead you to a page of resources that include direct links to some very useful websites.

What should I look at first?

Read the Statutory Framework first. This is the most important document as it sets out the legal requirements that you must adhere to. If you are short of time, I would suggest that you start by turning straight to the Welfare Requirements and check them through carefully. (We will be looking at these in more detail on pages 30–43 of this book.) Make sure that you are able to comply with them fully, especially the Organisation section (Statutory Framework, page 37). You should also think about how you might provide evidence that you are complying with the Welfare Requirements by, for example, your records, policies and procedures and other documentation.

Time for a quiz?

1   How many general Welfare Requirements are there?
2   What are the four Themes of the EYFS?
3   Where can you find out about the content of first aid training?
4   Which Theme is coloured orange?
5   On what page of the Statutory Framework are the legal requirements for 'Organisation'?
6   Which part of the pack contains the legal requirements for the EYFS?
7   How many *Principles into Practice* cards are there?
8   Are the six photographs of children on each of the covers of the documents the same?
9   How many pages are there in the Statutory Framework?
10 How many photographs are there on the poster?

Putting Themes into Practice

As you have seen there are four Themes that make up the EYFS. It is important that you are familiar with them, as you will be expected to incorporate them into all aspects of your work with children and their families. It might be tempting to skip out this section and focus only on planning for the early learning goals, but I would caution against this as your policies, routines and even the way in which you plan your activities need to reflect that you are using the Themes.

To help you navigate your way through this section, the colours of the Themes have been used to highlight the relevant sections.

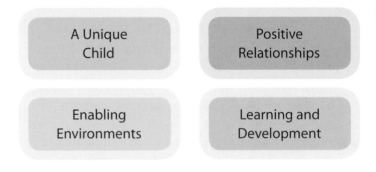

| A Unique Child | Positive Relationships |
| Enabling Environments | Learning and Development |

A Unique Child

> **'Every child is a competent learner from birth who can be resilient, capable, confident and self-assured.'**

The Principle behind this Theme is easy to understand. It is about the way in which you need to support each child so that they can become confident. The focus of the practice you will need to show is that you are able to understand that each child you care for is unique and that you are aware of and are meeting children's individual needs.

There are four Commitments for A Unique Child. Each one is detailed on a *Principle into Practice* card. They are quite diverse.

1.1 Child Development

> *'Babies and children develop in individual ways and at varying rates. Every area of development – physical, cognitive, linguistic, spiritual, social and emotional, is equally important.'*

If you have worked with several children, you will already know that no two children are the same. Even identical twins have different interests, temperaments and ways of simply being! To work effectively with individual children, you have to know each child's characteristics, development, interests and needs. When you have got to know children, it means that you can communicate easily with them.

1.1 Child Development	1.2 Inclusive Practice
A UNIQUE CHILD	
1.3 Keeping Safe	1.4 Health and Well-being

The four Commitments for A Unique Child

A major focus of the Child Development card is that children are 'competent learners.' While this term is used only on this card, it is a recurring idea throughout the EYFS. (If you have worked with the Birth to Three Matters pack, you will recognise this term.) It is essentially recognition that children from birth come primed and ready to learn, so as adults we need to make sure that our focus is not so much about teaching children but enabling them to learn.

What should I do?

Make sure that your child development knowledge is up to date

It is easy to forget what children are likely to be doing at different ages or the pattern of normative development. If you trained some years ago, it is worth knowing what new research has contributed to the understanding of child development. Consider attending training and keeping up to date by reading magazines, articles and books. Remember to keep any certificates of attendance or notes that you have made, so you can demonstrate your child development knowledge.

Make sure that you are aware of each child's development

You can do this through your observations of individual children, which are a statutory part of the EYFS in any case (see also page 19 of this book). Make sure that as well as looking out for what a child can do, you also watch out for their interests, ways of communicating and individual quirks, for example the way in which Jayne, a three-year-old girl, always claps her hands onto her head if she is about to ask for a favour!

As well as observing individual children, you will also need to think about what the observation findings mean for your practice with them. For example, if you observe that a toddler is tetchy after waking from sleep, you might allow more time before expecting the child to join in with an activity.

Spend sufficient time communicating with individual children

This may seem obvious, but the only way to understand children's individual temperaments, likes and needs is by being with them. Time spent with children in this way is essential to their feeling secure and confident. In group care, this means thinking about the way in which routines can be tweaked to ensure that children spend enough time with their key person (see also page 16 in this book).

Links to Every Child Matters

Child Development supports the 'Make a positive contribution' outcome.

Links to the Statutory Framework for the EYFS

Welfare Requirements:

- *Suitable people* – 'Adults looking after children must have appropriate qualifications, training, skills and knowledge' (Statutory Framework, page 31).

- *Organisation* – 'Providers must plan and organise their systems to ensure that every child receives an enjoyable and challenging learning and development experience that is tailored to meet their individual needs' (Statutory Framework, page 37).

Examples of evidence of practice

- Observations of individual children with notes about their development

- Planning that shows how you are supporting individual children's learning

- Certificates of attendance of training courses

1.2 Inclusive Practice

'The diversity of individuals and communities is valued and respected. No child or family is discriminated against.'

The term 'inclusive' is gradually replacing the term 'equality of opportunity', although the Statutory Guidance asks you to have an equality of opportunities policy. There is a difference between the two terms:

- Inclusive practice is meant to be an indication of the way in which your practice should be all-encompassing. Children and their families should feel genuinely welcome and totally accepted regardless of their individual differences. Inclusive practice means being open-minded and ready to adapt the way in which you work or the routines of the setting so that a child can join in. For example, a snack time might be moved to an earlier time in order to support a child with diabetes, while photographs might be taken to show parents with limited English what their children have been doing during the day.

- Equality of opportunity is slightly narrower in focus and concentrates more on how you ensure that children are able to fulfil their potential.

Children and their families should feel genuinely welcome and totally accepted regardless of their individual differences

What should I do?

Make sure that your knowledge of inclusive practice is up to date

While treating children fairly and valuing families seems straightforward, ideas about how best to do this do change. A good example of this is the way in which some terminology relating to disability has altered enormously in the past ten years; even the term 'children with special needs' is under review. This means that you will need to be active in learning about anti-discriminatory practice. Look out for training courses and articles, and be mindful that posters and resources bought a while ago may no longer be relevant.

Check that your equality of opportunities policy is up to date

Having an equality of opportunities policy is a legal requirement. You need to make sure it is up to date and reflects the concept of inclusive practice.

Follow the SEN Code of Practice

The SEN Code of Practice is statutory guidance so you should make sure that you read and follow it. Under the Code, you will need to have an SEN policy.

Think about the resources that will help children to develop a positive self-identity

Mirrors, dressing-up clothes, toys and props for the home corner will all help children to explore identity. You can also provide books and resources with positive images of people from a range of cultural backgrounds to help children feel comfortable about their own identity.

Make sure that your setting and own practice is welcoming

Think about what your setting looks like and how you and others interact with parents, visitors and, of course, children. Read *Principle into Practice* card 1.2 for suggestions.

Communicate with parents regularly about their child's needs

Develop a system whereby you can gain information regularly from parents about their child's needs, as children's interests and needs can quickly change.

Support children with a different home language from English

To do this you may need to find out from parents which language(s) the child is learning and how they are progressing.

Observe children and recognise when further support might be needed

While sometimes it is parents who notice that their child may need extra support, there are also times when this is picked up through observations or simply by noticing that a child may need a referral.

Recognise that some children will need more support and time than others

Good inclusive practice does not mean treating children the same. There will therefore be times when some children require more of your time and help.

Build up contacts with other agencies

In order to support children and thereby develop inclusive practice, you will often need the help of other professionals. This may include the Early Years advisory team in your area as well as health professionals such as the speech and language service. Take some time to be aware of what is available in your area.

Ask for and listen to feedback from parents

Consider ways in which you can get feedback from parents. This might be a questionnaire or comments box if you work in a large setting, or by simply talking to parents if you work as a childminder or in home-based care.

Check through your policies to ensure that they reflect inclusive practice

It is worth reading through your policies with 'fresh' eyes. Look to see if the tone of what you have written is inclusive and think also about the content of your policies.

Links to Every Child Matters

Inclusive Practice supports the 'Make a positive contribution' outcome.

Links to the Statutory Framework for the EYFS

Welfare Requirements:

- *Safeguarding and promoting children's welfare* – 'The provider must take necessary steps to safeguard and promote the welfare of children' (Statutory Framework, page 25).

- *Organisation* – 'Providers must plan and organise their systems to ensure that every child receives an enjoyable and challenging learning and development experience that is tailored to meet their individual needs' (Statutory Framework, page 37).

Examples of evidence of practice

- Equality of opportunities policy, SEN policy and that other policies such as Admissions policy reflect inclusive practice

- Resources, books, toys and equipment

- Certificates of attendance at training

- Feedback from parents

- Planning that shows how you are meeting children's individual needs (including Individual Education Plans)

1.3 Keeping Safe

'Young children are vulnerable. They develop resilience when their physical and psychological well-being is protected by adults.'

From the title, you might think that this Commitment would be about safety gates and risk assessment. While this is true in part, the main focus is helping children learn to keep themselves safe. The idea is that children need to learn to control their own behaviour and actions. This focus is important, as over the past few years there has been a tendency for adults to overprotect children. An example of this is the way that few children have been allowed to play outdoors or that in some settings children have not been allowed to use scissors! Overprotection can hold children back as it can prevent them from developing confidence and skills.

In order to get to a point when children can begin to keep themselves safe, children will first need to have experienced being safe. This Commitment therefore includes appropriate protection for babies and toddlers as well as consistent boundary setting in terms of behaviour.

What should I do?

Make sure that you are providing an appropriately safe environment for children

You are of course required to keep children safe, but you must match carefully the amount of supervision, protection and safety measures to the age and stage of the children that you are working with.

Help children to learn about safety

Children can learn about how to keep safe from adults by, for example, hearing our thought processes – 'I'd better cover the sand pit now, because we don't want any cats to mess in it, do we?' As children develop language they can become increasingly involved in safety considerations. Your role is to help children think about dangers and ways of managing risk by, for example, encouraging them to provide solutions – 'You can play football, but you will need to find a good place to do it in.'

Look at how you supervise activities

Make sure that the amount of supervision is appropriate to the age and stage of development of children. While a baby must not be left unsupervised, a couple of three-year-olds happily playing with a huge cardboard box will not require an adult to stand next to them.

Make sure that children are given opportunities to be independent

Helping children to do the most they can for themselves should be the guiding principle of your work. This can be difficult as our inclination is often to do things for children as a way of showing our care for them or because we can do things quicker. While understandable, it is better to support children in learning to do things independently, as this is how they gain not only skills but confidence.

Provide opportunities for decision making

As well as learning to be independent, you should also make sure that your way of working encourages children to make choices. Again, these need to be age and stage appropriate and also right for the context. For babies this might mean providing treasure basket play as an activity so that they can choose and pick out the objects that are of interest to them. For a four-year-old, this might be about collecting a variety of resources to create a den outdoors.

Observe children's independence skills

A key way in which you can work out how best to support children in being self-reliant is by observing them first. Take time to notice what children can already do or what they are trying to do. This will help you to work out how much help they might need to do tasks such as feeding, dressing or choosing play materials.

Make sure that you have an up-to-date behaviour policy

You will need to show that your approach to managing children's behaviour is fair, consistent and developmentally accurate. Your behaviour policy should also demonstrate that you will always treat children with respect and dignity.

Make sure that children observe good role models

Young children can begin the process of learning about socially acceptable behaviour by seeing adults work in ways that later they can copy. It is also important to talk about why you are doing things, for example 'I will give this to Michael as it will make him happy.' Talking about the feelings of others is an important step in children's

learning about behaviour, although it is worth remembering that developmentally most children will find it hard to share and be cooperative with others until about three years old.

Use the adult to child ratio wisely

The higher levels of staffing required for the under-threes reflects the way in which these young children need significant amounts of adult support. In group care where there may be many under-threes, it can be worth subdividing children into smaller groups so that it is clear which member of staff is directly responsible for working with them. This makes it easier to provide consistent boundaries for behaviour and makes young children feel more secure.

Links to Every Child Matters

Keeping Safe supports the 'Stay safe' outcome.

Links to the Statutory Framework for the EYFS

Welfare Requirements:

- *Safeguarding and promoting children's welfare* – 'The provider must take necessary steps to safeguard and promote the welfare of children' (Statutory Framework, page 22); 'Children's behaviour must be managed effectively and in a manner appropriate for their stage of development and particular individual needs' (Statutory Framework, page 28).

- *Suitable people* – 'Staffing arrangements must be organised to ensure safety and to meet the needs of the children' (Statutory Framework, page 32).

- *Suitable premises, environment and equipment* – 'Outdoor and indoor spaces, furniture, equipment and toys, must be safe and suitable for their purpose' (Statutory Framework, page 33).

Examples of evidence of practice

- Plans of activities that show ways in which children are making choices

- Behaviour policy
- Safeguarding children policy
- Routine of your setting that demonstrates how children are helped to gain independence

1.4 Health and Well-being

'Children's health is an integral part of their emotional, mental, social, environmental and spiritual well-being and is supported by attention to these aspects.'

While childhood obesity and reduced levels of activity in childhood have been of recent concern, so too has children's mental health: it is now recognised that young children and even babies can become depressed. There are many aspects of practice that link to Health and Well-being, including the routine of your setting, the food that you serve and the way in which you help children to feel that they belong. Health and Well-being also covers child protection, although you might have noticed that increasingly this is referred to as 'safeguarding children'.

What should I do?

Make sure that your Safeguarding Children policy is up to date

You will need to have an up-to-date Safeguarding Children policy (this term is now used instead of child protection policy) that reflects the procedures put in place by your Local Safeguarding Children Board. You will need to make sure that you and anyone working in your setting knows what they should do if they have concerns about a child's well-being.

Have a good understanding of nutrition

Nutrition is quite complex, but there are many first-rate materials that will help you to plan meals and snacks for children and provide advice to parents, if appropriate. It is also worth looking at portion sizes and checking that they are correct for the age of children. This is important as children can become overweight even if they are being fed 'healthy' foods.

Look at the routines of your setting

Although it may be difficult to arrange, make sure that your routines reflect the varying needs of children, especially in terms of sleep and rest. Your routines should also allow time for outdoor play for all ages, including babies. In addition, routines have to be flexible enough so that there is opportunity for toddlers to spend time doing up their own coats or for four-year-olds to finish playing a game, for example.

Think about what children hear and see

The term 'emotional' environment is often used to describe the 'feeling' of a setting. Try listening hard to the sounds of your setting and get down to a child's level and think about what they would be seeing.

Think about the quality of interactions

While relationships are the focus of the second Theme, it is important to consider them in relation to Health and Well-being. How are children spoken to in the setting? If you were taping the sounds of the setting, would voices sound harsh or would they sound mostly warm and welcoming?

Observe children's physical development and skills

You are required to observe children as part of the EYFS framework. Make sure that you observe children's physical development and note the skills that they are showing or that are emerging. Think about ways in which these skills can be supported, for example by providing new activities, toys or simply encouragement.

Work closely with parents

Your relationships with parents and the information that is shared between you can support children's health and well-being. As well as finding out from parents about children's care needs, you could also think about ways of providing information on topics such as sleep, toilet training and nutrition.

Links to Every Child Matters

Health and Well-being supports the 'Be healthy' outcome.

Links to the Statutory Framework for the EYFS

Welfare Requirements:

- *Safeguarding and promoting children's welfare* – 'The provider must take necessary steps to safeguard and promote the welfare of children' (Statutory Framework, page 22); 'The provider must promote the good health of the children, take necessary steps to prevent the spread of infection, and take appropriate action when they are ill' (Statutory Framework, page 27).

- *Suitable people* – 'Staffing arrangements must be organised to ensure safety and to meet the needs of the children' (Statutory Framework, page 32).

- *Suitable premises, environment and equipment* – 'Outdoor and indoor spaces, furniture, equipment and toys, must be safe and suitable for their purpose' (Statutory Framework, page 33).

Examples of evidence to show practice

- Admissions and settling-in policy

- Routine that shows how children are helped to become independent

- Menus showing snacks, meals and drinks

- Certificates of training to show knowledge of food and nutrition

Positive Relationships

> **'Children learn to be strong and independent from a base of loving and secure relationships with parents and/or a key person.'**

This Principle is about the importance of having good relationships with children and their families. While this is the starting point for Positive Relationships, there is also a focus on the way in which practitioners work with other professionals.

There are four Commitments for Positive Relationships. Each one is detailed on a *Principle into Practice* card.

2.1 Respecting Each Other

> *'Every interaction is based on caring professional relationships and respectful acknowledgement of the feelings of children and their families.'*

Although the Commitment statement above appears to focus on children and their families, the *Principle into Practice* card is more extensive. Its emphasis is on the way in which we communicate with team members and other professionals. This is now considered to be essential as the way that adults communicate and work together around children can affect both the smooth running of the setting and the emotional environment that is created. As well as the focus on working relationships, the *Principle into Practice* card also

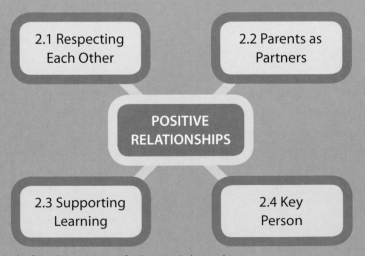

2.1 Respecting Each Other	2.2 Parents as Partners
POSITIVE RELATIONSHIPS	
2.3 Supporting Learning	2.4 Key Person

The four Commitments for Positive Relationships

considers the importance of helping children develop friendships with one another.

What should I do?

Observe children's social development

Observation is a legal requirement of the EYFS and some of your observations could note children's social development. If you are working with babies and toddlers, you might note whether they are starting to recognise other children and respond to them. With older children, you might observe whether children are seeking out other children to play with and to what extent children are able to be cooperative.

Plan activities that help children with turn-taking and sharing

Children under three years or so find it very hard to be cooperative and share, but can do so when an adult is helping them. For older children, look at providing activities that will encourage problem solving together.

Think about how the routine supports children's friendships

For children to develop friendships, they need to spend enough time together. Consider whether your routine supports opportunities for children to get to know each other. If some of the children you work with are sessional, you might also need to think about how they can be included by the other children.

Make sure that you are working effectively with parents

This is the major focus of the next Commitment, so you will need to refer to the 'What should I do?' section on page 14.

Look at ways in which the staff team can be helped to communicate more easily

In most settings where there is a staff team, communication between members can make or mar relationships. If you are responsible for the management of the team, think about ways in which staff members can recognise and value each other, for example at staff meetings.

Links to Every Child Matters

Respecting Each Other links to the 'Make a positive contribution' outcome.

Links to the Statutory Framework for the EYFS

Welfare Requirements:

- *Safeguarding and promoting children's welfare* – 'The provider must take necessary steps to safeguard and promote the welfare of children' (Statutory Framework, page 22).

- *Organisation* – 'Providers must plan and organise their systems to ensure that every child receives an enjoyable and challenging learning and development experience that is tailored to meet their individual needs' (Statutory Framework, page 37).

Examples of evidence to show practice

This Commitment does not easily lend itself to 'paper' evidence, but you could consider the following:

- children's records showing friendships and social development

- records of staff meetings.

2.2 Parents as Partners

'Parents are children's first and most enduring educators. When parents and practitioners work together in early years settings, the results have a positive impact on children's development and learning.'

As the title suggests, this Commitment is about the way in which you work with parents and the relationships that you form with them. The term 'Parents as Partners' is about more than just information sharing. To deliver this Commitment requires finding ways of including parents in some of the decision making, for example planning, contribution to children's records and – as suggested in the *Principle into practice* card – policies. There is also a significant link between this Commitment and Inclusive Practice (1.2). This is because if you are making parents feel that they are part of the setting rather than just users of it, you will be demonstrating inclusive practice.

What should I do?

Think about how welcoming your setting is for a new parent

Some parents can find it hard when meeting practitioners for the first time. If you are working in a nursery, pre-school or school, think about the initial impressions that new parents would have when coming in for the first time. If you are a childminder, think about how hard it might be to meet someone for the first time in their home. (Some childminders therefore arrange to meet new parents in a more open place such as in a parent and toddler group or the local children's library.)

Consider the information that you provide for parents

Read through your policies and look at your notice board and letters that are sent out, and consider how friendly and inviting they seem. Are they easy to read? Do they reinforce a 'them and us' approach or a more collaborative one?

Look at the routines of the setting

How easy would it be for a parent to talk to you about their child at the start or end of a session?

Think about the way you share information about children with parents

Sharing information about what children have been doing and what you have observed is essential. Think about when and how often this is done as ideally there should be many informal as well as formal opportunities to do this. You might also like to think about using modern technology to share information, for example digital photographs, voice recording using MP3 and maybe even sending e-mails (see also Section 3, page 244).

Make sure that parents are involved in observing and making assessments of children

As well as sharing information, you will need to show how parents contribute to their own children's records. This is good practice and should be useful – you might find that parents have a different view of their children as they see them in a variety of situations.

Think about how you communicate with parents who you rarely see

There might be some parents who you do not see very often, for example because another family member or au pair brings the children to and collects them from your setting. This makes it a little harder to form a relationship and to share information with parents. Think about phoning the parents, using e-mails or having a notebook that moves with the child.

Ask for feedback from parents

To find out more about what parents need and how well you are working with them, you will need to gain feedback from them. This can be done in a variety of ways. You could organise a questionnaire, talk informally to parents or carry out a structured interview. A structured interview is where you might ask parents a series of questions and note down their responses as an alternative to sending out a form. It can also be useful to ask parents whose children are about to leave your setting to give you some feedback about how you could improve your service in the future.

Provide information for parents

Parents can sometimes find it helpful to gain information about other services in the area. Some settings have a table, rack or notice board with information about leisure opportunities, benefits, and job and education opportunities. Some settings also run information sessions for parents about the curriculum or how children learn. When looking at providing information, think about asking parents what information they would like. This would be an example of how parents can be included in decision making.

Look out for training

Two types of training can be useful. First, a 'working with parents' course might be provided by your local authority. Second, consider a basic counselling course. While your role is not to counsel parents, learning some of the techniques of listening and communication are invaluable.

Links to Every Child Matters

Parents as Partners links to the 'Make a positive contribution' outcome.

Links to the Statutory Framework for the EYFS

Welfare Requirements:

- *Safeguarding and promoting children's welfare* – 'The provider must take necessary steps to safeguard and promote the welfare of children' (Statutory Framework, page 22).

- *Organisation* – 'Providers must plan and organise their systems to ensure that every child receives an enjoyable and challenging learning and development experience that is tailored to meet their individual needs' (Statutory Framework, page 37).

- *Documentation* – 'Providers must maintain records, policies and procedures required for the safe and efficient management of the settings and to meet the needs of the children' (Statutory Framework, page 38).

Examples of evidence to show practice

- Children's records that show parents' contributions

- Feedback from parents, including letters and questionnaires

- Policies and letters to parents, etc., that show a friendly, warm and respectful tone

- Certificates of attendance at training

2.3 Supporting Learning

'Warm, trusting relationships with knowledgeable adults support children's learning more effectively than any amount of resources.'

This Commitment is about the way in which good relationships between adults and children can support children's learning. It focuses on the skills that you need to have when talking and listening to children and how, by observing children, you might know how best to approach and work with them. This is because children need to feel relaxed and comfortable with adults in order to participate well and because children can learn a lot by being with adults who share their thinking with them.

Sharing your thinking with children helps them to gain 'metacognition' skills. These are the skills involved in

learning. An example of a metacognition skill is to make connections between new information and information that already exists, for example 'your new blue jumper is similar to the blue in my shoes'. Metacognition is also about using information that you have to make decisions, for example 'I won't put my drink there in case someone knocks it over.' Metacognition skills in children develop over time as the brain develops, but being with adults who put thinking into words can help children significantly.

What should I do?

Observe children's interests and ways of communicating

Every child, even when a baby, has slightly different interests and ways of reacting to situations. Some children may appear 'sad' when in reality this is their way of thinking, while other children may become excited easily. It is important to get to know each child and their individual ways, and to make sure if you are working alongside other staff that this information is shared with them.

Talk to parents about children's interests

Parents are often keen observers of their children and watch them develop and change over time. Parents may often tell you about situations in which their child thrives. Listening and talking to parents about their children will help you learn how best to communicate with them.

Think about group size and group dynamics

All children need time for one-to-one attention or to be in very small groups. The adult to child ratio for the under-threes makes this easier if you are working in group care. If you are a childminder, you might find the differences in the ages of children that you mind means that they need you in different ways and at different times. Thinking about group size and group dynamics is important as some children need more time to respond, and in a large group another child might take over while other children (often older) can spark off each other.

Record the way in which you interact with children

It can be helpful to record yourself during some sessions or an activity with an MP3 player or other audio device. You need to be brave to do so, but it is worth it – many practitioners report that they then realise they do not always give as much time for children to respond as they had thought or that they are asking very closed questions.

Use children's play and opportunities

There is always a balance to be struck between giving children opportunities to play by themselves and playing with them. Playing with children and using their activity as a basis for 'thinking aloud' is very valuable, although you will need to tune into children's activities rather than take them over.

Plan some problem-solving activities

Children enjoy activities when adults play and work on something alongside them. Making a den together is a good example of the way in which an adult might be able to encourage children's thinking skills through questions, suggestions and 'what ifs…'

Links to Every Child Matters

Supporting Learning links to the 'Make a positive contribution' outcome.

Links to the Statutory Framework for the EYFS

Welfare Requirements:

- *Organisation* – 'Providers must plan and organise their systems to ensure that every child receives an enjoyable and challenging learning and development experience that is tailored to meet their individual needs' (Statutory Framework, page 37).

Examples of evidence to show practice

- This Commitment does not easily lend itself to 'paper evidence' but you might like to use recordings of the way in which you interact with children

- You could also include children's records that show how you are planning to meet children's individual needs and interests

---

2.4 Key Person

> 'A key person has special responsibilities for working with a small number of children, giving them the reassurance to feel safe and cared for and building relationships with their parents.'

The focus of this Commitment is to provide a key person for each child within a setting. The idea of a key person is for the child to know that one adult in particular is taking especial care of them and that this person goes on to develop a close and genuine bond with them.

The concept of young children needing a key person in order to cope with the temporary separation from their parents or main carers is not new – it has been good practice for some time, although the extent to which settings have taken it on board has varied. As well as being a Commitment, it is essential for all staff to realise that it is also now a legal requirement (see page 37 of the Statutory Framework for the EYFS). In my view, this is wonderful news for children, although it will mean that many settings may have to work hard at incorporating it into their practice. The benefits for each child of having their own key person are immeasurable. We know that children's behaviour is sometimes a response to stress and feeling unsettled, and that when they are not feeling totally secure their immune system comes under more pressure and children find it hard to concentrate and learn.

The benefits for each child of having their own key person are immeasurable

(For childminders, playing the role of a key person has never been a problem, although it will be a good idea to make sure that you have a settling-in policy that shows how you help individual children to settle in.)

What should I do?

Look at your settling-in policies

Separation from parents, even for a couple of hours, is hard for young children and they will become anxious and 'protest'. Protest, as it is known, will show itself through loud cries and tears, tantrums, running to the door and eventually, when the child is tired, simply sadness and withdrawal. This is not necessary if children have established a strong enough relationship with their key person before their parent or main carer leaves. Your settling-in policy should be based on the principle that parents or main carers leave only when the child is likely to be happy.

Make sure that your settling-in procedures reflect individual children's needs

There are many factors that will affect how quickly a child will settle in and separate from their parents.

- *Experience* – a child who has never been separated from their parents will need more time than a child of the same age who has had many 'successful' separations. In the same way, a child who has had an 'unhappy' separation has learnt from this and may be clingier and need more time.
- *Age* – in general terms, children from three years onwards find it easier to separate than toddlers, but again experience can play a part.
- *Siblings and friends* – children may settle in more quickly if they already know a member of staff or have a sibling or friend there.
- *Parental confidence* – children pick up anxiety from parents. A parent who has never left their child may be anxious and you will need to settle in the parent as much as the child! A parent who has already left a sibling with you may be more confident and the child may pick this up.

Produce individual settling-in plans for parents

As each child will need different amounts of settling in, it is useful to draw up a plan with parents. This can in itself help some parents to feel more confident. When drawing up a plan, it is essential to find out about any previous separation experience that the child has had. It can also be useful to help parents know what they should do when they bring the child into the setting.

Some parents feel awkward and unsure and this can transmit itself to the child. Ideally, you need parents to be present but to 'step back' a little so that the child is able to interact with their key person.

Organising a key person system

This is not always straightforward, particularly if you have part-time staff and children who come in for different sessions. It is important, though, to make sure that no member of staff has too many key children in any one session, otherwise they will not be able to work effectively. In some situations, for example in day care when staff work shifts, it might not be possible to allocate just one person. In this case, the *Principle into Practice* card suggests that it is possible to provide a second key person.

Once a key person is allocated, it is important that they are available to settle in the child. You should therefore look ahead to avoid situations where a child might just have become used to the key person only to find that this person is about to go on holiday. Where a second key person is used, it is essential that this person also has a strong relationship with the child in order for the child to be settled. A second key person can be introduced at any time.

Look at the routine of the setting

A key person can only develop a bond with the child if sufficient time is spent with the child. This means that the routines of the setting will need to be organised so that key persons spend time with their key children. This might be for certain activities, such as tidying away, greeting at the start of the session, cooking or for certain care activities, for example nappy changes, feeding and meal times.

Involve parents in the key person system

The key person system will only work well when parents are involved. As you have seen from Parents as Partners (2.2), you are meant to be working closely with parents. This means that they should know who their child's key person is and have regular contact with this person. They should get to know their child's key person during the settling-in period.

Observe children

You can recognise whether there is a strong relationship between the key person and child. Children very quickly should become pleased to see their key person at the start of the session and during activities may look across to check where their key person is.

They may also go to their key person to ask for help, seek physical reassurance or simply to chat. When their key person goes out of the room or is away, it will be a good sign if the child notices their absence. (This is why a second key person is often needed as a back-up.)

Links to Every Child Matters

Key Person links to the 'Stay safe' outcome.

Links to the Statutory Framework for the EYFS

Welfare Requirements:

- *Suitable people* – 'Staffing arrangements must be organised to ensure safety and to meet the needs of the children' (Statutory Framework, page 32).

- *Organisation* – 'Providers must plan and organise their systems to ensure that every child receives an enjoyable and challenging learning and development experience that is tailored to meet their individual needs' (Statutory Framework, page 37).

- *Documentation* – 'Providers must maintain records, policies and procedures required for the safe and efficient management of the settings and to meet the needs of the children' (Statutory Framework, page 38).

Examples of evidence to show practice

- The easiest way to ascertain if a child has a strong relationship with a key person is through observation. It should be fairly clear to see an extra level of warmth and genuine pleasure in the interactions

- Admissions and settling-in policy

- Children's records completed by the children's own key person

- Copies of letters and correspondence between key person and parents

- Planning showing how individual children's needs are being met

- Routines of the setting that show how children can spend time with their key person

Enabling Environments

'The environment plays a key role in supporting and extending children's development and learning.'

The Principle of Enabling Environments has its roots in the concept that children are essentially competent learners who need an environment that will stimulate them.

There are four Commitments for Enabling Environments. Each one is detailed on a *Principle into Practice* card. It is important to look at each Commitment carefully because Enabling Environments is more complex than simply putting out appropriate equipment for children to play with.

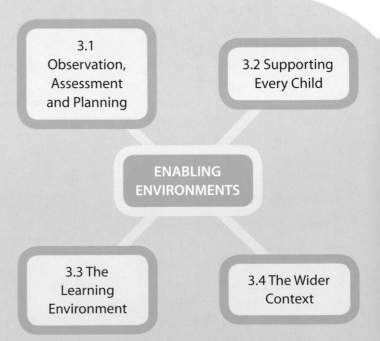

The four Commitments for Enabling Environments

3.1 Observation, Assessment and Planning

'Babies and young children are individuals first, each with a unique profile of abilities. Schedules and routines should flow with the child's needs. All planning starts with observing children in order to understand and consider their current interests, development and learning.'

The idea behind the focus on observation is that unless you know what children enjoy doing and their current level of development, it is hard to know what activities, equipment or approach will work best with them. Observation is also a statutory requirement and you should read page 37 of the Statutory Framework for the EYFS carefully in this regard. Observations are no longer just good practice; they have to be regularly carried out on children. You are also asked to involve parents in the observation process. They will need to contribute to observations and you will also need to share with them your observations. In this book, we look at ways of observing children and involving parents.

Once you have observed children, the next step will be to draw some conclusions from what you have seen – that is, to make an assessment. Most of the time you can do this by adding in some comments about what you have seen, but you will also need once in a while to write an overall summary of the child's development with some reference to the areas of Learning and Development within the EYFS. This is sometimes referred to as a summative assessment, although most parents will think of it as a 'report'. How often you should do this is not specified, but I would say that it needs to happen at least once a year and if possible every three or four months.

After observing and then assessing children, you will also need to make sure that your planning reflects individual children's needs and interests. If you are a childminder this is likely to be straightforward, but if you work with large groups of children this will be more of a challenge. This is further considered in Part 3.

What should I do?

Make sure that your knowledge of child development is up to date

It is essential that your knowledge of child development is current as otherwise your assessments may not be accurate. Look out for a child development training course or get hold of a book such as *Child Development: An Illustrated Guide* (2nd edition) by Carolyn Meggitt (Heinemann, 2006).

Work out a system for observing children regularly

Where you are working with groups of children, it is essential to establish a system whereby you observe each child regularly. If you are working in a team, it is also important to talk about who is observing what, who and when. The key people should observe their key children so that they can feed back to parents and because they need to know as much about their key children as possible. As well as observing individual children, it is also useful to observe groups of children, for example during an activity.

Consider a rolling programme for summative assessments

While schools tend to produce 'reports' or summative assessments for all the children at the same time, it might be worth avoiding this if you are working in other settings. A rolling programme can mean that you write one summative assessment every fortnight rather than having to write several all at once. The key person is again the best person to complete a summative assessment. Before writing the assessment, remember that it is essential to have contributions from parents.

Make sure that you have sufficient opportunities for child-initiated play

The guidance suggests that most of your observations should come from child-initiated play. To gain information about a child across all the areas of development, you will need to make sure that children have very varied opportunities to play.

Involve parents

It has always been good practice to involve parents in the observation and assessment process. Make sure that parents know that you need to observe children and talk to them about the range of methods that you will be using and what you will be observing. For some types of observation, such as photographic or recorded observations, you might need parental permission. Encourage parents to bring in photographs from home and to write down comments about what they have noticed about their children. Children's records will need to show evidence that you have been involving parents.

Make sure that your short-term planning reflects children's interests and needs

Children's interests can change quickly, so the best place to reflect them is in short-term planning.

Make sure that children's Individual Education Plans are reflected in the planning

Some of the children you work with might have an Individual Education Plan (IEP) to support their special educational needs. If you are working in a group setting, you should already have someone who is nominated as the coordinator for Special Needs – a SENCO. This person should be able to help you integrate children's IEPs into your planning. If you are a childminder, you should talk to your network organiser about supporting children with special needs and how to draw up a plan for them.

Links to Every Child Matters

Observation, Assessment and Planning links to the 'Enjoy and achieve' outcome.

Links to the Statutory Framework for the EYFS

Welfare Requirements:

○ *Organisation* – 'Providers must plan and organise their systems to ensure that every child receives an enjoyable and challenging learning and development experience that is tailored to meet their individual needs' (Statutory Framework, page 37).

Examples of evidence to show practice

○ Examples of observations

○ Children's records that are up to date and contain formative and summative assessments

○ Children's records that show how parents have been involved in the collation of them

○ Planning that shows how children's individual needs and interests have been taken into consideration

○ Notes of staff meetings that show how observations and assessments are influencing practice

3.2 Supporting Every Child

'The environment supports every child's learning through planned experiences and activities that are challenging but achievable.'

The idea behind this Commitment is that every child is an individual and, as such, will have unique interests and needs. To incorporate this into your practice, you will need to show that even when planning and working with groups of children, you still make sure that you view each child as an individual. The *Principle into Practice* card also gives examples of the way in which some of the everyday routines with individual children can be turned into learning experiences; an example is counting buttons when encouraging a four-year-old to put on a coat.

This Commitment clearly links to Observation, Assessment and Planning (3.1) and also Child Development (1.1) and Inclusive Practice (1.2), as these particularly focus on the needs of individual children.

What should I do?

Make sure that your planning takes account of individual children's interests and needs

You will need to find a way of incorporating children's interests and needs into your planning. In group settings, you might do this by putting children's initials next to certain activities that you have planned with them in mind. (You might also like to look at the 'Response Planning' sheet in the Appendix.)

Look at the routines of your setting

The routines of a setting need to work for each child. It is a good time to look at what you currently do and re-evaluate it. Observe how children react and which parts of the routine are working well, but which parts seem to create problems.

Be flexible when working with children

In group situations, it is important to remember to be flexible. At story time, for example, consider whether all the children really have to come and listen or whether a child who is engrossed in the sand tray can finish off playing there. With children under three years old, being flexible in this way should be straightforward as the adult to child ratio is high (this reflects the way in which the under-threes find group situations hard).

Child-initiated play provides an ideal opportunity to observe children's interests and development

Share information about children with others who work with them

One of the main focuses of the EYFS is to ensure that different agencies are collaborating. This means sharing information across teams, although you should remember that permission may need to be sought from parents and also that confidential information must be handled carefully.

Have regular contact with parents

Parents need to understand how you are working with their child and you have to collaborate with them so as to meet their child's needs and interests. (See also 2.2 Parents as Partners on page 13.)

Links to Every Child Matters

Supporting Every Child links to the 'Enjoy and achieve' outcome.

Links to the Statutory Framework for the EYFS

Welfare Requirements:

- *Organisation* – 'Providers must plan and organise their systems to ensure that every child receives an enjoyable and challenging learning and development experience that is tailored to meet their individual needs' (Statutory Framework, page 37).

Examples of evidence to show practice

This Commitment is clearly about what you actually do when you are with children, although you can show some 'paper' evidence of the way in which you are supporting individual children, as follows:

- Special Educational Needs policy

- Children's records that show how you have identified individual's interests and needs

- Planning that shows how individual children's needs are being met

3.3 The Learning Environment

'A rich and varied environment supports children's learning and development. It gives them the confidence to explore and learn in secure and safe, yet challenging, indoor and outdoor spaces.'

The title of this Commitment makes it very clear that it is about how we provide for children. The term 'environment' does not simply refer to what is put out or the layout, it also refers to the emotional environment that is created. You may remember that the 'emotional environment' was also considered in Respecting Each Other (2.1).

A major focus, and perhaps a change to some traditional early years provision, is the emphasis on being outdoors. This is more than just letting children play outdoors to let off steam; it is about looking at activities and ways of delivering the areas of development. This means that the odd fifteen minutes of outdoor playtime will not suffice! It is worth noting here that the guidance states 'Wherever possible, there should be access to an outdoor play area, and this is the expected norm for providers' (Statutory Framework for the EYFS, page 35). The *Principle into Practice* card for this Commitment also suggests that, where possible, children should be free to move between the indoors and outdoors. This is sometimes referred to as 'free flow'.

What should I do?

Think about the sounds, layout and overall feel of your provision from a child's point of view

Creating an emotional environment that is warm and welcoming links to suggestions that you will find in the Positive Relationships section above (see pages 12–18).

Make sure that the indoor environment is homely

All children enjoy times when they can relax, snuggle up or find a quiet area, so it is important in terms of creating an emotional environment that you find ways of making it feel homely. This is particularly essential with babies and toddlers and those children who may be spending many hours a day in your provision.

Observe children in and out of doors

Observing children playing and using the environment is a good starting point when revamping areas and materials. Think about which are most popular and identify those which are underused. Consider, too, how children behave with different materials and in different areas.

Look for ways of creating a flexible environment

Ideally, you will need to find ways of changing the environment so that children do not become bored. You could do this by putting out varied materials and equipment, but also by following children's ideas and interests. On the *Principle into Practice* card, it is suggested that children are involved in helping to plan the layout of the environment.

Make sure that children can 'self-serve' and tidy away

Both in and out of doors, children need to be able to access some equipment, toys and materials by themselves. This means looking out for shelving or boxes that children can access; for babies and toddlers, you will need to put a range of materials onto the ground so that they can choose for themselves. This helps children to gain in confidence and to feel that they 'belong' in the setting.

As well as being able to help themselves, children also need to learn to care for their environment. This means that you will need to find effective ways for children to do some of the tidying away. In some situations, this might mean simply encouraging children to pop one or two items into a box; with older children (assuming they are developmentally ready) it might mean putting things back in the place where they originally found them.

Look at the routine of your setting

Think about how much time children are currently spending outdoors and then find ways of increasing it. Babies and toddlers will also need to spend time outdoors.

Look at the storage that is available outdoors

Storage is often the key to providing equipment and activities outdoors, so think about investing in a shed or storage containers. When doing so, aim to find some storage that will allow children to access the equipment and to tidy it away at the end.

Provide information for parents

Some settings find that they have to explain to parents the benefits of going outdoors, especially on days that are damp or cold.

Provide protective clothing

Accessing the outdoor areas is easier when you have sufficient clothing for different weather conditions. Think about investing in a set of rain ponchos, wellies, spare gloves and jumpers.

Identify or create areas of shade

While the focus of concern can often be damp or cold weather, it is important to recognise the dangers of direct sunlight on children's skin. Aim to create some areas of shade within your outdoor area.

Consider creating areas of learning within the outdoor provision

Some settings find it helpful to separate their outdoor spaces into different areas so that children can experience different play types. These could include areas for role play, construction and painting, as well as an area for equipment to promote gross motor movements.

Links to Every Child Matters

The Learning Environment links to the 'Enjoy and achieve' outcome.

Links to the Statutory Framework for the EYFS

Welfare Requirements:

- *Suitable premises, environment and equipment* – 'Outdoor and indoor spaces, furniture, equipment and toys, must be safe and suitable for their purpose' (Statutory Framework, page 34).

○ *Organisation* – 'Providers must plan and organise their systems to ensure that every child receives an enjoyable and challenging learning and development experience that is tailored to meet their individual needs' (Statutory Framework, page 37).

Examples of evidence to show practice

In some ways the setting itself will show whether you have created good learning environments and those where children can feel at home. In addition, you can also consider using the following 'paper' evidence.

○ Routine of the setting showing how the outdoor space is used

○ Plans that reflect how the outdoor space is being used to deliver the areas of Learning and Development

○ Observations of children taken outdoors

○ Risk assessment showing that you have considered the hazards both indoors and out

3.4 The Wider Context

'Working in partnership with other settings, other professionals and with individuals and groups in the community supports children's development and progress towards the outcomes of Every Child Matters: being healthy, staying safe, enjoying and achieving, making a positive contribution and economic well-being.'

In some ways there are three elements to this Commitment.

- The first is about the way that you help children settle into your setting or transfer to another setting or carer. The term transition is used frequently to describe the process of helping children settle in.
- The second is about the importance of making professional and social contacts in the local and wider community. The term multi-agency working

is used to describe professional contacts where different people from a range of disciplines are supporting a child or a family, for example a social worker, speech therapist or doctor. It is important to recognise that multi-agency working is not just about children and families who are in crisis or have needs, but should take place to provide all children with a richer experience. This means that you should make contact with people such as the local librarian or leisure centre manager.

- Finally, the Wider Context is about helping children to learn about and from their local environment. This might mean organising trips out or using photographs of local buildings and areas. (This links quite nicely with some aspects of the 'Knowledge and Understanding of the World' Area of Learning and Development.)

What should I do?

Think about planning activities, events or visitors in relation to the local community

Look for ways in which you can involve the local community and make your provision part of the community. This will of course depend on your type of provision and, to an extent, where you are based. Note that no visitor should be allowed unsupervised access to children.

Provide information about what is going on in the local community

As well as using the local community as a resource, you might also like to have a community notice board so that parents can find out what is happening within the local area.

Make sure that you are building up professional contacts

It is important to build up a network of professional contacts over time; this makes multi-agency working easier. Keep a list of names and organisations, including details of the person's role and ways of contacting them.

Develop a transition policy

Your transition policy will be an extension of your settling-in policy. Your policy should show how you would support children and their families in making transitions, how and in what circumstances you would provide information (note that you will need to think about confidentiality and the Data Protection Act) and how you would prepare children to make transitions.

Make contact with other professionals who share the care and education of the children you work with

It is quite common for some children to spend different parts of the day or week with a range of professionals in child care and education settings. A child might be brought to school by a childminder, attend the Reception class and then go on to an after-school club. The child would experience three transitions and have three key people! It is therefore important, assuming parental consent, for each of the key people to work closely together.

Links to Every Child Matters

The Wider Context links to the 'Make a positive contribution' outcome.

Links to the Statutory Framework for the EYFS

Welfare Requirements:

- *Suitable people* – 'The provider must take the necessary steps to safeguard and promote the welfare of children' (Statutory Frameworks, page 23).

- *Organisation* – 'Providers must plan and organise their systems to ensure that every child receives an enjoyable and challenging learning and development experience that is tailored to meet their individual needs' (Statutory Framework, page 37).

Examples of evidence to show practice

- Correspondence that shows how you manage the transition process

- Settling-in and transition policy

- Children's records that show how they have settled in

- Planning that reflects how you are involving or using the local community, for example visits to the library, visits by a local artist

Learning and Development

'Children develop and learn in different ways and at different rates and all areas of Learning and Development are equally important and inter-connected.'

As might be expected reading the above, this Theme is about children's learning and development and links to the six areas covered by the early learning goals and educational programmes outlined in the Statutory Framework for the EYFS. The *Practice into Principle* card for Learning and Development (4.4) is subdivided to give information about each of the areas of Learning and Development.

There are four commitments for Learning and Development, and each one is detailed in a *Principle into Practice* card. While you might be tempted to skip looking at these, I think that it is important to consider them as they should be embedded in your daily practice.

The four Commitments for Learning and Development

4.1 Play and Exploration

'Children's play reflects their wide ranging and varied interests and preoccupations. In their play children learn at their highest level. Play with peers is important for children's development.'

The focus of this Commitment is valuing play and its benefits in relation to learning. The *Principle into Practice* card focuses on the way in which adults might provide for children's play and how they might become involved in play.

In order to deliver this Commitment, you will need to make sure that play is the key medium through which you are working to enhance children's learning. This needs to be remembered when planning activities to deliver the areas of Learning and Development, organising the routine and setting out the layout of the provision. This applies to all ages of children. With babies, for example, play can be delivered through the playful interactions of the adult during care routines such as nappy changing and feeding; for example, saying 'Look, here comes the spoon and it is flying along…' when feeding a baby.

For play to work for children, you will need to observe them and identify their interests and fascinations. As a result of the observations you may, for example, find ways of extending play by adding equipment, provide opportunities for children to revisit activities that they have enjoyed or find ways of linking their play to a learning outcome.

What should I do?

Provide sufficient time for children to play

This may seem obvious, but in some settings the routine can tend to dictate. This can mean that children have only just begun to get embroiled in their play

For play to work for children, you will need to identify their interests and fascinations

when it is time for them to tidy up, have lunch or be whisked off to an adult-led activity.

Be flexible

Children may not always play with materials in the way that is intended and may be inclined to 'mix up' materials, for example by taking cups of water over the to the role-play area. Mixing up materials is often children's way of enriching their play and being resourceful. Think hard before preventing this and, better still, find ways of allowing this to happen.

Observe children as they are playing

You are required to carry out observations of children and the focus for many of these observations is child-initiated play. Make sure that what you have learnt about children's play interests is then reflected in your planning and thereafter in the provision of play opportunities and activities.

Use children's play as a way of delivering the areas of Learning and Development

When you are watching children play, consider how their play links to the areas of Learning and Development and to the early learning goals. This is important as some adults assume that only during adult-led activities will children be learning!

Make sure that you provide information for parents

Parents need to understand that the educational programme is a play-led programme. You might need to show how children's play links to the areas of Learning and Development and the eventual early learning goals.

Make sure that resources meet children's play needs

Children need resources for their play, but these do not always have to be toys. A cardboard box is often more useful to a child than a ready-made plastic item that requires no imagination or effort. You might like to carry out an audit of your resources, thinking carefully about what is required to enhance children's play.

Make sure that the outdoor area is a learning environment

While physical play is important for children, the outdoor area should provide other play and therefore learning opportunities, such as role play and mark-making (see also 3.3 The Learning Environment).

Make sure that different play types are on offer to children

A varied range of resources is required to enable children to play in different ways, for example those for role play, mark-making, construction and wheeled toys. Each type of play primes children to learn different skills.

Links to Every Child Matters

Play and Exploration links to the 'Enjoy and achieve' outcome.

Links to the Statutory Framework for the EYFS

Learning and Development Requirements:

○ *2.5* – 'All the areas [of Learning and Development] must be delivered though planned, purposeful play, with a balance of adult-led and child-initiated activities.'

Welfare Requirements:

○ *Organisation* – 'Providers must plan and organise their systems to ensure that every child receives an enjoyable and challenging learning and development experience that is tailored to meet their individual needs' (Statutory Framework, page 37).

Examples of evidence to show practice

○ Plans showing how children's play interests are being reflected

○ Plans that show how the outdoor area is being used as a learning environment

○ Activity plans that show how play is being used to support learning

○ Routines that show how children are being given sufficient time to play

○ Observations of children that focus on how their play is linked to the different areas of learning

○ Children's records that show how parents have contributed with their knowledge of their children's play interests

○ Information for parents about the provision of play in the setting

4.2 Active Learning

'Children learn best through physical and mental challenges. Active learning involves other people, objects, ideas and events that engage and involve children for sustained periods.'

Active learning closely links to Play and Exploration (4.1). The difference is the focus, which is here about making sure that play is purposeful and challenging, so that children can actively learn. While children during child-initiated play tend to be very active in their learning, in the past the learning in some settings' adult-led activities has been somewhat passive. Active Learning prompts practitioners to remember that all activities need to be engaging for children.

The *Principle into Practice* card for this Commitment refers to 'personalised learning'. This term is also being introduced into schools. The concept is that practitioners need to plan for children as individuals and to ensure that activities are geared to their individual interests, style of learning and level of development. The *Principle into Practice* card also suggests that you should have learning plans for each child.

What should I do?

Plan adult-led activities carefully

The Statutory Framework for the EYFS requires that the educational programme is delivered using a mixture of child-initiated play and adult-led activities. It is important to think about how adult-led activities will be engaging and grounded in play. Look at some of your current adult-led activities objectively; observe children during them and consider whether the activities are engaging all the children.

Look at group size during adult-led activities

A key strategy in ensuring that adult-led activities are working is to consider the group size. Small group sizes allow you to listen more carefully to children, be flexible in your approach and encourage children to be active.

Use observations and assessments to create individual learning plans

We have repeatedly looked at the importance of observation in planning. Producing a learning plan is relatively easy. It requires that you consider what a child is currently interested in, their present abilities and then decide (with parents where possible) what their next steps might be. Some settings do this in relation to each of the areas of Learning and Development. The plan also needs to show how you support this learning.

Provide sensory opportunities

Sensory materials such as sand, water, dough, bark chippings and pasta are wonderful for sustaining children's concentration. Make sure that you are providing plenty of sensory materials and that they are also used during adult-led activities. Think too about the 'feel' of materials; for example, a metal teapot is likely to hold children's attention for longer than a toy plastic one.

Links to Every Child Matters

Active Learning links to the 'Enjoy and achieve' outcome.

Links to the Statutory Framework for the EYFS

Learning and Development Requirements:

- 2.5 – 'All the areas [of Learning and Development] must be delivered though planned, purposeful play, with a balance of adult-led and child-initiated activities.'

Welfare Requirements:

- *Organisation* – 'Providers must plan and organise their systems to ensure that every child receives an enjoyable and challenging learning and development experience that is tailored to meet their individual needs' (Statutory Framework, page 37).

Examples of evidence to show practice

- Plans for activities showing how children's interests and learning needs are met

- Learning plans for each child showing how children are to be supported

- Audit of resources that are accessible for children and challenging

- Routines showing the balance between adult led and child initiated activities

- Observations of children's play

4.3 Creativity and Critical Thinking

'When children have opportunities to play with ideas in different situations and with a variety of resources, they discover connections and come to new and better understandings and ways of doing things. Adult support in this process enhances their ability to think critically and ask questions.'

This Commitment looks at the way in which adults who work with children can support their thinking or metacognition skills. To do this you will need to look at the manner in which you interact with children and the type of activities available that help children to problem solve. Interestingly, problem solving and exploring are key tools in creativity as creativity is seen as being larger than just the 'arts'. The *Principle into Practice* card for this Commitment uses the term 'sustained shared thinking.' This reflects the importance of finding solutions with children through a process of thinking aloud, questions and speculations. It is a great phrase!

What should I do?

Make sure that adults are free to play and work alongside children

Simply supervising children will not help them to gain more advanced thinking skills. Research shows that adults who ask open questions, think aloud and encourage children to join in can significantly support children's cognitive development. This links back to Positive Relationships, as children are more likely to gain in situations where they feel comfortable with the adult who is supporting them.

Ensure that there is a balance between child-initiated and adult-led activities

Child-initiated activities, where children are actively making choices and designing their own play, can be

Create opportunities for children to actively make choices and design their own play

very creative and are therefore an important way to support children. It is vital that adults take an interest when children are playing in this way, but that they do not change the nature of the play or seek ownership. Adults can support children by making comments and suggestions and asking questions.

Adult-led activities must engage children, as we have seen in Active Learning. They can be used to set up a problem for children to solve; for example, 'Teddy has lost his hat – where should we look for it first?' Good adult-led activities are flexible and will allow children to think and contribute.

Focus on the process rather than the end product

The process takes priority over the final result, especially when children are producing artwork, cooking or learning a song. Make sure that interactions with children help them to explore what is happening rather than just 'how to get it right'. Be aware that 'identikit' greeting cards, pictures and clay models in a setting will be viewed very negatively, as they show that staff are not giving children the chance to show their individuality.

Links to Every Child Matters

Creativity and Critical Thinking links to the 'Enjoy and achieve' outcome.

Links to the Statutory Framework for the EYFS

Learning and Development Requirements:

- 2.5 – 'All the areas [of Learning and Development] must be delivered though planned, purposeful play, with a balance of adult-led and child-initiated activities.'

Welfare Requirements:

- *Organisation* – 'Providers must plan and organise their systems to ensure that every child receives an enjoyable and challenging learning and development experience that is tailored to meet their individual needs' (Statutory Framework, page 37).

Examples of evidence to show practice

- Children's work, for example drawing, mark-making, photographs of models, that shows individuality and children's own thinking

- Planning that shows how adult-led activities will sometimes be open-ended and allow children to problem solve

4.4 Areas of Learning and Development

'The Early Years Foundation Stage (EYFS) is made up of six areas of Learning and Development. All areas of Learning and Development are connected to one another and are equally important. All areas of Learning and Development are underpinned by the Principles of the EYFS.'

As clearly stated above, this Commitment relates to the educational programme and the Practice Guidance for the EYFS. Included with the *Principle into Practice* card for 4.4 are six additional cards for each area of Learning and Development, as follows:

- Personal, Social and Emotional Development
- Communication, Language and Literacy

- Problem Solving, Reasoning and Numeracy
- Knowledge and Understanding of the World
- Physical Development
- Creative Development.

Ideally, you should see these additional cards as overviews of each area of Learning and Development and use the Practice Guidance to inform your planning.

However, it is worth making sure that you have read the legal requirements set out in the Statutory Framework that introduce each area of Learning and Development; these are shown below. The next section of this book looks at the Practice Guidance and each of the areas of Learning and Development in turn.

Learning and Development Requirements

Personal, Social and Emotional Development

2.7 'Children must be provided with experiences and support which will help them to develop a positive sense of themselves and of others; respect for others; social skills; and a positive disposition to learn. Providers must ensure support for children's emotional well-being to help them to know themselves and what they can do.'

Communication, Language and Literacy

2.9 'Children's learning and competence in communicating, speaking and listening, being read to and beginning to read and write must be supported. They must be provided with opportunity and encouragement to use their skills in a range of situations and for a range of purposes, and be supported in developing the confidence and disposition to do so.'

Problem Solving, Reasoning and Numeracy

2.11 'Children must be supported in developing their understanding of Problem Solving, Reasoning and Numeracy in a broad range of contexts in which they can explore, enjoy, learn, practise and talk about their developing understanding. They must be provided with opportunities to practise and extend their skills in these areas and to gain confidence and competence in their use.'

Knowledge and Understanding of the World

2.13 'Children must be supported in developing the knowledge, skills and understanding that help them to make sense of the world. Their learning must be supported through offering opportunities for them to use a range of tools safely; encounter creatures, people, plants and objects in their natural environments and in real-life situations; undertake practical 'experiments'; and work with a range of materials.'

Physical Development

2.15 'The physical development of babies and young children must be encouraged through the provision of opportunities for them to be active and interactive and to improve their skills of coordination, control, manipulation and movement. They must be supported in using all of their senses to learn about the world around them and to make connections between new information and what they already know. They must be supported in developing an understanding of the importance of physical activity and making healthy choices in relation to food.'

Creative Development

2.17 'Children's creativity must be extended by the provision of support for their curiosity, exploration and play. They must be provided with opportunities to explore and share their thoughts, ideas and feelings, for example, through a variety of art, music, movement, dance, imaginative and role-play activities, mathematics, and design and technology.'

Understanding the Welfare Requirements

Introduction

The Welfare Requirements have replaced the old Care standards and you must read and follow these to the letter. Ofsted will look at how you are meeting the new Welfare Requirements and it is clear from the wording in the overview to Section 3 of the Statutory Framework that no excuses will be allowed:

> 'This section sets out the welfare requirements that all early years providers must meet, regardless of type, size or funding of the setting.' (Statutory Framework for the EYFS, page 19, paragraph 3.1)

This means that if you are a childminder, a setting that is cash-strapped or even a school, no allowances will be made. This is why it is essential to get to grips with the Welfare Requirements as soon as possible. In some cases, settings may need to look at ways in which they are funded and staffed. If you are a childminder, you may need additional training to take you through the planning for the areas of Learning and Development.

While the Welfare Requirements may seem daunting, the good news for children is that they are designed to ensure that they are safe, emotionally secure and stimulated. The idea behind the Welfare Requirements is that children's needs must come first at all times.

Your Questions Answered

Do I need to read through all the Welfare Requirements?

If you work as a childminder or as part of the management team, you will need to familiarise yourself with all of the Welfare Requirements. If you do not hold this level of responsibility you can probably manage without reading them, but you will need to read pages 32 and 37 of the Statutory Guidance (covered on pages 38 and 40 of this book) as they significantly impact on your work with children.

Policies and procedures

All settings, with the possible exception of childminders, are meant to have written policies that reflect the Welfare Requirements. In practice, this means that you should have a range of policies covering everything from safeguarding children, equality of opportunity, admissions, behaviour, health and safety (which will include outings) and medicines through to data protection and confidentiality. For each policy you are likely to need a set of procedures.

Procedures are step-by-step guidelines for staff and volunteers. These are essential as they help everyone to follow the policy. It may be worth looking at each of the Welfare Requirements and thinking about whether your existing policies link into them or whether you may need to introduce a new policy, for example a key person policy, or update an existing policy.

Making sure staff and volunteers know about the policies

You must find a way of ensuring that each of your staff and even volunteers know about the policies and procedures in your setting. You may need to think about the way in which you organise your induction, for example. Make sure that each new member has a chance to read through and ask questions about each of the policies. Many settings ask new members of staff to sign a form so that they have evidence that policies have been shown. In addition, it may be worth going through some policies from time to time at staff meetings – it helps everyone to remember what is in them! Staff must also know where policies are kept, although do note that the Statutory Framework states that staff should be given copies of policies and procedures as part of their induction (page 20, paragraph 3.8).

Parents need to know about policies as well

The Statutory Framework also states that providers should explain and make accessible the setting's policies and procedures to parents (page 20, paragraph 3.8). You could explain these as part of the admissions process. You might also find it helpful to state some of the key elements of the policies in a brochure for parents.

Your Questions Answered

Do childminders need policies?

In theory, no – the Statutory Framework states that if you are a childminder you do not need to have written policies, providing that you know what you would do in any given situation (page 20, paragraph 3.9). In practical terms, however, you might find it helpful to have a folder of policies to show parents when they first come to you. These do not have to be wordy documents, but simply statements that outline what your approach is (the policy) and then what you actually do (the procedure). For more information on policies for childminders, contact your local childminding network or the National Childminding Association (www.ncma.org.uk). Remember that if you use other people's policies, you will need to adapt them to suit your own circumstances.

The general welfare requirements

The five general welfare requirements for the EYFS are shown in the spider diagram opposite.

Each of these is further broken down into:

- general legal requirements
- specific legal requirements
- statutory guidance to which providers should have regard.

Each general welfare requirement is broken down into its key aspects below.

Safeguarding and promoting children's welfare

The diagram on page 32 shows the three general legal requirements for Safeguarding and promoting children's welfare as well as the areas to which the specific legal requirements and statutory guidance apply.

'The provider must take necessary steps to safeguard and promote the welfare of children'

Safeguarding (page 22)

This requirement is all about child protection, and you will need to find out about the requirements of your Local Safeguarding Children Board (LSCB). There is an emphasis here on reporting allegations of abuse immediately, both to Ofsted and your LSCB. For group settings you must have a designated person who can liaise with the LSCB. Note that this person must attend a child protection training course.

In addition, Ofsted will expect to see that *all* staff have an up-to-date understanding of child protection, or what they refer to as 'safeguarding children issues'. This means that everyone should know what to do if there was a concern and also how to identify concerns.

General welfare requirements

Safeguarding and promoting children's welfare

General legal requirements

'The provider must take necessary steps to safeguard and promote the welfare of children.'

'The provider must promote the good health of the children, take necessary steps to prevent the spread of infection, and take appropriate action when they are ill.'

'Children's behaviour must be managed effectively and in a manner appropriate for their stage of development and particular individual needs.'

Areas to which specific legal requirement and statutory guidance apply

- Safeguarding
- Information and complaints
- Premises and security
- Outings
- Equality of opportunities

- Medicines
- Illness and injuries
- Food and drink
- Smoking

- Behaviour management

Points to consider

✳ Who is your designated person? Have they been on a child protection training course?

✳ Do you have a safeguarding children policy that is up to date?

✳ Are the contact details of the LSCB available to staff?

✳ Does every member of staff know what they should do if they suspect abuse?

✳ Does every member of staff know what to look and listen out for?

Information and complaints (page 23)

This section is quite substantial and needs carefully working through. The section begins with the requirement that settings should 'engage' with and provide information for parents. The term 'engage' is an interesting one and is designed to ensure that when parents are given information they have enough time to digest it and to ask questions. The list of information that parents should be provided with is substantial, and you will need to make sure that you have allocated sufficient time to go through it before a child starts at a setting. Some of the information could be provided in a prospectus or booklet about your setting. Some of the information is fairly obvious, but it is worth noting that parents should know what would happen if a child went missing and how they can contact Ofsted should they have a complaint. Parents should also know that they can have free access to their own child's developmental records and can apply in writing for the setting's personal files on their own children.

As well as providing information for parents, you are required to collect some information before a child starts at a setting which includes who has legal contact with the child and parental responsibility. You must also ask for written permission in the event that a child needs emergency medical treatment. In the unlikely event that a parent refused this written permission, it would be advisable to contact either Ofsted or your local early years advisory team.

You will also need to have a written complaints procedure and copies must be available for parents. Your complaints procedure must reflect some further legal requirements that are set out on page 23.

Points to consider

❋ What is your system to ensure that parents know about the policies and procedures in your setting?

❋ Have you asked parents for feedback as to how you could improve your admissions procedure?

❋ How do you ensure that parents are aware of how to contact Ofsted?

❋ Does your complaints procedure comply with the legal requirements set out on page 23 of the Statutory Framework?

❋ How do you make sure that information is regularly exchanged with parents?

❋ How do you exchange information with other providers?

❋ Are all members of staff aware of how to maintain confidentiality?

Premises and security (page 24)

The focus here is on safety in the premises and on ensuring that children cannot go missing or be taken by an unauthorised person. The legal requirements are quite straightforward with the emphasis on security. Note, though, that any changes to the facilities that

may affect the children must be immediately brought to the attention of Ofsted.

Points to consider

❋ What are your procedures when children leave the premises?

❋ How do you ensure that doors, gates and other areas are secure?

❋ How do you help parents and staff to remember to close doors?

❋ Do you obtain written permission from parents when children are to be collected by another adult? (You could provide slips for parents to sign.)

❋ Do all staff remember that visitors must sign in and out of the setting?

Outings (page 24)

The focus on outings is about ensuring that children are safe. You will need to provide a full risk assessment for every type of outing and, although not stated, it would be sensible to do so in writing. Before going on an actual outing, you should check that the risk assessment for its type is still valid. For example, a risk assessment has already been done for taking children out to the local shop to buy ingredients, but on the day you notice that a diversion is in place and there is more

You will need to provide a full risk assessment for each type of outing

traffic which will mean that additional staff might be needed.

It is left completely to the setting to decide whether there should be an increase in adult to child ratios. This is a positive move but make sure that adult–child ratios are considered in your risk assessments. It is also important to read the statutory guidance; while much of this is commonsense, it is worth noting that you are expected to have records about the vehicles that you are using, insurance details and named drivers.

Points to consider

* Do you have a risk assessment form for outings?

* Are risk assessments carried out for each type of outing and in advance?

* Does your risk assessment form contain a statement about adult to child ratios?

* Are you keeping records of vehicles, insurance details and drivers?

* Do you check that drivers using their own cars have adequate insurance cover?

Equality of Opportunities (page 25)

This requirement is about ensuring that every child is given the opportunity to flourish and that policies and procedures are in place to meet each child's needs. To meet the legal requirements for this, you will need to have an equality of opportunities policy and, if you receive any government funding, a Special Educational Needs policy based on the SEN Code of Practice. (You can obtain a SEN Code of Practice by telephoning 0845 602 2260 or 0845 600 9506 and asking for reference DFES 0581/2001 or by going to http://publications. teachernet.gov.uk/ and using the reference number in the search box.)

Points to consider

* Do you have an up-to-date equality of opportunities policy?

* Does the policy include the information required by the statutory guidance on page 25?

* Do your activities, routines and other policies link to your equality of opportunities policy?

* Do you need to follow the SEN Code of Practice?

* Do you have a policy on Special Educational Needs?

'The provider must promote the good health of the children, take necessary steps to prevent the spread of infection, and take appropriate action when they are ill'

Medicines (page 26)

You will need to have a policy on administering medicines, and it is clear that as part of the policy the needs of children must be taken into consideration. (This is to avoid situations whereby children might be discriminated against on the basis of 'we're not allowed to give medication.' This is the type of information that parents will need to know during the admissions process.)

You will need to ensure that some medicines are easily accessible at all times during the session

Points to consider

✳ Do you have an administering medicines policy?

✳ Is the policy up to date so that it conforms to the statutory requirements and guidance?

✳ Are medicines that need to be easily accessible, such as inhalers, available at all times during the session?

✳ How do you prevent non-authorised access to medicines that are being stored in the fridge?

✳ Do parents know and understand your policy on medicines?

✳ Are you keeping records that show which medicines are stored and when medicines are administered?

✳ Do you have written permission from parents for each medicine that a child takes?

Illnesses and injuries (page 26)

The requirements for illnesses and injuries are straightforward, although you will need to read the section carefully. One point to note is that you will need at all times, including outings, a member of staff who has a paediatric first aid certificate. It is therefore important in group care settings that several members of staff are trained so that outings, illnesses, holidays and shift patterns do not leave the setting without a trained member of staff. For details as to what the paediatric training must include, you should read Appendix 1 of the Practice Guidance (page 21).

In the event of a serious accident, illness or death of a child in your care, you would need to notify Ofsted and local child protection agencies. You also need to make sure that parents know what the procedure is when children are ill or infectious; you are therefore likely to need a policy for this. (Interestingly, notifiable diseases come under the food and drink specific legal requirements; see below.)

On a positive note, there is no ban on animals in the setting, provided that they are safe and do not pose a health risk to children.

Points to consider

✳ Do you or other staff have a current paediatric first aid certificate that covers the content listed on page 21 of the Practice Guidance (Appendix 1)?

✳ Is there a first aid box on the premises?

✳ Are the contents of the first aid box appropriate to meet the needs of children?

✳ Do you have a policy about illnesses and injuries and how you would deal with these in the setting?

✳ Do you have an accident book and a way of notifying parents about minor injuries and any treatment given?

Food and drink (page 27)

As suggested in the title, the focus of this requirement is food and drink, although watch out for the need to alert Ofsted if two or more children have food poisoning or notifiable diseases. (A list of currently notifiable diseases is included in the appendix of this book, on page 255.)

To comply with the requirements, you must make sure that children have access to fresh water at all times and that if you are providing food it is healthy, balanced and nutritious. You should also be preparing food in line with the latest food hygiene legislation. A good source of current information is the Food Standards Agency's website (www.foodstandards.gov.uk) – the site is easy to navigate and will help you determine what is healthy food and how to comply with food legislation.

Points to consider

✳ Is food handling included as part of your induction of new staff?

✳ Are you aware of current food hygiene legislation?

✳ Is your menu balanced and based on the nutritional needs of the children?

※ Do you have records of children's dietary needs and how do you ensure that these are considered when providing food and drinks?

※ How do you ensure that children have access to fresh drinking water?

Smoking (page 27)

This is fairly straightforward – children have to be in a smoke-free environment. The statutory guidance also makes it clear that smoking will not be allowed in any play areas.

Points to consider

※ Are 'no smoking' signs put up in play areas to prevent parents and other adults from smoking there?

※ Do your policies on smoking comply with the latest legislation in England?

'Children's behaviour must be managed effectively and in a manner appropriate for their stage of development and particular individual needs'

Behaviour management (page 28)

This requirement is about the way in which behaviour is managed. There are several points that are worth picking up on. First, you must have a behaviour management policy and in group settings a named member of staff who will be responsible for behaviour issues. Your policy should incorporate the specific legal requirements about corporal punishment. The essence of the legal requirements is that not only must you not use corporal punishment, such as smacking, but you should also avert its use by others who care for the child. This is quite significant and means that in theory you should intervene if you were to see a grandmother slap a child or you knew that this was taking place.

You will need an effective behaviour management policy that reflects the specific legal requirements

Points to consider

※ Do you have an effective behaviour management policy that reflects the specific legal requirements?

※ In group settings, do you have a member of staff who is responsible for behaviour issues and can support other staff?

※ Do you cover behaviour management as part of your induction?

※ Are parents aware of your behaviour management policy and in particular the requirement for you to intervene should you see their children being subjected to corporal punishment?

Suitable People

The diagram opposite shows the three general legal requirements for Suitable People, as well as the areas to which the specific legal requirements and statutory guidance apply.

General welfare requirements

Suitable people

General legal requirements

'Providers must ensure that adults looking after children, or having unsupervised access to them, are suitable to do so.'

'Adults looking after children must have appropriate qualifications, training, skills and knowledge.'

'Staffing arrangements must be organised to ensure safety and to meet the needs of the children.'

Areas to which specific legal requirement and statutory guidance apply

- Safe recruitment
- Alcohol and other substances

'Providers must ensure that adults looking after children, or having unsupervised access to them, are suitable to do so'

Safe recruitment (pages 29–30)

This requirement is about ensuring that anyone who will come into unsupervised contact with the children you are caring for is safe to do so. You will need to ensure that you have read each of the points and, ideally, incorporate them into your recruitment and safeguarding children policies. The crux of these points is to ensure that anyone coming into unsupervised contact with children must have been CRB checked and that you have kept records of doing so. CRB stands for Criminal Records Bureau and information about the checking procedure can be found on its website (www.crb.gov.uk). In addition, there is a list of circumstances in which you must contact Ofsted to inform them of any changes. These include changes to staffing, people living with childminders and changes to premises (see page 30).

Points to consider

❊ Do you keep up-to-date records of staff details and CRB checks?

❊ Do you take up references of all members of staff?

❊ Do your recruitment and safeguarding children policies reflect the legal requirements?

❊ Are you aware of the qualification framework when you are recruiting?

Alcohol and other substances (page 30)

Not surprisingly, the legal requirements state that you must not be under the influence of alcohol. This does not just mean not drinking while children are present, but ensuring that you are 'free' of alcohol if alcohol had been taken in the preceding hours. The legal requirements also look at other substances. These might be illegal drugs or over-the-counter remedies such as hayfever tablets and prescription drugs. The key is to ensure that any other substances are not affecting the ability to work with children.

Points to consider

✳ How are staff informed about the requirements regarding alcohol and other substances?

'Adults looking after children must have appropriate qualifications, training, skills and knowledge' (page 31)

This requirement is about the minimum levels of training and qualifications that are mandatory in settings. Note that if you are a childminder, it is essential that you have a current paediatric first aid certificate and that you keep your training up to date. If you are currently working as an unqualified member of staff, you will need to think about completing a qualification that will give you a full Level 2. The term 'full' is used because some courses and qualifications are longer than others; a full Level 2 or 3 is likely to be a qualification which covers more knowledge. To check which qualifications are considered 'full', visit the following website www.cwdc.org.uk.

Points to consider

✳ If you are a childminder, do you have a current paediatric first aid certificate?

✳ Do you have a staff appraisal programme?

✳ Do you have an induction training programme and handbook?

✳ Do you have a staff training programme or, if you are a childminder, a professional development plan?

✳ Do you keep records of training that has been completed?

'Staffing arrangements must be organised to ensure safety and to meet the needs of the children' (page 32)

The main focus of this section is adult to child ratios and how they should be applied. The thrust is also to make sure that staffing arrangements are built around the needs of the children rather than those of the organisation. You must read this section in conjunction with Appendix 2: Specific legal requirements for ratios of adults to children, on pages 49–51.

The key when reading this section and Appendix 2 is the need for adults to be working directly with children, except when they are sleeping. It is worth reading the third bullet point on page 49 as it is made clear that sufficient staff must be available to cover staff breaks and working with parents. The requirement for adults to be working directly with children in order to be in ratio may mean that an overhaul of routines will be required, for example if 20 three-year-olds are grouped together for a story while the other staff tidy away equipment. The need to use staff to work directly with children will in the long term produce results. Young children desperately need the attention of adults and when the right adult to child ratios are used, it creates a win-win situation for everyone. Children's behaviour improves and adults usually find their work more rewarding.

Points to consider

✳ Do you have policies for how to deal with unexpected emergencies such as staff absences?

✳ Are you planning group activities with adult to child ratios in mind?

✳ How are staff breaks covered?

✳ How would you manage to stay in ratio if a parent needed to talk to their child's key worker or see their child's records?

Suitable premises, environment and equipment

The diagram opposite shows the general legal requirement for Suitable premises, environment and equipment, as well as the areas to which the specific legal requirements and statutory guidance apply.

General welfare requirement

> Suitable premises, environment and equipment

General legal requirement

> 'Outdoor and indoor spaces, furniture, equipment and toys, must be safe and suitable for their purpose.'

Areas to which specific legal requirement and statutory guidance apply

> • Risk assessment
> • Premises

'Outdoor and indoor spaces, furniture, equipment and toys, must be safe and suitable for their purpose'

Risk assessment (page 33)

A key way in which children can be kept safe is by adults being aware of the risks in the environment. You will need to conduct an overall risk assessment of your setting at least once a year. The risk assessment will need to be a full one and the statutory guidance states that it will comprise 'anything with which a child may come into contact'. Your risk assessment will also show which aspects of the environment will need to be regularly checked, such as toilets and the sand tray. Once identified in your risk assessment as requiring regular checks, you will then need to set up a recording system that shows that these checks have been carried out.

It is worth remembering that outings will need their own specific risk assessment (see page 24). You will also need a health and safety policy which must take account of the latest health and safety and food hygiene legislation.

A key way in which children can be kept safe is by adults being aware of the risks in the environment

Points to consider

✳ Do you have an up-to-date health and safety policy that takes account of recent legislation?

✳ Does your staff induction training and handbook help staff to understand their role and responsibilities?

✳ Do you have a full risk assessment?

✳ Is this reviewed at least once a year?

✳ Do you have records to show how you are checking specific areas?

Premises (pages 34–36)

As the title suggests, this requirement is about premises. It is also about ensuring that settings have good evacuation procedures.

The first point on page 34 is about the need to notify Ofsted of any significant changes to the premises or something that might affect the smooth running of the setting, for example repair work. You also have to let Ofsted know about any changes to the outside areas. This might mean that if you redesign your outdoor area by adding a large piece of equipment, pond or changing the fencing, you would need to let Ofsted know.

The rest of the requirements on page 34 are about fire precautions and procedures for fire. You are required to keep records of fire drills which must include details of any problems encountered and how they are to be avoided.

Points to consider

✳ Do you need a fire prevention officer to visit your premises? This might be worth doing if it has been a while since your last visit.

✳ Do you have the necessary fire detection and control equipment?

✳ Do you have a system in place for testing alarms and checking that fire doors work?

✳ Do you have a procedure written down and displayed to ensure that everyone knows how to safely evacuate the premises?

✳ Do you have records of your fire drills?

✳ Are your fire exits identifiable and does your layout take them into account?

Pages 35 and 36 on premises look at the physical space and how it is to be used. It is important to read through each of the requirements carefully, although if you are a childminder you will find that not all apply to you, for example the number of toilets available.

You should be aware that the requirements on page 35 state that you should 'as far as is reasonable' be organising your premises and equipment to ensure that they are suitable for children with disabilities. It is also worth noting that while in group care settings babies should have their own room and they should also be able to mix with older children. This is something that I am pleased to see since it means that siblings can see each other and also that babies and toddlers are not isolated from the rest of the group.

Another welcome note in the statutory guidance is the requirement to provide an area for children to sleep and rest, which needs to be either separate or partitioned off from the play space. You may also note that each child who sleeps will need their own bed linen.

The requirements on premises are not only about the indoor environment, as there is an obligation to provide either an outdoor play area or, in settings where this is not possible, a daily outing to an outdoor play space.

Points to consider

✳ Is your lighting sufficient in view of the statutory guidance?

✳ How are you ensuring that children have access to an outdoor play space?

✳ Are babies and toddlers able to have contact with older children?

✳ Are you displaying your current public liability insurance?

✳ Is there a space set aside where records can be stored and a space where parents can talk to staff in private?

Organisation (page 37)

There is one general legal requirement for Organisation: 'Providers must plan and organise their systems to ensure that every child receives an enjoyable and challenging learning and development experience that is tailored to meet their individual needs.' While Organisation covers one meagre page, its significance should not be underestimated. Here in some ways is the heart of the EYFS.

'Providers must plan and organise their systems to ensure that every child receives an enjoyable and challenging learning and development experience that is tailored to meet their individual needs'

There is a huge amount to unpick in the specific legal requirements and statutory guidance. Most of this is about good practice that some settings were already showing but had not previously become a legal requirement. It is important to read each one of the statements carefully. The focus is about meeting children's individual needs, and this is reflected in the need to observe and plan for them, meet their emotional needs for care and attention, and provide them with appropriate stimulation. Watch out for these key points.

Key person

Each child has to have a key person and this is not just about reporting and recording. A key person is meant to develop a genuine bond with the child. This might mean that group settings will need to think about their routines to ensure that children spend enough time with their key person.

Points to consider

- Do you have a settling-in plan for individual children?

- How do you manage if a child does not seem to respond to their key person?

- How do you check that a child has developed a strong relationship with their key person?

- How much time do children spend with their key person?

Observations

You will need to observe children regularly and keep records of the observations. The records should show how children are making progress towards the early learning goals.

Points to consider

- Are you observing children in a range of different play situations?

- Are you observing children during child-initiated play?

- Do you share your observations with parents?

- Do you encourage parents to contribute towards the observation process?

- Do your observations link to your planning?

Planning

You will need to have a comprehensive planning system which is based on the observations from children, the EYFS and, if appropriate, children's individual education plans.

Points to consider

- Do your plans reflect children's individual needs and interests?

- Does your planning show how you are going to work towards the early learning goals?

- Do you have plans that are medium or long term as well as short term?

- Are parents aware of your planning system?

Indoor and outdoor play

You are required to provide activities and play both in and out of doors.

Points to consider

- Are a range of play activities planned for outdoors (not just physical play)?

- Are outdoor activities shown in the planning?

Activities

You will need to plan for activities that are adult-led (I think of these as 'Delia Smith' activities where adults are clearly leading the way because they are telling children what they need to do and maybe even how to do it) and child-initiated or free-play activities. The activities and routine of the setting must be enjoyable and challenging – not just for the children as a whole but for each child. This may mean a reorganisation of how you work. Being flexible and trying to do many small group activities including story time is probably the key to managing this. Once children are in large groups, it is likely that one or two of them will not be as interested or will not find the activity as stimulating.

The activities and routine of the setting must be enjoyable and challenging – not just for the children as a whole but for each child

Points to consider

✳ Are your activities planned around individual and groups of children's interests?

✳ Do you have a balance of different types of play activities?

✳ What is the balance of adult-led to child-initiated play?

✳ How do you adapt group activities to ensure that they meet individual children's needs?

Documentation

The diagram below shows the general legal requirement for Documentation, as well as the areas to which the specific legal requirements and statutory guidance apply.

General welfare requirement

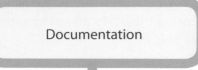

Documentation

General legal requirement

'Providers must maintain records, policies and procedures required for the safe and efficient management of the settings and to meet the needs of the children.'

Areas to which specific legal requirement and statutory guidance apply

- Data
- Providers' records

Linguistic diversity

In the statutory guidance for Organisation, you are required to find ways of 'developing and using [children's] home language in their play and learning' (page 37). This might seem at first glance to be impossible unless you speak the child's home language or there are groups of children who are speaking the same language. On reflection, I suspect that the way to manage this is to work closely with parents. It might be that parents can repeat some play activities at home so that children are able to enjoy them in their home language. You may also be able to find DVDs, CD-ROMs, toys and books that are based in the child's home language.

'Providers must maintain records, policies and procedures required for the safe and efficient management of the settings and to meet the needs of the children'

Data (pages 38–39)

This requirement is straightforward – you simply have to read this through and check that you are collecting the correct and sufficient information. Whether you need to keep information for the Early Years Census depends on whether children are being funded by the local authority for their early years place.

Points to consider

✳ Are you collecting the information set out on pages 38–39?

✳ Do you make it clear to parents that they do not need to indicate their child's ethnicity unless they wish to?

Providers' records (page 40)

This section deals with the records that you must keep. It needs to be read very carefully. Remember that in addition to the records stated, you will also need other records such as administration of medicines, accidents as well as policies. It is important, too, that you are up to date with the Data Protection Act; this concerns the storage of personal information, whether on computers or on paper. For more details about the Data Protection Act visit the Information Commissioner's Office website (www. ico.gov.uk).

Points to consider

✳ Are you displaying your certificate of registration?

✳ Are your records easily accessible?

✳ If you are working in a group setting, do other members of staff know where to find key documents and records?

✳ Are you keeping confidential records secure?

✳ Is your knowledge of the Data Protection Act 1998 up to date?

Practice Guidance

Introduction

This section looks at the Practice Guidance, the areas of Learning and Development within and some sample activities that might be useful.

The structure of the Practice Guidance for the EYFS

Before you come to the actual pages containing the areas of Learning and Development, there are three sections. Each section is quite short, but probably worth a quick read to help you absorb the ethos and direction of the EYFS. The idea is that you read these sections in tandem with the Statutory Framework.

Section 1 – Implementing the EYFS

This gives you a general overview and some issues to think about when planning for the EYFS, such as partnership with parents and flexible provision.

Section 2 – Learning and Development

This section briefly explains how the guidance relating to the areas of Learning and Development has been put together. The real substance of the educational programme is surprisingly not at this point but is a few pages later in the appendix!

Section 3 – Welfare Requirements

This gives a little more guidance as to the Welfare Requirements. It is important that you read this in tandem with the Statutory Framework, but do not read it by itself otherwise you will fail to gain a complete understanding of your legal obligations.

Appendix 1

This lists the criteria for effective paediatric first aid qualification.

Appendix 2: Areas of Learning and Development

For most of you, this is the section that you are probably most interested in, although it seems amazing that it has been put in the appendix! While it might be tempting to only look at this section, you should take on board the ethos of the EYFS (its Themes and Principles) while looking at this section.

Starting out

I am a great fan of making documents easier to navigate through, so I would suggest that you find some stickers or page markers and begin by separating the guidance into the areas of Learning and Development.

The areas of Learning and Development

There are six areas of Learning and Development. For those of you who have previously worked with the Foundation Stage, they may already seem familiar.

- Personal, Social and Emotional Development (PSE)
- Communication, Language and Literacy (CLL)
- Problem Solving, Reasoning and Numeracy (PRN)
- Knowledge and Understanding of the World (KUW)
- Physical Development (PD)
- Creative Development (CD)

Each area of Learning and Development is subdivided further into what were referred to in the old Foundation Stage as 'aspects of learning'. The table opposite shows the aspects of learning within each of the areas of Learning and Development.

Early learning goals

For each area of Learning and Development, a list of goals known as early learning goals (ELGs) has been devised, so that children's progress can be measured. The aim is that by the end of the Reception year, most children will have reached these goals.

If you are working with babies or toddlers, the early learning goals should be used to give you a sense of direction as to what children later on will need to achieve, rather than for you to plan against. The early learning goals for each area of Learning and Development are listed in the Appendix of this book (pages 256–7).

Personal, Social and Emotional Development

- Dispositions and Attitudes
- Self-confidence and Self-esteem
- Making Relationships
- Behaviour and Self-control
- Self-care
- Sense of Community

Communication, Language and Literacy

- Language for Communication
- Language for Thinking
- Linking Sounds and Letters
- Reading
- Writing
- Handwriting

Problem Solving, Reasoning and Numeracy

- Numbers as Labels and for Counting
- Calculating
- Shape, Space and Measures

Knowledge and Understanding of the World

- Exploration and Investigation
- Designing and Making
- ICT
- Time
- Place
- Communities

Physical Development

- Movement and Space
- Health and Bodily Awareness
- Using Equipment and Materials

Creative Development

- Being Creative – Responding to Experiences, Expressing and Communicating Ideas
- Exploring Media and Materials
- Creating Music and Dance
- Developing Imagination and Imaginative Play

Looking at the structure of the Practice Guidance

The structure of the Practice Guidance is similar for each of the areas of Learning and Development.

- The initial page gives some introduction about the area of Learning and Development and some general points about how it should be provided for.
- Next, you will find the pages that break the aspect of Learning and Development down into stages. The diagram below shows what you are looking for.

Effective practice

These are suggestions as to how you should practically work with children; do not feel that you have to do every one in turn. It is a good idea to read them through in order again, to get a flavour of what you should be doing.

Planning and resourcing

These are ideas for activities or resources that you might need in order to deliver the aspect of learning and development.

Creative Development

Being Creative – Responding to Experiences, Expressing and Communicating Ideas

	Development matters	Look, listen and note	Effective practice	Planning and resourcing
Birth–11 months	■ Use movement and sensory exploration to connect with their immediate environment.	■ Expressions of emotion shown through the movements of fingers, arms and bodies.	■ Use gentle touch to trace 'Round and Round the Garden' or to pat hands for 'Pat-a-Cake' with young babies.	■ Make available resources such as soft feathers, silk squares and pom-poms which offer sensory interest to young babies.
8–20 months	■ Respond to what they see, hear, smell, touch and feel.	■ Young children's favourite materials, music, lights and aromas.	■ Maintain the calm atmosphere of a light room or area by playing quiet music so that young children can rest from stimulation for short periods.	■ Vary sensory experiences by placing herbs such as basil, parsley or sage in muslin bags for babies to squeeze or catch with their fingers.
16–26 months	■ Express themselves through physical action and sound. ■ Explore by repeating patterns of play.	■ The ways that young children may repeat actions or make tuneful sounds as they climb steps, or step up and down from a stool.	■ Support children's patterns of play in different activities, for example, transporting blocks to the sand area.	■ Introduce young children to light fabric curtains, full-length mirrors and soft play cubes for hiding in, peeping at and crawling through.
22–36 months	■ Seek to make sense of what they see, hear, smell, touch and feel. ■ Begin to use representation as a form of communication.	■ Word plays, signs, body language and gestures that young children use in response to their experiences, for example, a child may jump up and down or whirr around when they are excited, or eagerly engaged.	■ Help children to value their creative responses by your interest in the way they move, represent or express their mood.	■ Provide props such as streamers for children to wave to make swirling lines, or place shiny mobiles, made from unwanted CDs, in the trees to whirl around in the wind.
30–? months	■ Use language and other forms of communication to share the things they create, or to indicate personal satisfaction or frustration. ■ Explore and experience using a range of senses and movement.	■ The ways children capture their experiences by, for example, finding materials to make wings from large pieces of red paper after watching some ladybirds in the garden.	■ Provide appropriate materials and extend children's thinking through involvement in their play, using questions thoughtfully and appropriately. ■ Encourage children to describe their experiences.	■ Ensure that there is enough time for children to express their thoughts, ideas and feelings in a variety of ways, such as in role-play, by painting and by responding to music.

Age groupings

These replace the old 'stepping stones' of the Foundation Stage; in fact, the term 'stepping stones' has totally disappeared. While you might find it frustrating that there are no definite age suggestions for what to do with children or what to look out for, this is deliberate. There was a lot of concern that some practitioners might look up the age of the child on a chart and then robotically follow the suggestions without thinking about the child's needs. You will therefore need to work out from the Development matters column, where you think that the children you work with 'fit'.

Development matters

This is the column on the left-hand side. At the very bottom of the column are the early learning goals. They are printed in bold and placed in the 40–60+ months section. This is deliberate because they are intended for children at the end of the Early Years Foundation Stage.

Throughout this column are statements that you should look at and consider how they relate to the children that you are working with. From this you can then go on to think about activities and opportunities that will be appropriate for them. Note that you might find that the Development matters statements may not be a perfect fit for the children that you are working with; they are designed to be a guide only. You may also find that in some aspects, your children seem to be more 'developed' than in others.

Being Creative – Responding to Experiences, Expressing and Communicating Ideas

	Development matters	Look, listen and note	Effective practice	Planning and resourcing
30–? months	■ Capture experiences and responses with music, dance, paint and other materials or words. ■ Develop preferences for forms of expression.	The ways in which children explore materials and the effects they can create, for example, making swirling lines with scarves and streamers by twirling round.	■ Be interested in children's responses, observing their actions and listening carefully.	■ Encourage children to discuss and appreciate the beauty around them in nature and the environment.
40–?+ months **Early learning goals**	■ Talk about personal intentions, describing what they were trying to do. ■ Respond to comments and questions, entering into dialogue about their creations. ■ Make comparisons and create new connections. ■ **Respond in a variety of ways to what they see, hear, smell, touch and feel.** ■ **Express and communicate their ideas, thoughts and feelings by using a widening range of materials, suitable tools, imaginative and role-play, movement, designing and making, and a variety of songs and musical instruments.**	■ The connections children make as they respond to different experiences, for example, remembering being cold at Diwali and seeing the cheery lights may inspire one child to begin to dance like the flames of the Diwali lamps. ■ How children respond to new experiences and how they respond differently to similar experiences, for example, a child may run around moving their arms rhythmically when they see or hear a train, or run along calling "train, train" as if they are trying to catch up with it, while another day they may want to draw, paint or represent the power of the train. ■ How children design and create, either using their own ideas or those of others.	■ Support children in expressing opinions and introduce language such as 'like', 'dislike', 'prefer' and 'disagree'. ■ Be alert to children's changing interest and the way they respond to experiences differently when they are in a happy, sad or reflective mood.	■ Introduce language that enables children to talk about their experiences in greater depth and detail. ■ Provide children with examples of how other people have responded to experiences, engage them in discussions of these examples and help them to make links and connections. ■ Provide and organise resources and materials so children can make their own choices in order to express their ideas. ■ Be sensitive to the needs of children who may not be able to express themselves easily in English, using interpreter support from known adults, or strategies such as picture cards to enable children to express preferences.

Look, listen and note

These are ideas for things that you may look out for when working with children. They are not intended to be a checklist, but are useful pointers, particularly if you find yourself working with an age group for the first time. Read them through to get a feeling of what you might be able to observe.

Creative Dev...

Using the Practice Guidance pages

It is essential to use commonsense when looking at the Practice Guidance pages. They were not designed as a step-by-step guide, so you must work out what your children need and what feels right to do with them. It is important, though, that you understand the 'flavour' of what children need to be doing in each of the aspects of learning and development.

A guide to working with the areas of Learning and Development

In this section we look at each of the areas of Learning and Development in turn, along with more detailed suggestions about how you could deliver them.

Personal, Social and Emotional Development

This is an important area of every child's development. Research has clearly shown that children who are secure, confident and know how to manage their own behaviour are more likely to develop friendships as well as achieve and cope with life's setbacks. This area of Learning and Development should be taken very seriously, so it is essential in my view to stress its importance when working with parents, particularly those parents who tend to see achievement only in terms of 'what their child can do'.

This area of Learning and Development is subdivided into six aspects, as shown in the spider diagram below.

Embedding Personal, Social and Emotional Development into routines and activities

While there are specific activities that you can plan for this area of Learning and Development, most of a child's journey towards the early learning goals will be taken because the way you work with them and your routine allows them to develop. The starting point for every aspect is that children, regardless of age, and their parents feel comfortable about being in the setting and have a key person with whom they have a strong relationship.

Settling in without tears – the key person

I feel strongly that no child should start their care and education by being distressed. Settling in and therefore transition must be a priority. All children, including babies, need to be familiar and have made a relationship with their key person before they should be expected to separate from their parents or carers. This might mean that settling in will take a little longer, but the pay-offs for children, their parents and staff are immense.

I see settling in as an individual process rather than an event. Below I have described the rough process that is likely to work best when children need to separate from their parents or main carers. The same process can be adapted when there is any sort of a transition, for example when a baby moves to a toddler room or when a childminder takes a child to a pre-school.

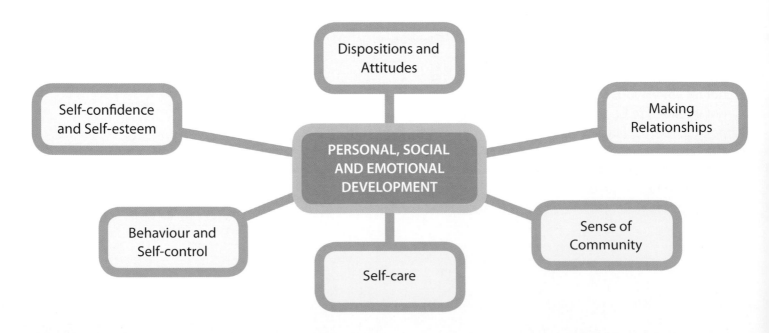

1. Understanding the individual needs of children and their parents

It is always worth doing some research in order to develop an understanding of the needs of the child and quite often their parents. A good starting point is to find out what any previous experiences of separation have been like for the child and their parents. In general terms, children who have been distressed, even if later on they have eventually settled, are likely to need more support as trauma memories run quite deep and quickly re-emerge. You might also like to talk to parents about their feelings – it is normal for parents to feel unsure about leaving their children as they have a strong attachment. Reassuring parents that they are not 'silly' because they are worrying can go a long way to reducing anxiety, and this in turn can help parents not to transfer their anxiety to the child.

It is also worth finding out how many different transitions the child has experienced. For example, a two-year-old who has already had three au pairs, two nannies and is about to start with a childminder may be cautious of a new relationship for fear that the person may disappear again!

2. Building a relationship with the key person

Once you get a feel for the child's and parents' needs, the next step is to begin the process of helping the child to feel comfortable with their key person. This is in some ways a two-part process. The key person must 'step forwards' to get to know the child, while the parents or current carer should take a slight 'step backwards' to allow this to happen. It is often worth explaining this to parents, so that when they bring the child to you they know what they need to do. I also believe that children need to associate coming into the setting with playing or being with their key person rather than coming to the conclusion that this is a place 'where I play with mummy or daddy'.

Everyone has their own way of 'making friends' with children; for me, I find that a puppet is useful, particularly for children whose stage of development or personality means that they are wary of 'strangers'. The puppet tends to be so attractive that children cannot help but be curious and so they tend to forget about me!

Once the child has started to get to know you, it is then important to see whether the developing bond between you is sufficient for them to cope while their parent or carer is absent for a moment. This is a test

run for the actual separation. For some children, they will need several visits before they will be ready, while others will be happy after ten minutes or so.

Your Questions Answered

How will we know when children have made an attachment with their key person?

Checking that children are developing a relationship with their key person should be something that you actually look out for in observations when children first join you. Once children are starting to show signs of feeling confident and comfortable with their key person, then is the moment when parents or their current carers can leave. For many toddlers particularly, the time spent away from their parents or current carers will need to be built up.

Signs that children have made an attachment include:

- showing visible joy when they see their key person
- disappointment and even distress when their key person is absent
- acute awareness of where their key person is at any time, for example a toddler may go outside to join their key person
- seeking reassurance and support from their key person even if another adult is closer
- being physically relaxed when alongside their key person and seeking physical reassurance by 'snuggling in'.

Aspects within Personal, Social and Emotional Development

Dispositions and Attitudes (pages 24–26)

This is an important aspect as it is about interest, perseverance, levels of engagement and concentration. Embedding this into the way you work means making sure that you are providing sufficiently stimulating opportunities for children and giving them the time in order to settle down and focus their attention. Child-initiated play is particularly essential in helping children work towards the early learning goals for this area.

Self-confidence and Self-esteem (pages 27–29)

Research carried out as far back as the 1960s demonstrated a link between self-esteem and children's achievement. Embedding this into the way you work means more than just praising children; it also means helping them learn that they 'can do' and supporting them to express feelings and to become thoughtful in relation to others. This might mean creating opportunities for children to help each other as part of the routine and, of course, child-initiated activities. The key person also plays an essential role here, as the child should feel valued by their key person and accepted for who they are rather than just for what they can do.

Making Relationships (pages 30–32)

This aspect needs to start with ensuring that children have a settled and close relationship with their key person. Not only will this fulfil the statutory guidance, it will also help children to develop the socialisation skills needed to make relationships.

It is important to understand that there are other factors that will influence children's ability to cooperate with others and take turns, etc. Language in particular seems to be important and this often means that until this is developed, toddlers and in some cases older children may find it hard to understand the need to share and play cooperatively. Embedding this into the session entails supporting children with emerging language and providing opportunities for them to play freely with each other. You will also need to stand back sometimes and gauge whether children can resolve their own difficulties, for example whose turn it is, through negotiation.

Behaviour and Self-control (pages 33–34)

This is a good example of an aspect that must be embedded into the way you work. Children can only show wanted behaviour when they feel secure and settled – the starting point is therefore a strong relationship with their key person. As with Making Relationships, language and cognitive development are factors that influence behaviour and self-control. This requires working on some children's language first in order that they can begin to show wanted behaviour and self-control. In terms of your sessions, it means that children, even babies, need opportunities to help and take responsibility as this extends their locus of control. For example, a baby may hold a rattle while you change their nappy, while an older child might put out the beakers ready for a snack.

Self-care (pages 35–36)

This is often about ensuring that adults have built sufficient time into the routine in order to allow children to practise and develop self-care skills. Children can only learn to dress themselves if they are given the opportunity to practise and are supported by encouraging adults. Self-care skills are a good example of the way in which parents and practitioners can work together, as they can be learnt and developed at home as well as in settings. Parents may therefore be able to contribute towards your observations and planning by talking to you about what their child can manage at home.

Sense of Community (pages 37–38)

This is another aspect that is interdependent with other areas of a child's development, particularly language but also feelings of self-confidence. Embedding this into practice requires checking that your way of working with children, parents, staff and others is inclusive. This is because children tend to learn their value system from key adults who interact with them. In practical terms it is also important that your routines, activities and resources reflect and value differences, for example including nursery songs in a child's home language, different types of cooking utensils in the home corner and food that widens children's palates.

This aspect links to Communities within the Knowledge and Understanding of the World area of Learning and Development.

Communication, Language and Literacy

While all of the areas of Learning and Development are interrelated, this along with Personal, Social and Emotional Development is one which I feel contributes greatly to children's later success both academically and socially. Children who have strong language or languages find it easier to control their behaviour, organise their thinking and process information in 'word format', for example instructions. This means that providing children are emotionally secure, they will find it easier to control their behaviour. Language also affects relationships and so children with good language skills, again assuming they are emotionally secure, will often quickly be able to cooperate with other children and develop friendships. Finally, language significantly impacts on children's ability to learn to read and write. In my experience, children

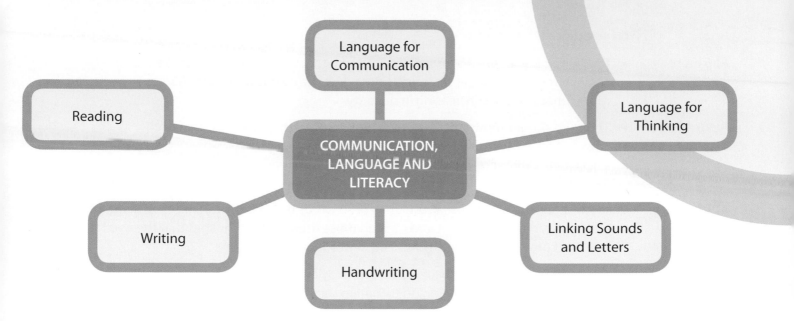

need to be fluent speakers of English when they start in Reception class so that they can 'crack' the code of phonics and go on to be able to write.

This area of Learning and Development has six aspects, as shown in the spider diagram above.

Embedding Communication, Language and Literacy into your practice

Early language is learnt through relationships. Babies, toddlers and children who have a good relationship with their key person will be motivated to communicate with them. This is why building good relationships from the beginning is so important. Language cannot be 'taught' as such, instead it is 'caught'. To help children of all ages 'catch' language, you have to create the time to interact properly with them. This means settling down with them, making eye contact and acting as a language partner rather than an instructor. Language and communication should be a fun, spontaneous and shared experience rather than something that 'has to be done'.

Points to consider

Supporting children's language development

✳ How much time is available for one-to-one interactions?

✳ Is the style of interaction instructional and functional or social with shared thinking?

✳ Are everyday tasks seen as language opportunities, for example getting ready to go out, changing nappies, tidying up?

Assessing children's language development

Because language plays such a critical role in children's development, it is essential to assess its development. This is particularly important if you are working with children under three years old or so. I have found it helpful to use an MP3 player to assess children's language as this is quite discreet and you can 'capture' the intonation as well as the grammatical aspects of emerging language. It can also provide you with a record of how speech is developing. You do not need to record for long periods of time – a burst of a minute or so is often sufficient. Parents can also contribute by recording at home.

Once you have recorded speech, it is important to assess it. While the 'Look, listen and note' section of the Practice Guidance provides you with various ideas to reflect on, the statements are not linked to ages. While I can happily accept that there is a variance between children when it comes to language, it can also be useful to have some milestones to look out for. Checking a child's development against these will help you to decide whether the child might need additional support or an assessment from other professionals.

Age	Developmental milestone
At 6 months	• Check that babies are making eye contact and that they enjoy being spoken to. • Listen out for babbling and sounds. Check over the next few months that these are becoming more tuneful and are increasing in quantity.
At 10 months	• The child should show great interest in pointing to attract adults' attention. • Look out for gestures such as 'bye, bye'. • Check that babies have some words that they clearly understand the meaning of, for example 'bottle', 'mum'. Most babies should understand around 15 or so words by 10 months.
At 18 months	Children should be able to speak about 10 or so words that adults working closely with the child can recognise. When counting words, add in those from other languages that the child is using. Expect that some children may have 50 or so words at this point.
At 2 years	• Children should have plenty of words, probably around 200. • Check that children are beginning to join up some words to form mini-sentences.
At 3 years	Most of the child's speech should be understood by someone who does not know the child.
At 4 years	Check for fluency – complete sentences that are grammatical. There should be the odd error remaining and the odd sound not being produced correctly. There should be no 'babyish' speech.

Above is a table that shows some milestones that you might find helpful.

Supporting children who will be learning English alongside another language

It is increasingly common to find children whose home language is not English. In Wales, of course, bilingualism is increasingly becoming the norm. My own children had French as their home language, learning their English 'outside' the home from carers, teachers and other children. Supporting children who will be learning more than one language is essential so that they can go on to make friends and cope in the education system.

Understanding the context for language

The starting point is to understand that the contexts for children who will be learning more than one language vary enormously. This means that a 'one size fits all' approach to supporting children will not meet all needs. It is worth finding out from parents what languages are spoken, for how long and when. Exposure to language is a key factor in fluency, so even though a child might be exposed to three languages at home, the chances are that one or two of the languages will be stronger than the third.

Separating the languages – essential for babies and toddlers

One of the potential problems when children learn more than one language as a baby or toddler is that

their brain may take a while to understand that more than one language is being used. This can result in speech delay, unclear pronunciation or a mixing of languages. To prevent this from occurring, the received wisdom is that a 'one language, one person' approach should be used. This means that the child associates a language with a person and that all communication between them is in one single language. The adult can of course talk to others in another language, but must be consistent when talking directly to the child. In my situation, this meant talking French to my children, even when we were out and about shopping and I was talking in English to others. (Once children are fluent in the construction and sounds of languages, starting a conversation in one language and finishing it in another is not problematic.)

While some families are bilingual, other families have three or more languages. For these families it might be that children will hear one language from the mother, another from the father and the third from grandparents or as a receptive language that they are not addressed in but overhear.

If you are working with a family who has more than one language and the child's progress in language is slower than expected, it may be that some 'sorting out' of the languages needs to take place. Do not forget, though, that speech delay could be linked to other factors such as hearing loss or a special need.

Supporting children who are new to English

Some children have already had quite a lot of exposure to English, so while they may not be fluent they have made a start. Other children may come into the setting with another language but be total beginners when it comes to English. The good news is that these children can soon pick up English, assuming that their home language is already developed. The starting point with these children is again to find out which languages are being used at home and how fluent the children are before they arrive. Once they come into the setting, you should focus initially on making them feel secure. It is a lonely and potentially frightening experience for a child to come into a setting and not be able to express themselves. This is why the key person system is so important. The process of language learning will be similar to that of how a baby learns, although much faster. In the same way that a baby relies on an adult for breaking into language, so too will the child. At first the child will 'tune in' to the sounds of the language and learn to understand key terms and phrases. Within a couple of weeks or so, if the key person is working effectively to make them feel comfortable, the child is likely to show that they are understanding some key phrases such as 'snack' or 'thank you' or 'home time'. This is a bit of a breakthrough, but it is important not to rush the child as it takes more time still for the child to start to actually say some of these words. First words are often single words, like those of a baby, but look out also for the way that the child might join in with rhymes and songs. Once the first words start to appear, the child usually picks up the grammar and phrases quickly. However, this can only happen if there is sufficient adult–child interaction. Children who have to rely on playing with other children for learning English are often much slower to break into the code.

Aspects within Communication, Language and Literacy

Language for Communication (pages 41–46)

This aspect is about helping children use language as a way of socialising and expressing their needs. To embed this into your practice means making sure that there is sufficient interaction between yourself and children. As children get older, you will need to ensure that there are also plenty of opportunities for them to use language between themselves, for example in role-play areas and during meal times.

Language for Thinking (pages 47–49)

This aspect is about looking at ways to help children use language to express their thinking, to predict and to reason. This is particularly important once children's speech has developed as it means that they can learn to use language to 'figure things' out; for example, 'If I put this here, the blocks might fall down'. One of the ways to embed Language for Thinking into your practice is to ensure that you draw children's attention to specific details and label things up for children, such as 'That's a spotty looking dog. I think it's a Dalmatian.' You can also help children learn how to use their language for thinking by modelling your own thought processes – 'I know that Mark has had his lunch, but I had better check that Bekir has not forgotten.'

Linking Sounds and Letters (pages 50–52)

This aspect is at first about helping babies and toddlers tune into the sounds of English and then eventually helping older children, once they have English, to link sounds with actual letters. Embedding this into your practice means doing plenty of rhymes and songs with children of all ages, and then with children who are ready, starting to draw their attention to letter shapes and sounds through games and activities. The Letter and Sounds pack produced by the Primary National Strategy team (ref. 00281–2007 FLR–EN) is a particularly good resource (see www.teachernet.gov.uk/publications for details).

Reading (pages 53–56)

At all ages, reading is about helping children learn to love books and become motivated to look at and eventually read them. Embedding this into practice requires making sure that children have daily opportunities to share stories and books with adults. It is essential that this is a pleasurable experience, so matching children to the language level of books is important as is keeping an eye on the size of groups. The best stories are of course ones that you can have when snuggled up comfortably with an adult. This means that parents play a vital role by reading books at home, especially at bed time.

Writing (pages 57–58)

Writing is at first about mark-making and gaining pleasure from seeing how marks can be made using a variety of materials. For older children writing is something that they can be motivated to try because they have seen adults in the setting writing in front of them or scribing for them. To embed writing into your practice you will need to make sure that there are always pleasurable materials available for marking. You will also need to incorporate marking and writing into the play opportunities both in and out of doors, for example by putting out clipboards and large white boards outdoors, shopping lists in the home corners and notebooks on the dough table.

Handwriting (pages 59–60)

This is interestingly not at all about tracing letters and being instructed! Even for babies it is about gaining control over the hands and, over time, being able to use tools so that eventually mark-making and drawing can be composed of more controlled movements. Embedding handwriting into your practice links closely with self-care skills in the Personal, Social and Emotional Development area of Learning and Development. Children will need opportunities to feed themselves and tidy up, etc., as this requires fine motor movements. There are also links to other areas of Learning and Development such as Designing and Making (Knowledge and Understanding of the World) and Using Equipment and Materials (Physical Development).

Problem Solving, Reasoning and Numeracy

The title of this area of Learning and Development has changed since the Foundation Stage Curriculum. The title reflects the importance of working on children's problem-solving skills rather than just their ability to do some early mathematics. It also reflects changes to the way children are being taught mathematics in schools. There is currently more emphasis on the importance of thinking skills and learning about how numbers work rather than on just doing sums.

This area of Learning and Development has three aspects, as shown in the spider diagram below.

Embedding Problem Solving, Reasoning and Numeracy into your practice

As with the other areas of Learning and Development, some of the requirements in this area need to be done through the way in which you are working. All children, including babies, need to hear you count, use numbers and talk about sizes and shapes of objects. They also need to see the way in which 'one to one' matching takes place, for example the way in which you point to objects as you count them or you put out a banana for each child. Embedding this area of Learning and Development also means ensuring that there is plenty of child-initiated play so that children can learn from the materials and equipment that are around them, such as trying to squeeze sponges, building dens or knocking down stacked beakers. It also means that when these 'mathematical moments' arise, you could either use them for the basis of further planning or draw children's attention to what is happening at the time.

Aspects within Problem Solving, Reasoning and Numeracy

Numbers as Labels and for Counting (pages 63–66)

This is the starting point for learning about numbers. It means that children of all ages need to hear you sing counting rhymes and watch you count. It also means that as children get older you start to draw their attention to written numerals by writing them in front of them, for example 'Teddy wants me to write a 5 to make sure he does not lose any of his apples'. You will also need to help older children recognise numbers by playing games such as simple snakes and ladders.

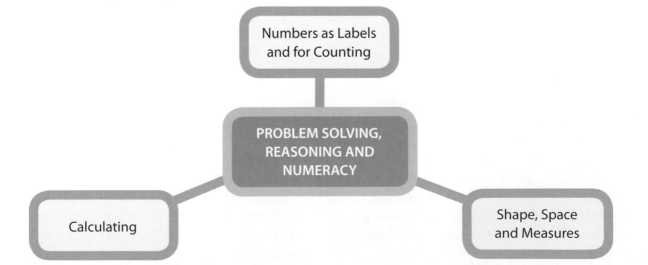

Calculating (pages 67–69)

It is important to stress that this aspect is not about sums, as some parents may assume that their babies are going to be taught their times tables! Calculating is at first about noticing reductions or increases, for example 'Only one more spoonful left' or 'Would you like an extra piece of banana?' The focus is also to ensure that children develop the mathematical vocabulary that they will need to talk about differences between numbers and groups, such as more, less and same. Again, this should happen during the everyday routines whenever possible.

Shape, Space and Measures (pages 71–74)

This is a lovely aspect of learning, since all children can benefit from exploring at first hand shapes and sizes through practical activities. For babies this might be treasure basket play, while for toddlers this could be watching how the amount of liquid in their beaker becomes less when they drink. Again, learning about this area can easily be embedded into your practice and through play opportunities. Talking about clothes fitting, providing junk modelling and nappy changing are all ways in which children learn to experience this aspect of Learning and Development.

Knowledge and Understanding of the World

This area of Learning and Development will link in the long term to the National Curriculum subjects of Science, History, Geography, Design and Technology and ICT. Having said that, in the EYFS the focus is developing the language, skills and interests that children will need for these later subjects, rather than teaching them any specific facts. This is important to convey to parents as the title of this area of Learning and Development, I would argue, is misleading.

There are six separate aspects for Knowledge and Understanding of the World, as shown in the spider diagram below. These are actually quite diverse, so you will need to check that you are covering them all, especially if you are working with the older age ranges.

Embedding Knowledge and Understanding of the World into your practice

The main thread that combines each of these quite diverse areas of learning is actually language. Children need to gain language in order to be able to talk about things such as what they have been doing (Time), what they have discovered (Exploration and Investigation) and where they like going (Place). If you are working with babies and toddlers, you will find that some of the everyday care routines and popular activities such as heuristic play are likely to deliver this area of Learning and Development. For those of you working with the older age range, you will probably find that you need to combine a mixture of child-initiated play and adult-focused activities to cover all of the aspects.

Aspects within Knowledge and Understanding of the World

Exploration and Investigation (pages 77–78)

This aspect is about children learning by touching, feeling, observing and – in the case of babies – mouthing. It is a fantastic aspect and will eventually link to early science. With interesting materials, objects

and some everyday items, you will find that it is also an easy area of learning to cover, as children are naturally curious and keen to explore. It is worth noting that this aspect also links well to the Exploring Media and Materials aspect of Creative Development.

Designing and Making (pages 79–80)

This is another easy-to-deliver aspect, as children of all ages try and put materials together to see what they will do. Embedding this into practice might include doing some regular cooking activities with children as well as giving them plenty of child-initiated opportunities to use construction materials, sensory materials and loose parts such as cardboard boxes and fabric. For toddlers and older children, this aspect can link to the Using Equipment and Materials aspect of Physical Development.

ICT (pages 81–82)

ICT is part of our everyday world. In the early stages, this aspect is about sharing with babies toys and books which have microchips built in, such as books that make noises and toys that light up. Later, it is about helping toddlers and older children learn how to control and use some gadgets safely, such as turning on and using a programmable toy or noticing that a calculator will only work when it is near light.

Time (pages 83–84)

This aspect of Knowledge and Understanding of the World will eventually lead into learning about history. In the EYFS, it is about helping children develop sufficient language so that they can explore the concept of time. Babies and toddlers need, for example, to hear the past tense before they can use it, while older children need language in order to sequence events. It is easy to embed this aspect into your everyday practice because it is about talking about what you are doing and what you have done. It links nicely to ICT, because digital cameras can be used to show the way in which time has passed. Objects and artefacts are also useful for older children to look at, so they can learn about past and present.

Place (pages 85–86)

This aspect of Knowledge and Understanding of the World will eventually lead into learning about geography. As with Time, the earlier stages are about language development. Babies and toddlers, for example, will gradually understand and then use words such as 'in' and 'out', and will learn the names of places

that are important for them, such as 'at home', 'in your bedroom' and 'outdoors'. With older children, learning about Place is about thinking about what they can see, where they have been and what they like about their environment.

Communities (pages 87–89)

This aspect is about helping children to explore cultures and beliefs, so it may eventually link into Citizenship and Religious Education. Again, there is an early focus on language here, with children needing to be able to talk about themselves and their families before coming to understand the way in which people can lead different lives and have different beliefs to them.

Physical Development

Promoting physical development is about respecting natural processes that occur within children's bodies and providing the right environment for them. The physical development of children is a 'hot' topic in the media at the moment in view of the numbers of children who are not taking sufficient exercise and who are overweight. Physical development is closely bound up with feelings of self-confidence, as often children who are active and are given opportunities to practise their skills tend to feel positive self-regard. This applies to babies who become very excited when they master the skill of rolling over or being able to guide something that they have seen to their mouth.

There are three aspects to Physical Development, as shown in the spider diagram below.

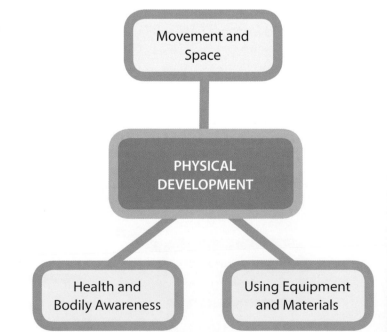

Embedding Physical Development into your practice

Embedding Physical Development within your practice means creating opportunities where children can do as many things for themselves as possible and also have plenty of time for child-initiated play, both indoors and outdoors, with a range of challenging and interesting materials such as sand, water, wheeled toys, paddling pools and trees to climb! It is also about thinking about role modelling physical activity and healthy attitudes towards food. In addition, you need to check that children are being given the opportunity to respect and think about their bodily needs, for example by going to the toilet when they need to rather than always being told.

Aspects within Physical Development

Movement and Space (pages 92–96)

This aspect is about children gaining an awareness of how to use their body and developing a sense of self in relationship to spaces (spatial awareness). This is fairly easy to embed within your practice, provided that you are giving children of all ages varied opportunities to experience and explore different types of spaces and sensations. A good example of this is height: all children need to feel what it is like to be higher than their bodily height. For babies this means lifting them up so they can see the world from an adult's height, while for toddlers this necessitates opportunities for climbing. With older children, this can range from climbing trees through to climbing up to the top of earth mounds. Interestingly, it is recognised that children with physical disabilities also need these experiences.

Child-initiated play, particularly outdoors where children may have more space and access to a range of equipment, is therefore essential in delivering this aspect of Physical Development.

Health and Bodily Awareness (pages 97–100)

This aspect of Physical Development is about eventually helping children to make good choices about keeping themselves healthy. It covers food, hygiene and safety, with the focus on children learning about making connections between what they do and eat and their overall health. It should not be about condemning families' lifestyles! In order to deliver this aspect, it is important that you provide nutritious food in the right portion sizes and encourage children to enjoy foods that are balanced and so good for them. It also means that you have to respect children when they say that they are full – this includes babies, who quite often will turn their head away when they have eaten enough.

Using Equipment and Materials (pages 101–103)

This aspect particularly focuses on the hand–eye coordination and fine motor skills of children. This should be embedded into most of the activities and play opportunities that are available for children, such as a baby playing with a rattle, a toddler trying to put a hat on Teddy or a group of children trying to make a hammock by tying fabric to a chain-link fence. Again, child-initiated activities are important here, as quite often this is where children will be ready to practise a skill over and over again and to persevere as they have set their own goal.

Creative Development

This area of Learning and Development is becoming of increasing interest as creativity along with problem solving are now considered to be essential in supporting both children's achievement and emotional well-being. This area of Learning and Development does require adults to feel that they can 'let go' a little, as young children are naturally curious and – given encouragement and resources – fairly creative.

There are four aspects to Creative Development, as shown in the spider diagram below.

Being Creative – Responding to Experiences, Expressing and Communicating Ideas

Exploring Media and Materials

CREATIVE DEVELOPMENT

Creating Music and Dance

Developing Imagination and Imaginative Play

Embedding Creative Development into your practice

This area of Learning and Development is particularly tied to adults' attitudes and assumptions about creativity. The focus should be experimentation, enjoyment and exploration rather than 'end product'. It may mean messy, original and sometimes 'gone wrong' movements rather than perfect adult-led activities and products. As with all the other areas of Learning and Development, there is a real need to make sure that children have plenty of child-initiated moments, including babies, who may, for example, spontaneously try banging a wooden spoon and a metal scoop together when given items during treasure basket play. For older children, resources will need to be provided so that more opportunities are available to make choices, try out new combinations and experiment.

Aspects within Creative Development

Being Creative – Responding to Experiences, Expressing and Communicating Ideas (pages 106–107)

This aspect is about the overall way that children might express themselves. It prompts us to make sure that children get a wide range of experiences, materials and resources so they can find a way to do this. In your planning, you should therefore have several types of provision available for children that will enable them to express themselves, for example paint, drawing, junk modelling, musical instruments and heuristic play, rather than a single adult-directed activity. It also means that you should avoid templates, colouring in or other potentially restrictive activities. A good test is always whether in a group setting there are ten virtually identical paper plate faces on the wall or whether it is clear that children have been able to try and find their own way of representing their face. The great thing about babies and toddlers is that they almost naturally have their 'own way' of doing things given the opportunity.

Exploring Media and Materials (pages 108–110)

This is a great aspect of learning which is easy to deliver through child-initiated play with a range of materials for them to explore. This means that sand, water, dough and paint are essential. Provision needs to be outdoors as well as many children will enjoy digging, mixing and mark-making with a range of materials. Interestingly, you are likely to see that some children will combine this with their imaginative play, for example by creating a meal with sand and sticks. Babies also enjoy trying out new experiences. This is partly during weaning with new tastes and textures, but also in terms of the sensory objects and materials such as gloop that you provide for them to explore.

Music and Dance (pages 111–112)

This is a lovely aspect of learning. It is about children of all ages, hearing and being able to respond to a range of music. Babies, for example, may wriggle on the floor to the sounds of a song that they like, while toddlers may bob up and down enthusiastically. This aspect of learning means providing ways of making sounds, such as shakers, rattles and more sophisticated tuned instruments such as glockenspiels, as well as responding to sounds. For this to be a creative experience for children, it is again essential for adults to be ready to take a step backwards and see what children want to do and how they respond.

Developing Imagination and Imaginative Play (pages 113–114)

This aspect is about making sure that children have plenty of opportunities to imagine and to use role play. With babies, it might be about laughing when they see a puppet popping up and then down. With toddlers, you may see the beginnings of them trying to make one thing stand for another, for example the toddler takes an empty beaker but pretends that it is full and 'drinks' from it or makes a mark and imagines that it is a dog running around. With older children you are likely to see a range of imaginative play including being 'at home', super-hero play and acting out stories that they have heard. You may also hear their imagination as they talk to each other about how they might play and what they can do. To provide for this aspect means looking at plenty of child-initiated provision where children can try out new things or play with equipment in ways that are unusual without fear.

A word about the activity pages in this book

The activity pages which follow are examples of adult-focused activities. They are of course not the only activities that would be useful to cover the areas of Learning and Development, but are samples that might be of use to you. While I have tied activities to the wide age groupings to reflect the EYFS, I would expect that some of the activities could be adapted for older children or children who need more challenge. I would equally expect that you might look at some of the activities and think that they would not be right for the children you are working with. This is where professional judgement comes in!

It is important to note that alongside some adult-focused activities, children should be able to choose what they want to do and follow their own interests. I call this 'free ranging' and imagine children happily clucking about in and out of doors, playing with materials that adults have put out, but also bits that they have chosen.

Group size

Group size matters enormously. The activities that I have written for the under-threes assume that babies and toddlers will usually be working individually with their key person. This is possible given that ratios for this age group are deliberately low and the Statutory Framework states that staff breaks should be covered. Note that if you are combining two-year-olds with three-year-olds, it is essential that they still get the one–four ratio in terms of adult attention. (I have sometimes seen some two-year-olds looking quite lost when this does not happen.)

For those of you working with children over the age of three years, I am assuming that you will work with small groups for short bursts of time. This allows for better interaction and will probably mean that both you and the children will enjoy the activity more.

Timing

You will see that no suggested timing is given. This is because the duration of the activity should be based on the engagement of the children.

Activities for the under-threes

If you are working with babies and toddlers and were hoping for 'big' activities, I am sorry but you may be disappointed. Although there are a few sensory activities, for the most part I have included some everyday activities. This is because delivering the EYFS

for the 0–26 month age group is about good practice, relationships and care. It is not about 'teaching'. For the children in the 22–36 month age group, there are more specific activities, but you will also need to remember that learning can take place as part of the everyday care routines.

Remembering that learning is holistic

While I have grouped the activities according to age and aspects of Learning and Development, it is important to remember that activities will always cover many areas. This is particularly true of Personal, Social and Emotional Development. As you become more confident and familiar with the aspects of Learning and Development, you will quickly become adept at knowing the links between various activities. This means that you will not necessarily need to plan adult-focused activities for each aspect separately, but rather work out the coverage gained from the really interesting ones that you and the children enjoy.

Your Questions Answered

We are a nursery and have been doing the Foundation Stage since it came in. Would we have to change anything?

That very much depends on how your systems are working. There are some subtle differences between the Foundation Stage and the Early Years Foundation Stage, for example there is a renewed focus on meeting individual children's needs and on outdoor play. This means that you will need to carry out an audit of your current practice and check that it correlates with the overall ethos of the EYFS (see Section 2 of this book, Putting the Themes into Practice) and the statutory requirements (see pages 30–43 of this book).

Personal, Social and Emotional Development

Personal, Social and Emotional Development underpins the ability to fulfil our potential in both personal and professional spheres. It is therefore a key area of development when working with babies and young children.

This area of Learning and Development includes the following aspects:

- Dispositions and Attitudes
- Self-confidence and Self-esteem
- Making Relationships
- Behaviour and Self-control
- Self-care
- Sense of Community

Dispositions and Attitudes

What do I need to do?

- Make sure that the baby and toddler has a secure bond with the key person.

- Recognise the signs that a baby or toddler is feeling overwhelmed.

- Expect that babies and toddlers will have varying levels of concentration.

- Provide items and toys that are tactile and can be mouthed.

- Be ready to reassure babies and toddlers when they encounter new people and experiences.

- Look for ways of helping babies and toddlers explore their environment.

- Talk to parents about what excites and also makes their child fearful.

Frequently Asked Questions

A baby that I am looking after will only go to sleep if rocked. Any ideas?

This baby has learnt to associate falling asleep with rocking. Try rocking intermittently so that the baby is not continuously being rocked, for example rocking for 10 seconds and then stopping for a second. Over a couple of days, increase the amount of time that the rocking stops, so that eventually the baby does not need to be rocked at all.

One of our toddlers has become quite fearful of new situations, especially meeting new people. What can we do?

Some children are more sensitive to new stimuli than others and can be easily overwhelmed. Avoid being impatient with the child and provide reassurance. Let the toddler explore people and new environments in their own time and way, and act as a safe base they can keep coming back to.

Fruits to handle

You need to encourage babies to be confident to explore new objects. While treasure basket play is good for this, you can also group some similar objects together for babies to touch and handle. Look out for some 'hard fruits' for babies to touch and mouth. Make sure that you have washed them first and consider looking for organic fruits as the skins should not have been exposed to pesticides. Examples of fruits that you could encourage babies to feel and hold include lemons, oranges, coconuts (remove hair), dragon fruit, unripe mangoes and hard pears. You will need to hold the fruit for young babies, while older babies who might be sitting or mobile should be able to manage unaided.

Observation

How does the baby react when touching the fruit?	→
Does the baby need help holding the fruit?	→
Does the baby try and mouth the fruit?	→

Planning

- Could this be repeated with vegetables?
- Could you take photographs of the baby exploring the fruit?
- Could you play a rolling game with some of the fruit?

0-11 months

Swinging

Babies and toddlers need plenty of pleasant new experiences so they learn not to be fearful in new situations. Look out for a baby/toddler swing that you can put up outdoors. It is important that you buy one that is correct for the age group and that you set it up according to the manufacturer's guidelines. Put the baby or toddler out in the swing. Gently push the swing so that the child can get used to the motion. Smile and encourage the child.

Observation

How does the child like this activity? →

Planning

Repeat this activity and over time increase the 'swing' by pushing more vigorously.

Make up a song or use the rhyme 'Bye, Baby Bunting'.

What other movements can you plan for babies and toddlers to experience, for example balancing, climbing?

8-20 months

Dispositions and Attitudes

What do I need to do?

- Look out for new learning opportunities and materials for toddlers to try out.

- Join in with activities so that toddlers have a role model.

- Expect that toddlers will have varying amounts of concentration.

- Provide sensory materials in the environment.

- Plan some activities based on toddlers' interests.

- Be flexible in your approach and ready to adjust according to toddlers' concentration levels.

- Talk to parents about their child's interests.

Frequently Asked Questions

I try to plan activities for the toddlers but they often will not come and take part. How can I make them?

There is no requirement in the EYFS for toddlers to do particular activities. Rather, the focus is on following children's interests and taking the lead from them. You may, for example, notice that a toddler is fascinated with moving things in and out of boxes and so put out toys and equipment to enhance this play.

Should we insist that toddlers sit down to do activities such as dough and mark-making?

Most toddlers prefer to do activities while standing up or down on the floor. Insisting that they should sit may result in toddlers leaving the activity very quickly. While you could put out some chairs, leave spaces at these tables for standing and do not make an issue out of those wanting to stand.

Out in the rain! 16–26 months

Familiarity with being outdoors is important for some children who literally lead sheltered lives. Going out when it is raining can be enormous fun for children who have not experienced the sound and feeling of rain. Begin by making sure that you plan this activity with the knowledge of parents. Make sure that you have sufficient rain wear so that children will not get wet. Look out for all-in-ones and Wellington boots. Take some containers out with you so that toddlers can also catch the rain.

Observation

How do the children react to being in the rain?

Planning

Repeat this activity and take out different equipment, for example rubber ducks to float in a puddle.

Take photographs of the children in the rain.

16-26 months

Soap flakes and whisks 22–36 months

Sensory materials are generally popular with children and are a way of them learning how to adjust to new situations. Look out for some soap flakes and put them into a tray with some warm water. Put out whisks and spoons so that children can mix them up and see how the soap turns into a thick lather which is fun to play with.

Note that you should always check first with parents when using these types of activities in case children have a known skin condition or reaction to certain products. You should also buy products that are sensitive to skin. Children should also wash their hands afterwards.

Observation

Do the children enjoy this activity?

Do some children find this activity overwhelming?

Planning

What other sensory materials could you introduce to children?

Consider whether these children are more sensitive to sensory materials (see page 218).

22-36 months

Dispositions and Attitudes

What do I need to do?

- Look out for new learning opportunities and materials for children to try.
- Observe children's level of concentration during activities.
- Provide sensory materials in the environment.
- Look for ways of varying the layout and the provision.
- Talk to parents about their child's interests.

Frequently Asked Questions

During group circle time, the children fidget and some call out when they should be listening.

Developmentally, because of children's developing language and cognition, their thoughts tend to 'come out' and it will not be until many children reach around 6 years that they will be able to think internally. Consider whether circle times are appropriate for your children.

Some of the parents feel that their children will not learn to concentrate by playing.

You will need to show parents that when children are engaged in child-initiated play, their levels of concentration are actually quite high. You could do this by timing the duration of children's play and getting parents to score their child's concentration levels, with 1 representing easily distracted and 5 representing high levels of engagement. You may also need to show that behind many play opportunities there are serious learning intentions.

Parachute games

30–50 months

A transition that many children need to make is to move from playing alongside other children to playing with them and sometimes being part of organised games. Look out for some short games that children can play together which helps them to enjoy being part of a small group. Play a parachute game whereby one child has to run or crawl underneath the parachute and emerge out of the other side, while the other children holding the parachute are gently lifting it up and down. If you do not have a parachute, you can use a thin piece of fabric.

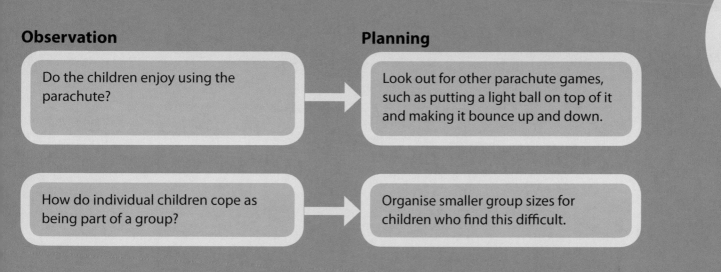

Observation

Planning

Do the children enjoy using the parachute? → Look out for other parachute games, such as putting a light ball on top of it and making it bounce up and down.

How do individual children cope as being part of a group? → Organise smaller group sizes for children who find this difficult.

30-50 months

Skittles

40–60+ months

Children need plenty of opportunities to try out new games. Skittles is a traditional game which encourages perseverance as well as throwing skills.

With a small group of children outdoors, fill up some empty plastic bottles with a mixture of materials – try gravel, some sand and water. The children can then experiment to see how much the bottles need filling up in order to stand when there is a breeze, but also to be sufficiently unstable so as to fall if a ball hits them. Set out the game and show the children how to play it, but then see if the children can organise the game for themselves.

Observation

Planning

Are there any children who seem hesitant or unsure of themselves? → Think about how these children can be given more responsibility in ways that they can handle.

Do the children enjoy this activity? → What other games could you show children, for example knocking bottles off the wall?

40-60+ months

Self-confidence and Self-esteem

What do I need to do?

- Provide opportunities for babies and toddlers to choose items to play with, for example treasure basket and heuristic play.

- Look for ways of giving babies and toddlers choices, for example putting out three different finger foods on the plate so the baby chooses which one to have first.

- Make sure that the key person relationship is strong.

- Create a relaxed and happy atmosphere.

- Greet children and their parents with a warm smile.

- Show through physical reassurance and smiling that you enjoy being with babies and toddlers.

Frequently Asked Questions

Why it is important to give babies and toddlers choices from such an early stage of their development?

Being able to select which finger food to take from your plate first or choosing the object from the pile that looks most exciting is actually about having a little control. People who have good levels of self-confidence inwardly believe that they 'can' do things rather than having to always depend on others.

On a course I was told that it is important to praise babies. What is the point as babies cannot understand the words?

Praise is not so much about the words but about the tone of voice and the facial expression. Babies and toddlers are very good at tuning into both of these – and so by praising them you help them to feel noticed and that adults who are with them approve of them.

Mirrors

0–11 months

Babies need to develop some sense of self-identity in order to develop self-confidence and self-esteem. A starting point in this journey is to find ways of helping babies recognise themselves.

Find a large mirror to take the baby towards. Sit or stand with the baby and point into the mirror. Take your time to let the baby look at the reflection and to explore it. Most babies will want to reach out or touch 'the baby' that they can see in the mirror, although occasionally some babies become distressed. If you decide to buy a mirror for babies and toddlers to look at themselves in, it is important to get the non-glass ones.

Observation

Is the baby interested in the reflection in the mirror?

Does the baby seem to recognise your reflection?

Planning

Keep repeating this activity.

Find other mirrors for the baby to look in.

Allow the baby to touch the mirror if it is safe to do so.

Show the baby photographs of you and of the baby.

Take a photograph of the baby looking at their reflection in the mirror.

0–11 months

Photograph flap book

8–20 months

This age range should be starting to get pleasure from books. Flap books are particularly popular as babies and toddlers are starting to enjoy the concept of peek-a-boo.

Take some photographs of the baby doing different things in the day. You might also like to ask parents if they will provide some photographs of them with their child. Stick the photographs onto sheets of card. Cover each photograph with a thin piece of card and attach this either above or to the side of the photograph. As this will be the flap that children will lift up to see the photograph, it is important that you attach it firmly – you can use tape or glue. Fold the card covering the photograph back and press down on the fold. This will make it easier for the toddler to lift up. Put the book together by punching holes through the sheets and attaching treasury tags. Take time to share the book with the baby or toddler – note that you should not leave this book around as babies may try to mouth it.

Observation

How does the baby or toddler respond?

Planning

What other ways can you help babies and toddlers to see photographs of themselves?

Does the baby or toddler enjoy using the flaps of the book?

What other flap books could you use with the babies or toddlers?

8-20 months

Self-confidence and Self-esteem

What do I need to do?

- Provide opportunities for children to take responsibility in the setting, for example by helping to set out activities in the setting and tidying away.

- Provide challenging activities that motivate children.

- Show unconditional love for children, for example smiles and approval.

- Encourage children to talk about their feelings.

- Do not over-react when children make mistakes.

- Recognise when children become frustrated and disappointed, and talk through how they can 'move on' from this point.

- Provide plenty of opportunities for self-care.

Frequently Asked Questions

One of the children hardly says a word to me, but according to his parents is quite chatty at home. He does talk to the other children.

The child's language is not an issue, but you need to focus on making him feel more relaxed with you. Think about using less words and showing approval through open body language. Some children relax when there is a puppet around, so you could try this.

We have a child who constantly gets the other children and adults to help her. What can we do?

You may need to work on this child's confidence and motivation. Use praise and even stickers when she starts to have a go, and be ready to go 'halves' at first, for example 'I'll start you off, but then you can just finish that bit.' Be firm but patient, as any sign of impatience will set this child back.

Hidden jigsaw pieces 30–50 months

Jigsaws are not only good at helping to develop children's mathematic and logical skills, they can also give children a great sense of satisfaction. However, some children have never experienced the satisfaction of completing a jigsaw. You can help children to gain the confidence to complete jigsaws by making them into a game.

Make up a complete jigsaw but remove two pieces. Put out a tray of shredded paper and hide the two pieces in it. Ask a child if they could find the missing pieces that Teddy has hidden. See if the child can put the final pieces in. Next time, hide two or three more pieces.

Observation **Planning**

| How much support does the child need? | → | Check that the jigsaw puzzle is at the right level for the child. |

| How interested is the child in completing the jigsaw? | → | Look out for puzzles that link to children's interests. Acknowledge children's frustrations and encourage them to complete the jigsaw puzzles. |

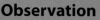

30-50 months

Making lunch 40–60+ months

Cooking activities can help children gain a lot of confidence as they make them feel 'grown up'. Look out for a range of cooking activities so that eventually children can work in small groups to produce a complete lunch, for example putting topping onto a pizza base, making a smoothie, making a fruit salad.

With a small group of children, say five or six, talk to them about making lunch. Encourage them to plan what they might do based on other cooking activities that you have already carried out in the setting. This can be quite an involved activity linking to many areas of the EYFS, for example the children may write a shopping list, go to get the ingredients with you, make a menu on the computer, lay the table as well as cook.

Observation **Planning**

| Do the children enjoy preparing the meal? | → | What other activities could this group of children take responsibility for? |

| How do the children manage the tasks? | → | Are there activities where individual children need practice and how can you help these children? |

40-60+ months

73

Making Relationships

What do I need to do?

- Recognise that the settling-in process will be individual.

- Make sure that the key person relationship is strong before separation takes place.

- Look out for some fun toys or activities that children can associate with your setting.

- Greet children and their parents with a warm smile.

- Think about activities that will help toddlers to be together.

- Expect that most toddlers will play alongside each other rather than cooperatively until around 30 months.

- Talk to parents about how children's social development progresses, so that they have realistic expectations.

Frequently Asked Questions

How can we prevent biting in our toddler room?

Biting is fairly common among young children – often from around 18 to 30 months. It is usually linked to frustration and jealousy and generally disappears once toddlers are talking well.

Providing sufficient sensory activities and adult attention can prevent bites. Where there are large groups of toddlers, it is best that they are kept in key person groups for much of the time so that an adult who is familiar with them is always near by and can intervene quickly. If a bite does occur, play it down and spend a moment with the victim. Telling the biter off will not prevent another bite as this age range is very impulsive. Rather, keep the biter 'busy' and ensure an adult is near them at all times otherwise there is a strong likelihood that the child will bite again.

Poor Teddy

While this age range are not yet playing with each other, they are starting to show caring skills by, for example, coming to hug an adult or pretending to give an adult a dough cake. Role play and making relationships are entwined, as to make relationships you have to imagine what someone else might be thinking. Role play can develop imagination and also language, another essential skill in communicating.

Take a teddy and wrap it up in a small blanket or sheet. Explain that 'Poor Teddy' is feeling sad. Could they look after Teddy as well?

16-26 months

Observation

Planning

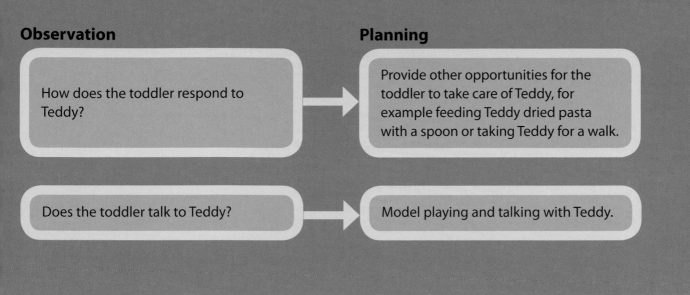

Observation	Planning
How does the toddler respond to Teddy?	Provide other opportunities for the toddler to take care of Teddy, for example feeding Teddy dried pasta with a spoon or taking Teddy for a walk.
Does the toddler talk to Teddy?	Model playing and talking with Teddy.

Hiding hands in the sand tray

One way in which you can help toddlers to make relationships with each other is by finding activities that they can do together alongside an adult. Sensory activities are particularly good for this age group as they allow children to come together but also play separately. Sensory activities also seem to help toddlers concentrate.

Provide a large tray of sand and bury your hands in it. Ask the toddlers to take turns burying your hands. See if you can bury their hands too! If you do not have a large sand tray, you could do this in smaller shallow trays – but give each toddler their own tray.

Note that it is important to supervise this age of children with sand as they may try to throw it or even eat it. Squabbles may also break out.

22-36 months

Observation

Planning

Observation	Planning
Do the toddlers make eye contact and enjoy this activity together?	Play other sand games together. Look for opportunities of doing other activities together such as sharing books or a simple cooking activity.
Do the toddlers enjoy burying?	Hide toys and other items in the sand for them to find.

Making Relationships

What do I need to do?

- Recognise that the settling-in process will be individual.

- Make sure that the key person relationship is strong before separation takes place.

- Look for opportunities where children can play cooperatively.

- Greet children and their parents with a warm smile.

- Encourage children to take an interest in each other.

- Provide opportunities for children with younger siblings to play together.

- Identify children who need more support in order to play with other children.

Frequently Asked Questions

We have a baby whose older brother is in another part of the nursery. Can we bring this child into the baby room?

Yes, provided that you will be in ratio and that you consider any risks, for example boisterous behaviour. It is actually essential that siblings play together, especially if they are away from their home for long periods of the day.

There is one child who does not seem to have any friends. What should we do?

Observe carefully and consider whether the child is being neglected or actually rejected by others. Rejected may mean working within the class on relationships and 'nice play'. If the child is being neglected, think about whether their language and social skills are an issue. You could try pairing the child up with children with similar interests, since these are often the key ingredient in friendships at this age.

Musical statues

30–50 months

Children in this age range are just starting to show cooperative play and learn to be part of a small group. Small group activities can help them to learn to take turns and develop a sense of belonging to the group. Musical statues is an example of such a group game.

Put some music on and then show the children how they must keep still when the music is turned off. You will probably need to practise this with them and demonstrate this several times. In this game there are no winners or losers – the children should just be having fun trying to keep still when the music stops.

Observation

Planning

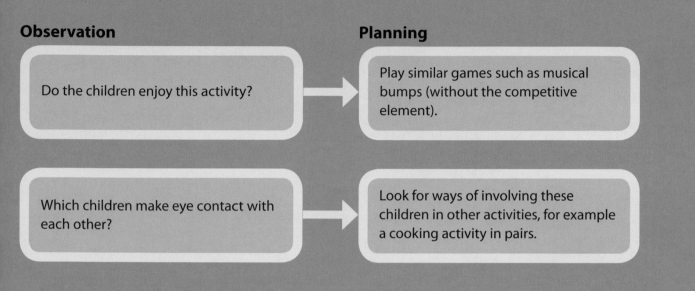

Do the children enjoy this activity? → Play similar games such as musical bumps (without the competitive element).

Which children make eye contact with each other? → Look for ways of involving these children in other activities, for example a cooking activity in pairs.

30-50 months

About me!

40–60+ months

Children need to learn to listen to each other and get to know each other. One way of doing this is to provide children with small boxes into which they put six or seven objects and photographs that reflect important things and people in their lives, for example photographs of their pets and favourite toys. Children can then share their box with you and one or two other children at a time. This is a lovely activity that can be used when a transition is taking place, as the new adult can learn a little about the child from looking at and talking about what is in their box.

Note that this is an activity that needs to be done in conjunction with parents so that they can help put the six or seven objects and photographs into the box.

Observation

Planning

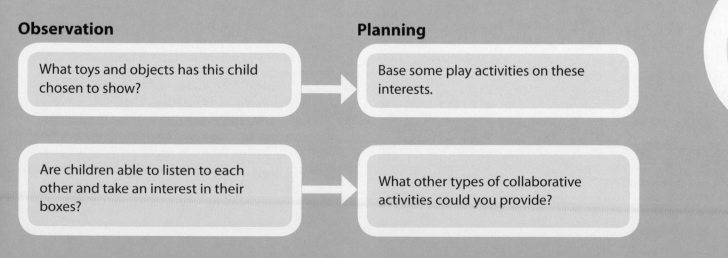

What toys and objects has this child chosen to show? → Base some play activities on these interests.

Are children able to listen to each other and take an interest in their boxes? → What other types of collaborative activities could you provide?

40-60+ months

Behaviour and Self-control

What do I need to do?

- Look for opportunities for babies and toddlers to show some independence, for example providing treasure basket play so a baby can choose what to play with or giving toddlers a spoon so they can start to feed themselves.

- Interact well with babies and toddlers so they start to develop language.

- Acknowledge babies' and toddlers' feelings.

- Make sure that the key person relationship is strong.

- Praise babies and toddlers and show that you enjoy their company.

- Share information with parents as learning to predict babies' and toddlers' needs can help babies and toddlers to be settled.

Frequently Asked Questions

We have a baby that cries for attention and then smiles if we pick her up. Won't this teach her that she can always get her own way?

No, babies need attention in order to flourish. Being held is nature's way of stimulating the brain and neural growth. Often, babies who do not get enough attention show more demanding behaviour later on. Give her plenty of attention now and she is more likely to become independent as a toddler.

I look after a toddler who is 15 months and who already has tantrums. Is this normal?

Toddlers' tantrums do start early, although often these first ones can be managed by distraction. Toddlers tend to grow out of tantrums once they can express their needs and reason, so it is essential to work on babies' and toddlers' language. Once the tantrum has passed, provide some physical reassurance.

I'm coming to get you...   0–11 months

The starting point for babies in terms of this aspect of learning is to learn to trust their key adults. Trusting others allows children eventually to build relationships and therefore be in a position to think about others.

Try saying a familiar line to a baby when you first hear them cry, such as 'I'm coming to get you!' in a musical way. Hearing a familiar voice should mean that the baby will stop crying once they have learnt that you are on the way to pick them up. Try this when a baby first wakes after sleeping. It is important that the baby does learn that someone is on their way.

Observation   **Planning**

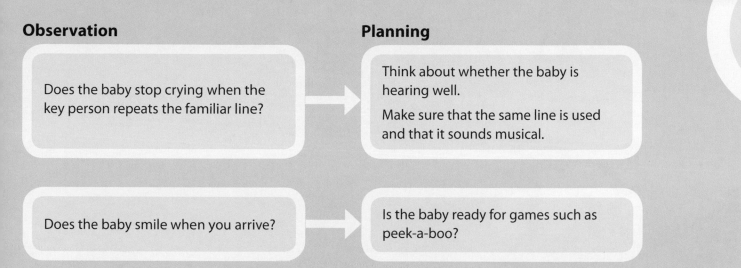

Observation	Planning
Does the baby stop crying when the key person repeats the familiar line?	Think about whether the baby is hearing well. Make sure that the same line is used and that it sounds musical.
Does the baby smile when you arrive?	Is the baby ready for games such as peek-a-boo?

Can you hold this?   8–20 months

Once babies are mobile or rolling over, nappy changes can become quite difficult. One way of distracting babies and toddlers is to involve them in the nappy change. Giving them something to hold is an effective solution and it also means that the baby or toddler is learning to help out. This is a good starting point for later activities such as tidying up, taking care of the environment and thinking about others.

Look out for something that the baby or toddler can hold that is safe. Babies and toddlers will often prefer items that are 'real' as opposed to toys. Toddlers, for example, may hold an item of clothing while a baby may like to hold a metal spoon. (It is important to choose items that are safe for a baby to mouth.) Remember also to talk to the child and that a swift nappy change may be important to prevent boredom.

Observation   **Planning**

Observation	Planning
Is the baby or toddler happy to cooperate?	In what other ways can babies and toddlers help out? For example, holding their socks before getting dressed or finding their shoes.

Behaviour and Self-control

What do I need to do?

- Understand that tiredness and hunger affect toddlers' ability to control their impulses and emotions.

- Make sure that your expectations are realistic for their stage of development.

- Keep toddlers busy with plenty of varying play opportunities.

- Praise toddlers frequently for showing wanted behaviour or joining in.

- Avoid using the word 'no' and keep it only for 'serious' occasions.

- Work with parents to understand their child's needs and to come up with some joint strategies.

Frequently Asked Questions

There are often tussles between toddlers. Why do they not seem to understand that they must share?

It is normal for children in this age group to see things and try and take them, even if someone else is holding them! This type of behaviour usually reduces once children can talk and use language for some reasoning. When a child snatches another's toy, calmly return the item to the original owner and distract the child with a similar or different toy.

If you tell a toddler not to do something, why do they carry on anyway?

Toddlers are keen for attention so you have to be careful not to fall into the trap of giving them attention for unwanted behaviour. Try ignoring unwanted behaviour and instead doing some amazing distraction, for example dancing with Teddy.

Watering plants

Carrying out simple tasks such as watering plants can help very young children to feel that they have some responsibility. Look out for containers with plants in them that toddlers can help to water – both in and out of doors. If you do not have plants that need watering, try planting a tray of cress or some runner beans. Put plenty of drainage holes and even some gravel at the bottom of the tray in case of over-watering. Fill up a small jug or a cup of water and pass it to the toddler. While the watering will not be up to a high standard, most toddlers are capable of pouring a cup of water into a pot. Expect, though, that they may also dip their hands and fingers in it first!

Observation

Does the toddler enjoy watering?

Planning

Look out for more play activities involving water, for example putting out sponges and water, scoops and water.

Is the toddler keen to help an adult with jobs?

Think about other 'helpful' activities that a toddler can undertake, such as filling up a cup of flour for a cooking activity or putting beakers out onto a table.

16-26 months

Washing and wiping

Look out for activities that encourage toddlers to learn to help others. The best activities are planned to be within the toddler's skill range and are also enjoyable.

As toddlers love water, encouraging toddlers to wipe tables with a damp cloth or wash dolls, duplo or other toys is likely to be a success. Do not worry about the standard of work – the idea is that toddlers become used to having some responsibility. Toddlers will enjoy helping out most when they are praised and are also doing the washing or wiping alongside an adult, as they love copying adults' actions.

Observation

Does the toddler enjoy this activity?

Planning

How can you incorporate washing and wiping activities into the setting out and clearing away of the session?

22-36 months

Behaviour and Self-control

What do I need to do?

- Think about children's age and stage of development and have realistic expectations.

- Model wanted behaviour including the way in which children are spoken to.

- Talk through with children the reasons why there are certain rules.

- Provide frequent reminders for children.

- Praise children when they show wanted behaviour.

- Work on children's language skills so that they can express themselves.

- Work with parents to ensure some consistency.

- Be aware of factors that can influence behaviour such as tiredness and hunger.

Frequently Asked Questions

If a child leaves the dough table to go and play elsewhere, then returns to it, why does she becomes upset to find that someone else is playing there?

This is quite normal – while the child is away from the table it is likely that she is not thinking about what is happening there in her absence. She is likely to assume that the table will be exactly as she left it, so coming back to it is a shock. Try and develop a 'putting away' routine – this seems to help.

Should we use stickers to promote wanted behaviour?

A tangible reward can be useful for children as it acts as a reminder of what they need to do. It is important, though, to keep them as an occasional treat. They also need to be distributed fairly – try giving stickers out to the whole group for 'playing well' or 'tidying up'.

Teddy's tidy-up games

Children need to learn to take on some responsibilities within their environment. One of the first things that children can learn to do is help tidy up. Tidying up needs to be built into the routine of the setting and individual activities. It is important that children know at the start of the activity what they must tidy up and when to do this. They can also be helped by playing a game.

In this game, Teddy comes to help the children tidy up. He whispers a number to the adult – this is the number of items to be put away. Sometimes he whispers to the adult a colour, and then anything which is that colour has to be put away. At other times, Teddy hides and the children and the adult have to put things away as quickly as possible before he reappears! These types of games can make tidying up fun.

Observation

| | |
| Do children enjoy this type of tidying up? |
| How much support do they need? |

Planning

| |
| Could Teddy help pairs of children work together? |
| Could Teddy be used to support other areas of behaviour and self-control? |
| What other ways can you make tidying up enjoyable for children? |

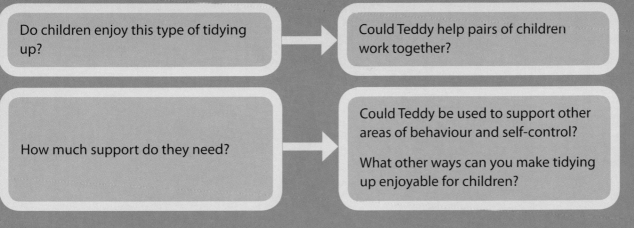

Tell Teddy

It is useful for children to learn to articulate the reasons behind some of the rules in the setting. This can help some children to moderate their own behaviour in the short term.

Give Teddy to a child who is having difficulty in one aspect of their behaviour. Ask the child to tell Teddy how to behave and to be 'in charge' of Teddy. Afterwards, praise the child for looking after Teddy and helping Teddy to be 'sensible'. This works best if the child is in charge of Teddy for a short and specific period. The aim is that the child is praised before any unwanted behaviour occurs.

Note that children (like adults) are fallible and will sometimes be able to say why they should not do something but then go on to do it, so it is still important to supervise and have realistic expectations.

Observation

| |
| How does the child cope with Teddy? |

Planning

| |
| Try using Teddy for other aspects of the child's behaviour. |
| Reduce the amount of time that the child 'looks after' Teddy if the child has found this difficult. |
| At what other times might Teddy be useful for helping this child? |

Self-care

What do I need to do?

- Meet babies' physical needs promptly.

- Talk to parents about how best to meet babies' and toddlers' needs.

- Observe how babies and toddlers start to help a little when you dress them, for example a baby might start to push his arm down into a jumpsuit while a toddler might go and find their shoes.

- Encourage babies and toddlers to feed themselves.

- Recognise when babies and toddlers try to become independent, for example a baby might turn her head when she has had enough to eat, while a toddler might say 'no more'.

Frequently Asked Questions

Some of the toddlers hate having their face wiped at the end of meals. Any suggestions?

Wipe downwards rather than upwards, so that the baby or toddler never feels that they cannot breathe. Try gentle dabbling motions and give the cloth to toddlers to see if they can wipe their own face. Avoid coming from behind so the child cannot see the cloth arrive, as this is quite scary.

One of the toddlers often asks for her dummy. Should we automatically give it to her?

The use of dummies is decided with parents, so check with them. If a dummy is not to be given, place it out of sight as otherwise it is unfair for the toddler. Extra physical reassurance may be needed, such as rocking and stroking, as dummies are often used when toddlers are feeling tired and unsettled.

Finger foods

From around 8 months, most babies start to be ready for finger foods. As with any aspect of feeding, it is essential that you talk to parents to ensure that they are happy with the type of food that you propose giving and also the timing. It is also essential to check that foods are appropriate for the age, for example no salt, honey or nuts. For the latest information about babies' diets, look on the Food Standards Agency website.

Put out some strips of finger food so that babies can have a choice, such as chopped banana and strips of bread. Note that babies must always be supervised to avoid choking incidents.

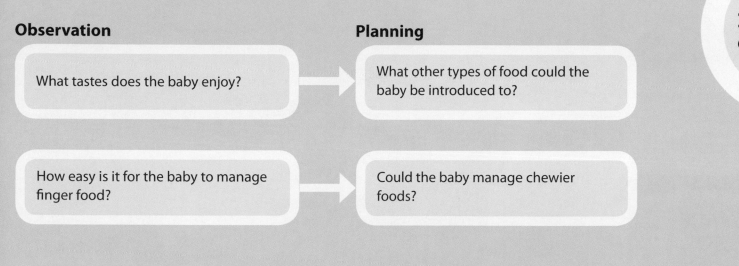

Observation

What tastes does the baby enjoy?

How easy is it for the baby to manage finger food?

Planning

What other types of food could the baby be introduced to?

Could the baby manage chewier foods?

0-11 months

Cups and beakers

Learning how to drink independently is an important skill for babies and toddlers to learn. At first babies will need beakers with lids that encourage them to suck, as this is similar to how they take fluid from the breast or bottle. They can then go on to use an ordinary beaker with a lid, before learning how to use a cup.

Try holding a cup for the toddler to take a sip from, then help the toddler put their hands around the cup. It will take several tries before a toddler learns how far to tip up the cup, so it is worth putting on an apron or bib with a tray. Next the toddler needs to learn how to pick up and put down a cup without spilling. This can be done through play on a low table with plastic cups and lightly coloured water. Keep a cloth to hand for the inevitable spills.

Note that at every stage, babies and toddlers must be supervised to avoid choking.

Observation

Is the baby or toddler happy to cooperate?

Planning

In what other ways can babies and toddlers help out, for example holding their socks before getting dressed or finding their shoes?

8-20 months

Self-care

What do I need to do?

- Help toddlers learn language relating to their bodies and their needs, for example head, toes, clean, tired, thirsty.

- Provide opportunities for toddlers to help with dressing.

- Support toddlers to move away from nappies (see also page 204).

- Encourage toddlers to feed themselves.

- Make sure that toddlers begin to help with washing their hands and face.

- Praise toddlers when they attempt to help themselves.

- Support parents by helping them to understand the importance of self-care skills.

Frequently Asked Questions

At what age can toddlers dress themselves?

This can vary quite significantly and depends partly on how much practice they have. Toddlers often find it easier to remove clothing rather than put it on. Most toddlers will need support as they are dressing, for example they may need you to put a pullover over their head but they can then put their arms inside.

Is it normal for toddlers to scream when having their hair washed?

Many toddlers go through a stage of disliking having their hair washed. It is important to use shampoo that does not sting and to use as little as possible. Find ways to encourage the toddler to be as involved as possible. Have a towel to hand so that the toddler can quickly wipe their eyes and a mirror so they can see what is happening.

Spoons and forks

By the age of 18 months, most toddlers have mastered the art of using a spoon to feed themselves. For children whose families use knives and forks, the next step is to introduce toddlers to using a fork alongside a spoon. Begin by putting a fork into the child's spare hand for them simply to hold. This helps the toddler get used to the feel of having something in their other hand. Once this looks comfortable, gently guide the toddler's hands so they can see how to use spoon and fork together to push food onto the spoon. Mastering this is an important skill.

Observation

Does the toddler seem to cope with holding a fork while using the spoon?

Is the toddler using the fork and spoon together?

Planning

Provide a fork for short periods at a time.

Eat alongside the toddler using a fork and spoon so that the toddler can see a role model.

Look for food stuffs that will be easy to use so that the toddler can practise, for example mashed potato and baked beans.

16-26 months

Teddy's hats and socks

Toddlers need practice at putting on and taking off clothes before they will be able to master this skill completely. Find a large teddy and some hats and socks that will fit the teddy – look out for hats and socks that will appeal to the toddler. Dress Teddy using some simple clothes and tell the toddler that Teddy wants to change his hat and socks. See if the toddler can take them off Teddy and choose some new ones for Teddy to wear.

Observation

Can the toddler take off Teddy's hat and socks?

Planning

What other clothes could be put on Teddy?

Put out some dressing-up clothes for the toddler to try on as well.

22-36 months

Self-care

What do I need to do?

- Ensure that enough time is available for children to practise self-care skills.

- Check whether the routine of your setting creates plenty of opportunities for self-care, for example wiping tables and hanging up coats.

- Praise children when they show self-care skills.

- Observe children and consider what else they may be capable of doing.

- Talk to parents about the benefits of self-care skills.

Frequently Asked Questions

Some parents take their child's coat off and then hang it up. Should we say anything?

Probably not. Many parents do this as an expression of their love and need especially to 'look after' their child at a moment of separation. Consider instead having a list of self-care skills that children can practise with their parents at home.

Some of our children cannot use a knife and fork at lunch time. Any suggestions?

Begin by putting knives and forks out with dough or even in a small tray of damp sand. Model their use so that children see how to hold a knife and fork. Remember that the use of knives and forks is cultural and so be sensitive rather than judgemental when talking about their use.

Shoe shop role play   30–50 months

Children in this age group are just starting to enjoy dressing up. Create a shoe shop with many different types of shoes for children to 'buy'. Choose shoes that have a range of different fastenings, including buckles and laces, as well as slip-ons. You might also like to include some boots. Take a role in the shoe shop so that children can learn the language of shoes, for example slip-on, lace-up, trainer and sandal.

This activity links very well to Problem Solving, Reasoning and Numeracy as you can talk about the sizes of different shoes as well as their price.

Observation

Planning

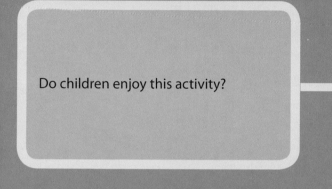

Do children enjoy this activity?

Think about other ways in which role play could be used to encourage children to develop their self-care skills, for example putting on coats and shoes or practising with knives, forks or other implements such as chopsticks or spoons.

30-50 months

Washing up   40–60+ months

Children love water and so learning to wash up can be great fun for them. At a meal or snack time, tell the children that they are going to do some of the washing up. Take children over to the sink or put out some washing-up bowls onto tables. Show children how to wash up and also dry up using a tea towel.

Note that you should check with parents that children do not have skin allergies and use only a small amount of washing-up liquid. Make sure that children rinse their hands afterwards. The items will also need to be properly washed later using hotter water.

Observation

Planning

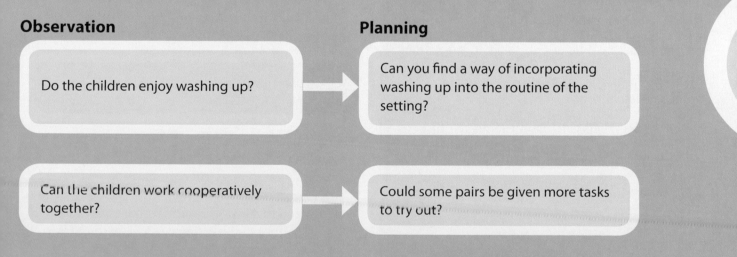

Do the children enjoy washing up?

Can you find a way of incorporating washing up into the routine of the setting?

Can the children work cooperatively together?

Could some pairs be given more tasks to try out?

40-60+ months

Sense of Community

What do I need to do?

- Provide opportunities for babies to see other children and adults.

- Take babies outdoors for walks, for example to the local shops.

- Create a warm and cosy environment for babies and toddlers.

- Look for ways of reflecting babies' and toddlers' home cultures in the setting.

- Use routines for babies and toddlers to feel settled.

- Put up photographs of babies' and toddlers' families and friends.

- Create a display showing photographs of other babies and children as well as the staff members working in the room.

Frequently Asked Questions

Our babies love seeing older children. Is it safe for different ages to mix?

It is actually very good for babies to see and be with older children, providing that you supervise the children well. It also has benefits for older children as it can help them to feel responsible. The Statutory Framework is clear that there should be opportunities for babies to spend time with older children.

We want to take the babies to the local shop. Do we need extra staff to do this?

You have to stay in ratio all the time, but you do not necessarily need extra staff if your risk assessment of this type of outing suggests that this is not required. On the day of the outing you will need to consider whether there needs to be any changes to the original risk assessment, for example because of the weather.

Baby display board

Babies often enjoy seeing photographs of other babies. Recognising other babies and enjoying seeing their pictures is an early start for developing a sense of community.

If you are working in a baby room, take some photographs of all of the babies in the room with a digital camera. Print them out on A4 paper and laminate them. Put them onto a wall so that babies can be picked up to look at them. If you are not working in a baby room, take some photographs of the baby and add photographs or posters of other babies to the display.

Lift the baby up and hold them close to you. Point out familiar faces to the babies and talk to them.

Observation

Does the baby seem to enjoy seeing other babies?

Does the baby point to or show in other ways that they are interested in the faces?

Planning

Build this into the routine of the day.

Add in new photographs of the baby.

If babies seem unresponsive at six months or so, consider whether they are seeing well.

0-11 months

Family treasure hunt

Sense of community begins with babies and toddlers feeling confident about their relationships with others. Laminate some photographs for babies and toddlers to look at. You could choose photographs of the people who care for them, including parents and family members. Hide these photographs by, for example, putting them in a basket with other items such as scarves and fabric or dried pasta. For older toddlers you might also hide the photographs in several small boxes.

Observation

How does the baby or toddler react when they find a photograph?

Planning

Find other ways of displaying photographs of family and key people who look after the toddler or baby.

Make a book of photographs and share it with the baby or toddler.

8-20 months

Sense of Community

What do I need to do?

- Talk to parents about what their child enjoys doing.
- Provide resources that help the child feel at home.
- Share books with children that have photographs or drawings of other children.
- Take toddlers on local outings so that they can become familiar with the area.
- Introduce small-world play when appropriate.
- Encourage the toddler to try out new foods.

Frequently Asked Questions

Our toddlers don't play together. How can we encourage a sense of community?

Toddlers are not really designed to play with each other – while they may notice other children, they tend to play alongside each other. A sense of community is about helping toddlers to feel part of the setting, which means trying to put together some routines so they feel settled.

There is one toddler who, when with their key person, becomes very upset and even aggressive if another child approaches. What should we do?

This behaviour is within normal development as toddlers tend not to enjoy sharing 'their' adults, and this toddler clearly has a good bond with their key person. For this age group, it is probably best to employ some distraction techniques or to reposition yourself so that you can accommodate a child on each side of you.

My favourite book

The starting point for learning about other people is for children to develop a sense of their own families and selves. Based on observations, photographs and talks with parents, produce a book about a toddler's favourite things and people. Laminate the book as it is likely to be handled quite a lot.

Look at the book with the toddler and talk to him or her about the photographs. Share other toddlers' books with the children to see if they can recognise each other.

Observation

Does this toddler seem to recognise the people and items in the photographs?

Planning

Can you put a box together of items that the toddler likes?

Produce another book after a few months as the toddler changes and develops.

16-26 months

Old Macdonald

Singing is a good way of children feeling that they are involved in a setting. Make up a song based on the tune of Old Macdonald that focuses on the children and, if relevant, the name of your nursery or playgroup. For example, 'Rainbow Playgroup had some children, Ee-i-ee-i-O. And all the children in the group came and played all day…' You can put out shakers and other simple instruments for children to join in with. Once you have devised your song, try and sing it quite often.

Observation

Do the toddlers enjoy this song and join in with it?

Planning

When can you use the song during the routine of the session, for example just before lunch or when getting ready to go out?

Can you personalise other songs, for example using children's individual names in a song?

22-36 months

Sense of Community

What do I need to do?

- Look for opportunities for children to talk about their own families, friends and events in their lives.

- Provide opportunities for children to talk to each about their lives.

- Make sure that you have a role-play area that reflects children's home culture.

- Look for ways of helping children to learn about shared differences, for example the way you celebrate birthdays, the food you eat, your favourite programmes.

- Provide resources that reflect cultural and other differences, for example toys from other countries, cooking utensils.

- Model respect in the way that you interact with children.

- Work with parents to ensure that you understand children's family contexts.

Frequently Asked Questions

Is there a list of festivals that we should be celebrating?

No, but you will need to help children learn that not everyone has the same beliefs, food or language and that other people may also celebrate events in different ways. Ideally, you should plan activities based on the children that you have in your setting.

We have been told that we should have a wider range of cooking utensils in the home corner. The problem is that children play with them in odd ways.

If children are to know how to play with objects such as chopsticks, woks and coffee pots, they need to see them being used. Think about asking a parent who uses them to show you what they are for or, better still, do some cooking with the children.

Take Teddy home   30–50 months

Take Teddy home is a popular activity in many settings. It is also a simple activity to organise. Children are given Teddy to take home for the night or the weekend. Some settings send home a digital camera or a diary so that a record of what Teddy has been doing can be kept by parents or children. This is a lovely activity as many children find it hard to talk about what they have been doing at the weekend, but holding Teddy or seeing the photographs can help them. It also helps other children in the setting to learn about another child's home and family life.

Note that some parents become very competitive when it is their turn to have Teddy! One way of calming this down is to have several teddies that go home fairly regularly rather than Teddy's visit being only once a year.

Observation

Do children enjoy this activity?

Planning

Send Teddy home with children when there is a special event, for example the child's birthday or a visit by grandparents.

Make 'Teddy' books with the children so that they have a record of his stay.

Encourage the children to talk in pairs about what Teddy would like doing in their home.

Children's day   40–60+ months

Most children learn that there is a Mother's day and a Father's day, but they may not know that many countries in the world also have Children's days. Children's days in the world vary enormously, although all celebrate the importance of children. In some cases children have parties and are given gifts.

Plan a Children's day with groups of children. Decide on what they would like to do on their Children's day. You might like to plan games and food with them. This activity would be good to help children learn to work together while also learning about the way in which other children in the world may have different celebrations.

Observation

Are children able to talk and cooperate together?

Planning

What other events could children be encouraged to think about and organise?

How can parents become involved with creating celebrations?

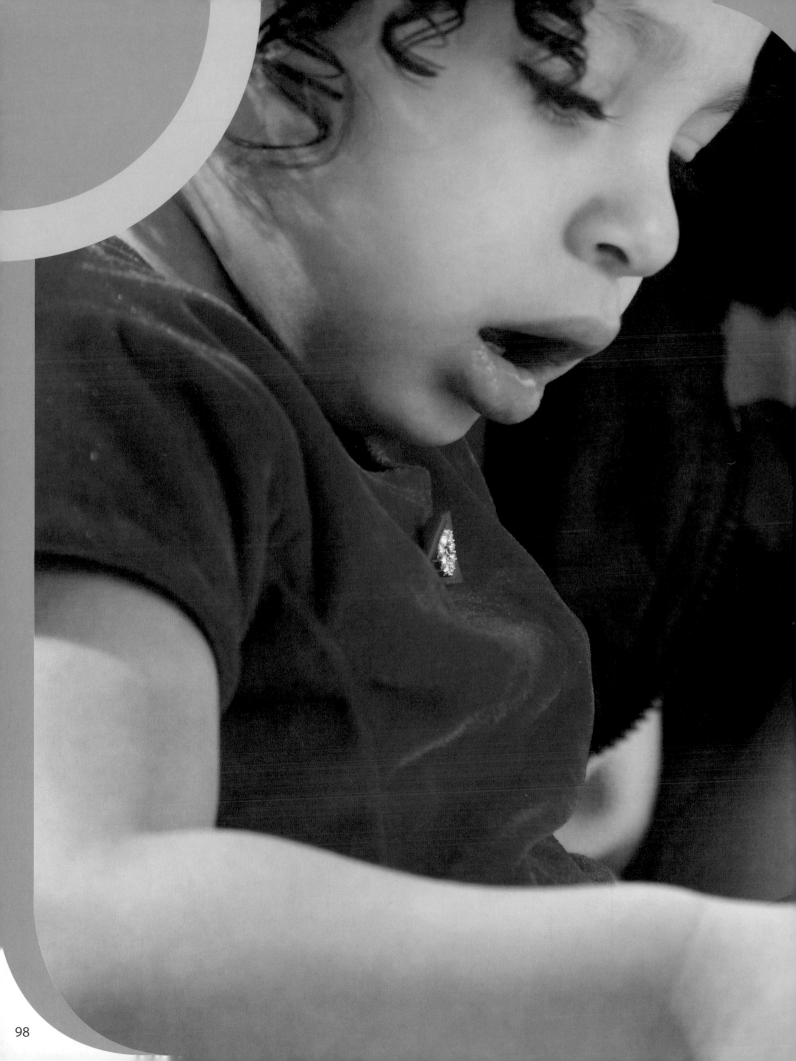

Communication, Language and Literacy

Being able to communicate and then later be able to read and write are life skills which begin at birth and require significant adult input.

This area of Learning and Development includes the following aspects:

- Language for Communication
- Language for Thinking
- Linking Sounds and Letters
- Reading
- Writing
- Handwriting

Language for Communication

What do I need to do?

- Recognise that babies and toddlers need to form strong relationships with their key person in order for language to develop.

- Provide sustained eye contact when communicating with babies and toddlers.

- Record babies' and toddlers' attempts at communicating and check that they are making progress in line with expected development.

- Acknowledge babies' and toddlers' attempts at communicating.

- Find out from parents how they communicate with their child at home.

Frequently Asked Questions

Why is the key person system so important?

To learn how to communicate, babies and toddlers have to tune into the language that they are being exposed to. Being with the same person allows this process to develop more easily. It also means that the key person can more readily 'tune' into the baby's or toddler's early attempts at communicating.

We have a baby whose parents are speaking Turkish to him at home. Is this all right?

Yes, it is lovely if a baby can learn another language early on. It is important, though, to encourage the parents to only use Turkish when talking directly with their baby, so that the baby learns to differentiate between the two languages. If a parent 'mixes' their communication, this can lead to the baby becoming confused about the sounds and structure of both languages.

Time to smile!

Making eye contact and gaining a smile from a baby is an important way to develop early communication. Most babies smile from about six weeks and will increasingly do so in response to seeing an adult smile.

Choose a time when the baby is settled and hold the baby. Smile and look directly at him or her while encouraging the baby to smile. When the baby returns the smile, acknowledge this by talking and smiling back.

Observation

Planning

0-11 months

| How long does the baby take to respond to the smile? | → | Take photographs of the baby smiling and laminate them. Make the photographs into a book. |
| When you stop smiling, does the baby try and make you smile? | → | See if the baby is ready to play games such as peek-a-boo or responds to rhymes such as 'Round and round the garden like a teddy bear'. |

Who's on the phone?

Very early on, toddlers take an interest in telephones. This means that it is worth looking out for a toy phone for toddlers to play with. To encourage chatter into the phone, it is important that you pretend to talk into the phone and also respond when a toddler attempts to communicate.

Observation

Planning

8-20 months

| Is the child interested in the telephone? | → | Look out for other toys that make sounds. Ask a familiar adult to phone the toddler and hold the phone to their ear. (Don't worry if the child does not respond.) |

Language for Communication

What do I need to do?

- Recognise that children will talk more to adults who they like and feel comfortable with.

- Make sure that children have opportunities to talk to each other.

- Look out for times when children can talk to adults individually or in small groups.

- Understand that children will often talk aloud when they are thinking.

- Find out from parents which languages are used at home.

Frequently Asked Questions

We have a child who hardly talks to other children, but enjoys adult company. Any suggestions?

It may be that this child needs adult attention or that they are not confident yet to play alongside other children. It is worth talking to parents first. Try organising games that require a pair of children and sit with them.

A child has started at the setting who does not speak any English. How can we help him?

The starting point is to make the child feel emotionally secure, so his key person will need to spend a lot of time with him. Take photographs of the toilets, drinks and key activities to help the child understand some of the essentials, and learn a few key words in the child's home language.

Time to talk: shelling peas

30–50 months

Children need opportunities to sit alongside adults and chat. This is best done when the adult is engaged in a simple activity that the child can either watch or join in with. It is important that the activity is repetitive and simple. One example of an activity that works well is to shell peas.

Sit at a table with a couple of bowls of peas and open them up. You will find that children will soon come and find you. They may ask what you are doing or if they can help. Invite them to join you. Do not feel that you must only talk about the peas – use this as an opportunity to chat to children and to let the children chat to you.

Observation   **Planning**

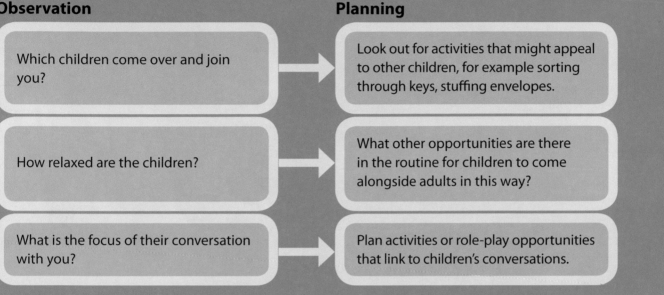

Observation	Planning
Which children come over and join you?	Look out for activities that might appeal to other children, for example sorting through keys, stuffing envelopes.
How relaxed are the children?	What other opportunities are there in the routine for children to come alongside adults in this way?
What is the focus of their conversation with you?	Plan activities or role-play opportunities that link to children's conversations.

30-50 months

What's Teddy been doing?

40–60+ months

Put three objects in a bag with a teddy bear. With a small group of children (no more than four), take out Teddy and the objects. See if the children can work out what Teddy has been doing.

You could make this activity easier by choosing three objects that are linked, for example a shopping list, a shopping bag and a purse. See if the children and you can make a simple story together. Once you have worked out the story, re-tell the story so that children can hear the language structure of a story with a beginning, middle and end.

Observation   **Planning**

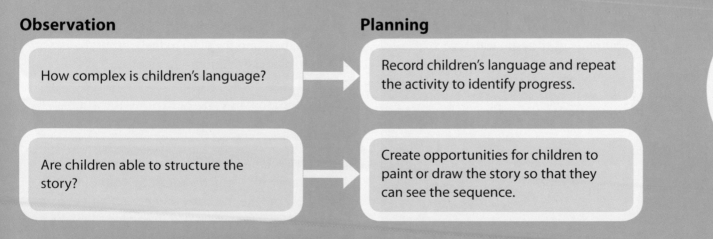

Observation	Planning
How complex is children's language?	Record children's language and repeat the activity to identify progress.
Are children able to structure the story?	Create opportunities for children to paint or draw the story so that they can see the sequence.

40-60+ months

Language for Thinking

What do I need to do?

- Draw children's attention to objects in the environment and label them.

- Make comments and use questions as part of a conversation, for example 'I wonder what happened to that? Perhaps it fell down.'

- Make sure that there are interesting items in the environment so that you have a focus for communication.

- Use the outdoor environment for toddlers to explore and use this as an opportunity to model language.

- Remember that toddlers need time to organise their thoughts and then to respond.

- Reflect on the way you use language to check that you are giving children opportunities to respond.

Frequently Asked Questions

Are there any particular words that toddlers should be learning?

No, but what you should find with this age range is that once they begin to use words, they are quickly able to learn new ones. At around two years, many children suddenly acquire words at an astonishing rate. They can only do this, though, if someone is talking to them and drawing their attention to things in their environment.

We have been told not to use baby language with toddlers and to use proper words. Is this correct?

Try to give toddlers as many words as possible rather than restricting them to the more simplistic words. For example, once a toddler knows what a coat is, try and use the word for the type of coat that they are wearing, such as an anorak or raincoat. In this way toddler's language can be extended.

Scooping and finding   16–26 months

Toddlers are more likely to remember words for objects if they are interested in them and are excited to have found them. This is an outdoor activity that could be adjusted for indoors. The focus on taking toddlers outdoors is important as it creates a more sensory environment.

Line a car or tractor tyre with polythene sheeting then fill it up with bark chippings. Hide some items inside it (towards the top so there is more chance that the toddlers will find them.) It does not matter what type of objects are hidden, providing you think that they will be of interest to the toddlers, for example farm animals or a leather purse.

Start the activity by digging yourself with your hands or a scoop. Show the toddlers what you have found and let them look at it. See if the toddlers are interested to explore and chat to them about what is being found. Do not worry if a toddler decides to play with an item that has been found rather than continue with the activity.

Observation

How interested was the toddler in this activity?

Planning

Repeat this activity but vary the items.

Try putting in a variety of items of different sizes or of the same colour.

Put out boxes or containers so that toddlers can place their 'finds' inside.

16-26 months

A box of bits!   22–36 months

One way to stimulate children's thinking and language is by giving them opportunities to sort objects. This can be done both inside and outdoors.

Put a range of objects into a suitcase; include some large and some smaller items. Some of the items should clearly belong together, such as toy cars or other small-world toys. Begin to open the suitcase with the child, but let the child finish opening the suitcase so they can see what is inside. Talk to the child about what they are finding, but be sensitive to the child's need to explore independently. You may find that a toddler will want you to hold items that are of interest; this is a way of sharing interest with you.

Observation

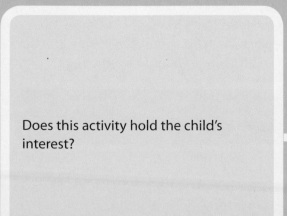

Does this activity hold the child's interest?

Planning

Repeat the activity using the same objects but add in some more.

Look out for ways of incorporating the objects that are of interest into other activities.

Take photographs of the child during this activity and show them to the child later.

Share the photographs with parents so they can repeat this activity at home if they wish.

22-36 months

Language for Thinking

What do I need to do?

- Use specific vocabulary wherever possible, for example 'daffodil' rather than 'flower'.

- Record children's speech to check that over time it is becoming more complex.

- Use language in context so that children can acquire new phrases and vocabulary.

- Make connections between what a child already knows and new information, for example 'that's called scarlet, your shoes are this colour.'

- Encourage children to use their language to explain their thinking and reasoning.

Frequently Asked Questions

We have a three-year-old who talks well, but it is hard to understand what she is saying. Any advice?

This is worth checking out as normally most children's speech at three years is intelligible to strangers. Begin by talking to parents and see if the child can be referred for speech and language support and a hearing test. (Note that a common cause of unclear speech in young children relates to difficulties in hearing. Also, children who have a conductive hearing loss can hear well on some days and not on others.)

At what age should children be able to pronounce all the sounds in words?

Speech maturity is linked to the development of the tongue, lips and teeth. Most children have all their sounds by seven years. Rhyme work and making sure that children eat chewy foods are ways in which you can support this development.

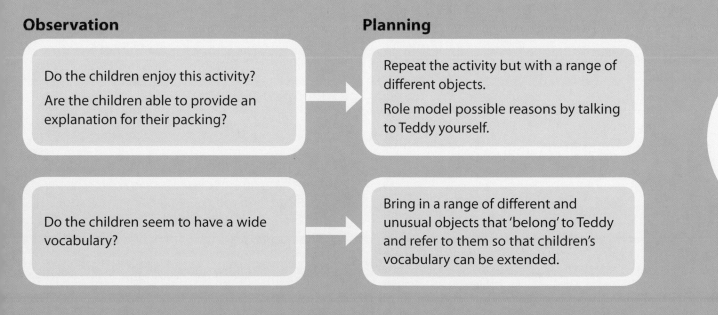

Same and different: Teddy's leaves 30–50 months

The ability to use language for explanation is an important linguistic and cognitive skill. It is also helpful if children can learn to look out for similarities and differences.

Give children a pile of leaves from different trees and bushes. Say that Teddy wants the children to sort them out. Make sure that each child has their own assortment. Provide boxes, containers or plastic hoops so that each child can find a way of sorting them. Pick up two leaves from the same group. Draw children's attention to the way in which they may still have differences, for example slightly different lengths and colours.

30-50 months

Observation

Does the child enjoy the sorting activity?

Can a child explain the reasoning for the grouping?

Planning

Provide other similar activities, for example Teddy's shells, Teddy's buttons or Teddy's stamp collection.

Repeat the activity but join in with the children as they are sorting. Role model the language and thinking.

Provide different objects to extend children's thinking.

Help Teddy pack 40–60+ months

Bring in a teddy, a toy suitcase, clothes and some strange objects (such as a shuttlecock or a packet of pasta). Tell a small group of children that Teddy is going on holiday and he does not know what he should pack. See if the children can pack his suitcase for him. Ask the children to tell Teddy why he cannot take some of the more unsuitable objects that he wants to.

40-60+ months

Observation

Do the children enjoy this activity?
Are the children able to provide an explanation for their packing?

Do the children seem to have a wide vocabulary?

Planning

Repeat the activity but with a range of different objects.
Role model possible reasons by talking to Teddy yourself.

Bring in a range of different and unusual objects that 'belong' to Teddy and refer to them so that children's vocabulary can be extended.

Linking Sounds and Letters

What do I need to do?

- Record babies' and toddlers' early vocalisations. Notice whether they are becoming more tuneful.

- Sing songs and rhymes with babies and toddlers.

- Let toddlers explore items that make different sounds.

- Acknowledge babies' and toddlers' attempts at communication.

- Consider whether babies and toddlers are responding to different sounds so as to ensure that they are fully hearing.

Frequently Asked Questions

Should we be introducing babies and toddlers to letter shapes?

No – at this stage the focus should be on promoting babies' and toddlers' overall communication skills and interests in sounds. This is the starting point for the children's later literacy development.

What's the point of singing rhymes if babies cannot join in?

Early rhymes and songs help babies and toddlers to tune into the sounds of language. They also help babies and toddlers to feel involved and emotionally secure. This is why rhymes and songs are traditional ways of soothing young children.

Why are rhymes and beats important?

There is some research to suggest that being able to hear rhymes and feel the pattern of beat within words is helpful later on when children learn to read.

Feel the beat

0–11 months

Babies are responsive to rhymes and songs and being rocked – this helps them to feel emotionally secure. Rhymes and songs can also help them to feel the pattern of beat within words, which can be helpful later on when learning to read (see FAQ).

Pick up a baby or put the baby securely in your lap. Sing a tune or say a rhyme that has a beat to it. Move or rock the baby in time with the beat. (Note the response of the baby and stop immediately if the baby is not enjoying this experience.) Repeat again, but change the pace in some way by, for example, repeating the rhyme more slowly or choosing a song with a different rhythm or beat.

Observation

Is the baby able to anticipate the beat?

Does the baby show that they prefer a song or rhyme?

Does the baby respond without prompting to tunes and rhymes?

Planning

Repeat with different songs and rhymes.

See if the baby is beginning to recognise certain tunes or rhymes and reinforce these.

Note which tunes and rhymes the baby enjoys and repeat these.

Try playing some recorded music.

0-11 months

Shakers and movers

8–20 months

Put out or make a range of shakers, for example an empty custard tin with some rice inside. The instruments can be presented in a basket or box to make them appear more attractive. Allow the toddler a free choice and watch carefully as they explore them. Toys that make sounds could also be included, although interestingly, many toddlers prefer the sounds made by natural materials such as wooden castanets or rain sticks.

(Safety note: make sure that homemade shakers cannot be opened by the child.)

Observation

Does the toddler have a favourite sound or shaker?

Does the toddler enjoy this activity?

Planning

Make larger or smaller shakers with the same filling inside.

Put on music and see whether the toddler reacts by playing with their shaker in time.

Provide other musical instruments so that the toddler can explore different sounds.

8-20 months

Linking Sounds and Letters

What do I need to do?

- Aim to teach a new rhyme or song every week.

- Make up rhymes that link to children's names.

- Put out musical instruments and play games to encourage children to hear and to respond to different sounds.

- Regularly check children's hearing by seeing if they can respond to sounds that take place out of sight.

Frequently Asked Questions

When should we start showing children letter shapes?

Most sound to symbol recognition work will take place in the Reception class. At this earlier stage, it is important to work on sound recognition skills (often referred to as auditory discrimination skills).

I have one child who does not seem to hear the beat in music. Any advice?

It is worth repeating games that involve a response to the beat several times. If you still feel that the child is not hearing the beat, consider whether they might need their hearing checked and talk to the child's parents.

Is it better to use traditional or modern nursery rhymes?

While modern rhymes often have more meaning, many traditional nursery rhymes have very strong rhythms and contain many alliterations (words beginning with the same initial sounds). Try using both types.

Sound wall   16–26 months

Toddlers love to explore sounds and ways of making sounds, so they will enjoy playing with a sound wall.

To construct a sound wall, first find a fence. Attach different objects to the fence that can be used to make a noise. These might include saucepans, filled plastic shakers, saucepan lids, metal colanders or dustbin lids. The aim is that children can make the objects touch each other or hit them with their hands or a stick. It is important that the objects are securely tied and that adults are on hand to supervise if children are given sticks.

Observation

Are the children interested in the different sounds?

Planning

Talk to the children about the sounds they are making.

Encourage children to find new ways of making sounds with the object.

Work with the children to find new things to hang onto the fence.

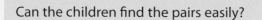

16-26 months

Sound pairs   22–36 months

Look for some identical small containers such as small boxes, opaque bottles or film canisters. Split the containers up into pairs and put identical materials in each pair, for example rice, dried peas, cat bells, buttons. Make sure that the containers are sealed. Put all the containers into a box or basket. Encourage the children to pick up the containers and shake them. Can they find any of the matching pairs?

Observation

Are the children interested in this activity?

Can the children find the pairs easily?

Planning

Make shakers with the children using the same materials that were used to make the sound pairs. Can they find which of their containers sound like the ones in the pair basket?

Make some new pairs, but choose materials that will make very similar sounds, for example rice and couscous.

22-36 months

115

Linking Sounds and Letters

What do I need to do?

- Plan games to help children hear and order sounds.

- Sing songs that have strong sounds patterns.

- Draw children's attention to sounds including those in their name.

- Plan a programme of rhymes.

- Teach older children an alphabet song.

Frequently Asked Questions

Why are rhymes so important?

Rhymes seem to help children focus on the sounds and patterns in words. Research has shown that children who have a good knowledge of nursery rhymes seem to find it easier to link sounds and letters. This is important for later reading.

We rarely put out musical instruments because the children squabble over them or make an awful sound. Any suggestions?

Musical instruments and activities are important in developing children's skills. The trick is to put instruments out more often so that children get used to them, and to put out similar instruments to start with so that children do not squabble over 'the best'. Think about making shakers with children so that each child has their own. At the start of an activity, give children the opportunity to explore what the instrument can do before attempting an adult-led activity.

The hot and cold game with sounds   30–50 months

Give a small group of children a shaker each. Ask a child to look away while you hide an object. When the child returns to the group, tell the child to start looking for the object. Ask the other children to help them by making loud sounds if the child is getting close to the hidden object (getting 'hot') and quiet sounds if the child is moving away from the hidden object (getting 'cold').

Observation

Planning

Do the children enjoy this game?

→

Vary the game by using a range of different shakers.

Vary the game by changing the sounds that the children have to make, for example fast shaking if the child is getting close and very slow shaking if the child is moving away.

30-50 months

Can you recognise these sounds?   40–60+ months

This is a fun activity that with modern technology is easy to organise. Using an MP3 player, record some everyday sounds such as turning on a tap, a dog barking, the sounds of children playing outdoors, a clock that ticks. Play the recording back through a laptop or computer. Can the children work out what sounds they are hearing?

Observation

Planning

Do the children enjoy this game?

→

Find ways of children choosing and recording other everyday sounds. (This links neatly to ICT within Knowledge and Understanding of the World.)

40-60+ months

Reading

What do I need to do?

- Encourage parents to share books with their child at home.

- Create pleasant opportunities for toddlers to share books with adults.

- Notice which books individual children enjoy.

- Encourage toddlers to look at the pictures and use this time to help them learn some new vocabulary.

- Respond to toddlers when they try and point out something in a picture to you.

- Make sure that individual children have opportunities each day to share a book with a member of staff.

Frequently Asked Questions

We find it hard to get the toddlers to come and sit down at story time. Any suggestions?

Group story time is not really appropriate for toddlers. They prefer to hold and look at books with an adult rather than as part of a group. Think about changing your routines.

Some of the older children choose baby books to look at by themselves. Should we stop them?

Children will often enjoy looking at books that they are familiar with. They may do this independently or may share these books with you. It does not matter which books children choose to look at independently – the most important thing is to build up children's interest in books and their understanding that print carries meaning.

Rhyme books

Rhymes are essential in helping children learn to differentiate between sounds. They are also popular with young children and you will find that they learn some of the rhymes quickly.

Choose an attractively illustrated rhyme book to share with a toddler. With the toddler on your lap or beside you, look at one of the rhymes. Read it through a couple of times while pointing to any pictures that act as illustrations. Some books use the same rhyme sequence throughout the book, for example *Peepo!* by Janet and Allan Ahlberg (Puffin). These type of rhyme books are particularly popular.

Observation

How interested is the toddler in sharing the book?

Does the toddler have a favourite page or rhyme?

Planning

Repeat this activity, although look out for signs that the toddler is losing interest.

Make a note of the book and make sure it is available again in the future.

Pass on information to parents about books that the toddler has enjoyed.

16-26 months

Teddy tells stories

At around this age, many children become interested in cuddly toys and role play. They also are beginning to like stories with simple, repetitive plots. This is a good time to introduce them to storytelling.

Think of something that the child enjoys doing and make it into a simple story involving the child and Teddy. For example, 'Once upon a time, Teddy and Darren decided to dig in the sand. They dug, and they dug, and they dug, until Darren found a…' Use traditional starts and ends to the story and try to include things that the child has done recently. Keep the story short so that the child does not lose interest.

Observation

Does the child enjoy hearing a story about their actions?

Planning

Repeat the story on another day and see if the child can remember it.

Look for ways of encouraging the child to join in.

Take photographs of Teddy doing different things, for example shopping, to act as a prompt for further stories.

22-36 months

Reading

What do I need to do?

- Share books with children.

- Encourage parents to read a bedtime story to their children.

- Point out words in the environment.

- Label objects, toys and other items of interest to children.

- Play matching games such as picture lotto and snap.

- Encourage children to tell stories from pictures.

- Provide opportunities to develop children's language.

Frequently Asked Questions

Should we be using a reading scheme with children?

Reading schemes are best used in the latter part of the Reception year. Formal teaching of reading works well only if children have developed sufficient pre-reading skills beforehand. Pre-reading skills include the ability to handle books, understand that print is read from left to right in English, being able to re-tell a story and being able to match.

What is the best group size for story time?

Small is always best, particularly for children who might not be read to at home, as children need opportunities to touch books, ask questions and make comments. This means that some children may need individual stories as well as group ones. Large groups are difficult to manage as children will have different interests and language needs.

Name Treasure Hunt   30–50 months

One of the first words that children learn to 'read' is their name. Names are useful because they help children learn the association between symbols and words. Children will need to see their name many times before they will be able to recognise it easily.

Hide two or three children's names outdoors in fairly easy places. Tell the two or three children that Teddy has been playing tricks and has hidden their names outdoors. Could they help you to find the name cards?

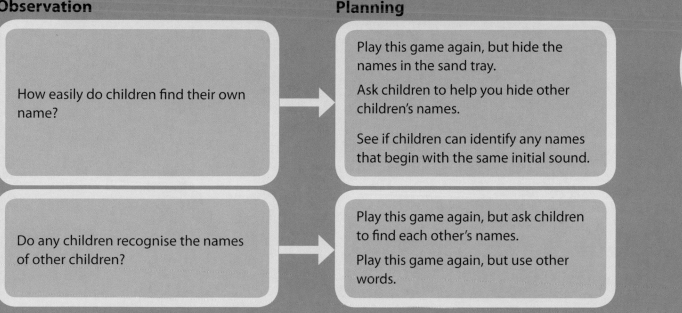

Observation

How easily do children find their own name?

Do any children recognise the names of other children?

Planning

Play this game again, but hide the names in the sand tray.

Ask children to help you hide other children's names.

See if children can identify any names that begin with the same initial sound.

Play this game again, but ask children to find each other's names.

Play this game again, but use other words.

30-50 months

Letters in the sand   40–60+ months

Children love receiving letters and this means that letters can be used as a way of stimulating interest in reading.

Write some simple letters, put them in envelopes and hide them in a dry sand tray. Aim for about ten words in each letter, for example 'Hello, I like playing in the sand. Love Teddy.' Tell the children that Teddy has been hiding letters for them to read.

Take the time to read the letters to the children. Make sure that you point at the words as you are reading them. Afterwards, the children can hide the letters again or they can be put out for the children to hold and read again.

Observation

Did the children enjoy finding letters?
Did the children look at the letters again?

Were any children pointing to words as they were looking at them?
Which words did they appear to know?

Planning

Play this game again using new letters.
See if the children would like to write back to Teddy.

Use similar words in other letters.
Make a word lotto game using some of the words in the letter.

40-60+ months

Writing

What do I need to do?

- Provide opportunities for babies and toddlers to make marks.

- Look for a variety of materials that will encourage babies and toddlers to use their hands.

- Draw and make marks alongside babies and toddlers.

- Talk about the marks that are being made.

- Observe which materials are the easiest for babies and toddlers to use.

Frequently Asked Questions

What's the point of doing writing with this age group?

The first stages of the EYFS are about preparing babies and toddlers for the later skills that they will need. The starting point for writing is a desire to make marks and to express oneself.

Will the babies and toddlers know that they are writing?

Not as such, but this does not mean that they are not enjoying themselves or learning about the link between self-expression and making marks.

What should the adult do to encourage mark-making?

The adult needs to role model mark-making by, for example, drawing or using the materials alongside the children. It is also important for the adult to talk to the babies and toddlers, as eventually they will need to learn that there is a link between speech and writing.

Spills!

0–11 months

One of the first ways in which a baby learns to make marks is by moving their hands through liquid and watching the effect that this has. This usually happens when the baby or the adult has spilt some milk or food onto the highchair tray.

Choose a time when the baby is not hungry. The baby should be at a stage when they can be propped up safely or can sit unaided. Put a bib on the baby and then place the baby in the highchair and pour some lightly coloured water into the highchair tray. See if the baby tries to spread the spill around. (It is important not to use highly coloured water as it may stain the baby's clothes.) Note how interested the baby is and be ready to change the activity if the baby becomes tired.

Observation

Planning

Is the baby interested in spreading their hands through the spill?

Look out for other liquids and materials that you could use to repeat this activity, for example cornflour and water or rice.

Look for large-scale opportunities for the baby to make marks with their hands and body, for example putting a spill out on a plastic mat.

0-11 months

Shaving foam

8–20 months

Early mark-making is about toddlers learning that when they move their hands, traces can be seen. One popular activity is to put out a layer of shaving foam.

Put out a layer of shaving foam onto a tray. Come alongside the toddler and make some marks within it. Encourage the toddler to do the same. Watch to see what types of marks are made. Do not worry if the toddler is not interested in making marks but instead just squeezes the foam to explore the texture.

Note that you should use shaving foam suitable for delicate skin which is not highly perfumed. You must also wash the children's hands carefully afterwards.

Observation

Planning

How interested is the child is exploring this material?

Try other types of sensory materials.

Repeat this activity on another day.

Take photographs of the child exploring the shaving foam to show parents and the child.

8-20 months

Writing

What do I need to do?

- Provide plenty of opportunities for toddlers to make marks in a variety of ways.

- Provide positive feedback about the marks that are being made.

- Act as a role model – draw and paint alongside toddlers.

- Talk about the marks that are being made.

- Observe the materials that seem to attract toddlers.

- Make sure that the focus is on mark-making rather than on 'writing'.

- Explain to parents the importance of early mark-making.

Frequently Asked Questions

Should we be showing toddlers how to write?

While you can encourage toddlers' interest in the process of writing by talking as you write and draw, it is too early for toddlers to be formally taught to write. They are at an earlier stage when they need to explore how to make marks and enjoy making them.

Does it matter that toddlers do not know what they are writing?

No, at this stage it is the process of trying to write and communicate that is important. You may find that some toddlers will be more interested than others in this process.

What types of marks should toddlers be making?

Many toddlers will be interested in making lines and circular shapes, although their main focus will be exploring the feel of the mark-making materials that have been provided.

Paint brushes and water

16–26 months

This is a wonderful outdoor activity that will engage toddlers. Put out a bucket of water, a range of paint brushes and some aprons. Put on an apron, take a brush and dip it in the water then make marks on the ground, fence or even a window. Doing the activity yourself is essential as toddlers tend to copy the movements and actions of adults. You can also make the water soapy. As with all activities involving toddlers, you may find that they may choose to dip their hands in the water instead of using the brushes – this is fine, but try repeating the activity another time.

As with any water activity, it is essential to supervise the children at all times.

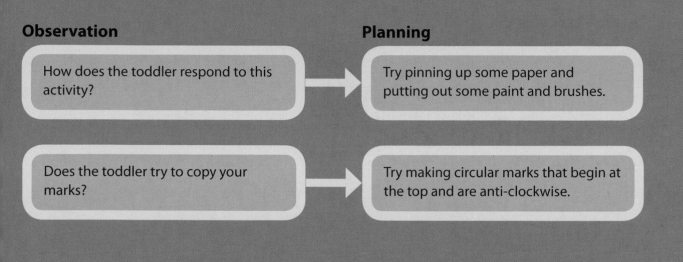

Observation

Planning

How does the toddler respond to this activity? → Try pinning up some paper and putting out some paint and brushes.

Does the toddler try to copy your marks? → Try making circular marks that begin at the top and are anti-clockwise.

16-26 months

Cornflour and water gloop

22–36 months

Combining cornflour and water produces a fascinating mixture. Put out a thin layer of gloop onto a baking sheet, plastic tray or other flat surface. In addition, put out some brushes or other tools that will help children make a mark, such as spoons or sticks. Model how you can make marks in the gloop with your finger or a stick. You might like to have your own tray and continue modelling in this way, as you may find that toddlers will copy some of your actions.

(As this activity will often be popular, you will need to provide several trays so that each child can explore mark-making without any squabbles!)

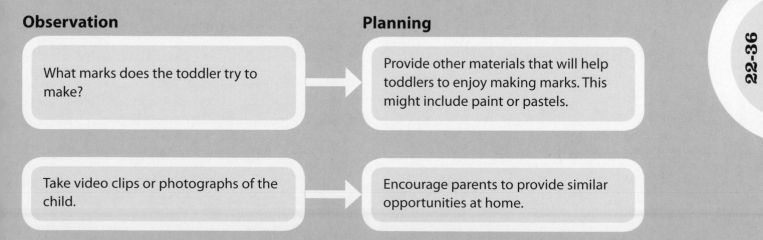

Observation

Planning

What marks does the toddler try to make? → Provide other materials that will help toddlers to enjoy making marks. This might include paint or pastels.

Take video clips or photographs of the child. → Encourage parents to provide similar opportunities at home.

22-36 months

Writing

What do I need to do?

- Provide enjoyable marking activities.
- Look out for opportunities to role model writing.
- Create opportunities for children to write with a purpose.
- Provide paper and writing materials alongside role play.
- Look for opportunities for children to write outdoors.
- Acknowledge children's attempts at writing.
- Avoid over-correction.
- Help parents understand the stages in mark-making and writing.

Frequently Asked Questions

Some parents see early mark-making as scribble. What can we tell them?

Explain to parents that children will need at first to explore marking, and that letters and recognisable words will appear later. It is worth showing parents the way in which mark-making does develop, for example when letters first appear.

Should we force children to write if they are not interested?

No, as this is likely to put them off and affect their future confidence. It is important to look for ways of incorporating writing into play activities, such as a pad of paper for the 'police' to use. Role modelling writing is one of the best ways for children to become interested.

Does it matter if children cannot write their name before they join Reception class?

No, providing that they are motivated to mark, recognise their name and have practised the early handwriting skills.

Painting wall
30–50 months

Children will often enjoy making marks on a large scale. At first, mark-making and drawing can be entwined, and so providing opportunities for large-scale painting can be wonderful for children.

Protect a wall by putting up plastic sheeting with masking tape. (You can use a plastic shower curtain for this.) Put paper on top of the plastic sheet – you could use brown paper or the back of wallpaper. It is worth leaving generous borders to avoid paint getting onto the wall. Give each child a small tray of paint and a paint brush so they have a mini palette. You can paint a dividing line onto the paper if children need 'their own' space in which to paint.

Observation

Do children talk as they are painting?

Are children ascribing meanings to their drawing and marks?

Planning

Do some painting yourself and role model writing as you paint.

Work out a story with children and then together paint and write the story.

30-50 months

Teddy letters
40–60+ months

Children are more likely to write when they can see a purpose. This is a way of combining writing with imaginative play.

Carry out an activity with Teddy. Afterward, ask the children whether they would like to write Teddy's mum or dad a letter, telling them how Teddy got on. Tell the children that Teddy's mum or dad can read all sorts of children's writing so they do not need to worry about what to put down.

Put out paper, pens and a bag for the letters to go in. Once a child has finished a letter, wait for a moment and then give the child a reply. The letter that you write back from Teddy's mum or dad needs to be short (around ten words). This will allow the child to remember what it says and help them to match the words to the print. Many children will then go onto write another letter immediately as they will be keen to get another reply!

Observation

How confident are children when they write?

Is a child using the reply letter to help them write back?

Planning

Think about other ways in which children can be encouraged to write when they know that they will not be corrected.

Look at ways of varying the response so as to increase the store of letters that a child is using.

40-60+ months

Handwriting

What do I need to do?

- Provide opportunities for babies and toddlers to develop gross motor movements.

- Give babies and toddlers materials to assist with their hand–eye coordination.

- Provide opportunities for babies and toddlers to handle objects.

- Talk to babies and toddlers as they are making marks.

- Look out for activities that will strengthen muscles in the hand.

Frequently Asked Questions

Why is there an emphasis on physical development in relation to handwriting?

The starting point for handwriting is physical movement, both fine movements with the hand and larger arm movements. In this way you can prepare children for the very small movements required in handwriting.

Should we be thinking about pencil grip?

No – babies and toddlers are not likely to be using pencils, and in any case their hands and wrists are too immature to be ready to hold pencils using a traditional tripod grasp.

Does it matter if babies and toddlers enjoy using the same materials?

No, because this means that they are constantly strengthening their coordination muscles. It is important, though, to provide some variety in the materials that are used, both to prevent them from becoming bored and to help them develop different skills.

Playing with handled objects

0–11 months

Early handwriting for babies is partly about supporting the development of their hand–eye coordination. Providing opportunities for babies to explore objects with handles is therefore useful. Look out for a range of objects which have handles, such as a scoop, a soft bristle make-up brush and a teaspoon. Choose objects that are made from natural materials as these give babies more sensory feedback and therefore pleasure. Make sure when choosing items that they are safe and not a choking hazard.

Pass each object to the baby. Do not worry if they explore it with their mouth as well as with their hands – this is normal in terms of their development.

Observation

Does the baby have any objects with which they are particularly fascinated?

What material are these objects made of?

How easily does the baby handle the objects?

Planning

Choose similar objects on another occasion or objects that are made out of the same materials. For example, a child who enjoyed a metal teaspoon might be interested in a metal scoop.

Think about whether the baby needs more challenges or would prefer materials that are lighter or smaller in order to explore them.

0-11 months

Sponges in water

8–20 months

Most toddlers love playing in water. Many different types of water play will encourage fine motor movement, especially those involving filling, scooping and pouring. In addition to materials that support these types of movements, it can also be useful to put out sponges for toddlers to squeeze.

Choose sponges of different sizes and textures so that the toddlers can find one type of sponge they can manage. If you play with the water alongside the toddlers, they will quickly learn how to manipulate the sponges. Talk to the toddlers about what they are doing and how the water is being released from the sponge.

Observation

Is the toddler able to squeeze out some water?

How easily can the toddler squeeze out the water?

Planning

Colour the water so that the child can see the amount of water that is being released from the sponge.

Put out cups and beakers so that the toddler can fill them up with the released water.

Look out for a range of different types of sponges.

8-20 months

131

Handwriting

What do I need to do?

- Provide opportunities for children to develop fine motor skills.

- Provide opportunities for children to make marks on a large and small scale.

- Provide activities that encourage children to make a variety of hand movements.

- Role model mark-making.

- Provide opportunities for painting.

- Note whether children are developing hand preference.

- Help parents to understand how physical skills relate to handwriting.

Frequently Asked Questions

Should children be doing tracing activities?

No, this is not required and is likely to be too difficult for children of these ages. Hand control is gained at this age by being given opportunities to use tools, make marks and playing. Tracing too early can put children off writing and can encourage poor pencil grip.

Should we be correcting the children's pencil grip?

It is normal for children in these age ranges to be using a palmar grip or simply experimenting. These children need plenty of different experiences of using tools. If you have concerns that a child is consistently holding a pencil incorrectly, it may be better to give them a different marking tool such as a paint brush or a much fatter pencil.

Spoons and scoop in damp sand
16–26 months

Put out some cat litter trays or other trays. Fill them with clean, damp sand. Put out a selection of spoons and scoops as well as plastic beakers, cups and other small containers. Sit with a tray and role model scooping and filling the beakers. You could also make mini sandcastles. The children are likely to come over and start to copy you! Make sure that each child has their own tray as sharing at this stage might be difficult for them.

Note: it is advisable to have a dustpan and brush to hand so that you and the children can sweep up if necessary.

Observation   **Planning**

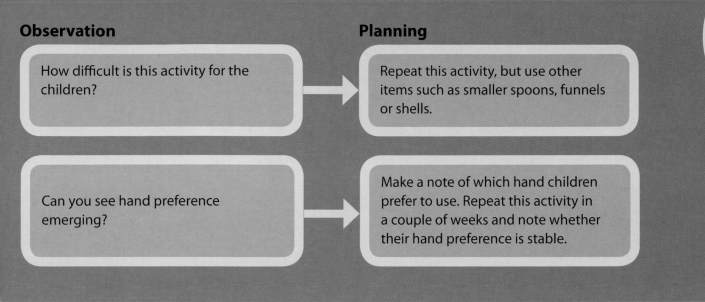

How difficult is this activity for the children? → Repeat this activity, but use other items such as smaller spoons, funnels or shells.

Can you see hand preference emerging? → Make a note of which hand children prefer to use. Repeat this activity in a couple of weeks and note whether their hand preference is stable.

16–26 months

Threading macaroni
22–36 months

This activity will help strengthen hand preference as children have to use two hands.

Put out some macaroni and some string. Tell the children that Teddy wants them to make him a necklace using the macaroni. See if the children can thread the string through the macaroni. If this is too difficult, look out for cotton reels or large beads. Encourage the children to work out how long the necklace needs to be in order for it to fit Teddy.

Observation   **Planning**

Can the child thread the macaroni? → If yes, try putting out some other materials for threading which require greater hand–eye coordination.

If a child has difficulty, try putting out larger shapes. Consider, too, whether the difficulty is linked to fine motor movements or to eyesight.

22–36 months

Handwriting

What do I need to do?

- Provide opportunities for children to develop fine motor skills.

- Provide opportunities for children to make marks on a large and small scale.

- Show children how to make anti-clockwise rotational movements.

- Look for activities that encourage two-handed movements.

- Plan activities that will encourage pincer movements.

- Check that children have developed a hand preference and provide activities that will strengthen hand preference.

- Role model handwriting.

Frequently Asked Questions

What should we do if a child has not developed a hand preference?

While you cannot determine hand preference, you can provide activities that might strengthen a hand preference. Look out for two-handed movements where one hand acts as a stabiliser and the other hand is actively engaged. An example of this is peeling a banana – one hand holds the banana while the other hand peels it. Other two-handed movements include threading, washing up and pouring drinks.

Should we correct letters?

Yes, but very sensitively and only when you have worked first on the underlying writing skills. These include anti-clockwise rotational marks (oooo), bouncing movements (*uuuu; mmmm*) and vertical lines starting at the top (llll).

Teddy's tweezer game

30–50 months

Pincer grasp can be developed by encouraging children to pick small items out of rice, buttons or pasta. You can also put out tools such as tweezers to develop this further.

Put some rice in different containers and add in some chick peas. Tell the children that Teddy has dropped some chick peas into the rice and now wants them to come out. Could they help Teddy? Give each child a set of tweezers, a container of rice and chick peas, and a bowl to put the chick peas in when they have pulled them out.

Observation

Do the children enjoy this activity?

How difficult is this activity for the children?

Do the children show a clear hand preference?

Planning

Repeat this activity, but add in other items based on the needs and interests of the children, for example confetti, beads, buttons, sequins.

If not, plan two-handed activities such as spreading butter on bread, washing duplo with a toothbrush or pouring water through a funnel.

30-50 months

Brushes and rice

40–60+ months

Children will need to practise certain movements before they learn how to form their letters (see FAQ opposite). This activity works well as it is a sensory activity and may appeal to children who are uninterested in mark-making ordinarily.

Colour some rice by adding a couple of teaspoons of food colouring to some dry rice in a bag. Shake the bag and then spread out the rice to dry. Put the rice onto a tray so that it is one-grain deep. Put out a soft brush, such as a make-up brush or a paintbrush. With an individual child or pairs of children, show how you can make the pre-writing shapes in the rice.

Observation

Can the child easily make the pre-writing movements?

Planning

If the child needs more practice, put up large sheets of paper on a wall and play a follow-my-leader game using markers. Show the children how to make the pre-writing movements as large movements.

If the child can make these movements, choose a letter in their name and show them how to form it correctly.

40-60+ months

Problem Solving, Reasoning and Numeracy

Problem Solving, Reasoning and Numeracy will help babies and young children take their first steps towards learning about mathematics by helping them to develop confidence and thinking skills.

This area of Learning and Development includes the following aspects:

- Numbers as Labels and for Counting
- Calculating
- Shape, Space and Measures

Numbers as Labels and for Counting

What do I need to do?

- Look for everyday opportunities for toddlers to hear you count, for example counting buttons as you fasten them up, counting stairs.

- Sing counting songs and rhymes and sometimes use props.

- Draw children's attention to groups of objects during personal care routines, for example sing 'This little piggy went to market' after a bath.

- Draw toddlers' attention to quantity by talking about 'less' and 'more'.

- Look for activities where toddlers can find the 'odd one out', for example a cuddly toy hidden in the box of bricks.

Frequently Asked Questions

At what age should toddlers be able to recognise numbers?

It is unlikely that toddlers will be able to recognise numbers, although you will start to hear some of them counting. Counting is an important first step as it shows that children have learnt the sounds of numbers, although it does not mean that a child knows that 'three' is a smaller number than 'five'. This is why it is important to show children how to count objects so they can link the 'sounds' of counting to quantities.

We have been told that worksheets are not to be used. Why is this?

Because of the way young children process information, they learn concepts better at this age through doing. You may also find that when children are engaged in playful activities they will concentrate for longer and be more enthusiastic.

Posting things

16–26 months

Posting things is an activity that many toddlers of this age enjoy. It is also mathematical in terms of learning about shape, size and quantity. Look out for posting toys, but also think about making your own opportunities by, for example, using a cardboard tube (the longer the better) and objects such as balls, cars and even small cuddly toys. It is useful if some of the objects will not fit as this will help teach toddlers about size.

As the child is dropping things down the tube, use the opportunity to count them.

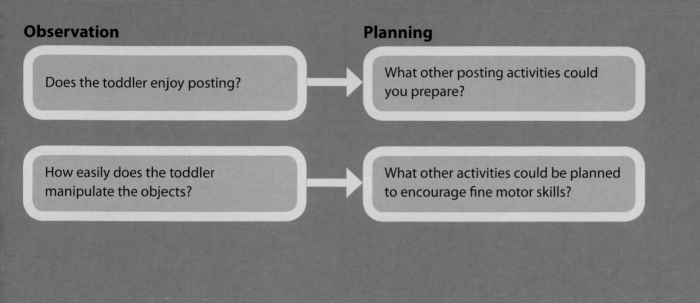

Observation

Does the toddler enjoy posting?

Planning

What other posting activities could you prepare?

How easily does the toddler manipulate the objects?

What other activities could be planned to encourage fine motor skills?

Hidden objects

22–36 months

Children like discovering things that have been hidden. This activity can be used to help toddlers match single items.

Put six objects into a tray of sand or rice. Put out a tray with six indentations such as a muffin tin or empty chocolate box. See if the child can find the objects and put each object in its own 'slot'. Children's ability to do one-to-one matching is an important skill to observe.

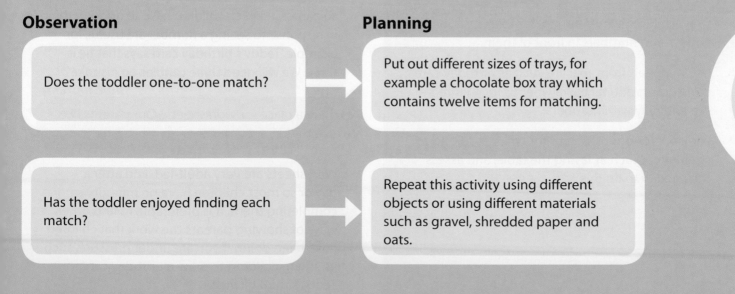

Observation

Does the toddler one-to-one match?

Planning

Put out different sizes of trays, for example a chocolate box tray which contains twelve items for matching.

Has the toddler enjoyed finding each match?

Repeat this activity using different objects or using different materials such as gravel, shredded paper and oats.

Calculating

What do I need to do?

- Talk to babies and toddlers and use the language of counting and quantity during everyday routines.

- Sing counting songs and rhymes and sometimes use props.

- Draw babies' and toddlers' attention to the objects around them.

- Play games such as peek-a-boo so that babies and toddlers learn about things disappearing and then re-appearing.

- Talk about more and less as you feed babies and toddlers.

Frequently Asked Questions

Do we need to plan specific mathematical activities for babies and toddlers?

No – providing that you think about the way in which you play and talk to babies and toddlers, everyday activities and ordinary toys can provide mathematical experiences for them.

What do we do if babies are not interested?

It is essential to follow babies' interests by watching their reactions closely. Babies show when they are bored by looking away or even crying; when they are interested they stare intently or smile. Interestingly, researchers have noticed that babies are aware of quantity: if you show them two toys then take them out of view only to return one, they are quite puzzled. This means that talking to babies and playing with them is important as it builds on what seems to be their innate mathematical abilities.

Jack-in-the-box

A significant developmental step in babies' cognitive development is when they know that objects they have seen but are removed still exist (object permanence).

Find a jack-in-the-box or a puppet on a stick that can pop up and down to use with the baby. Choose a time when the baby is alert. Hold the baby on your knee and gradually show them the toy. Take your time and do not rush any actions, to avoid the baby becoming startled. Talk to the baby about what you are doing and draw the baby's attention to the jack-in-the-box or puppet as it appears. Repeat this game several times so that the baby can anticipate what is about to happen.

Observation

Does the baby respond to seeing the jack-in-the-box-reappear?

Does the baby enjoy finding things?

Planning

Repeat this game over a period of time. Look out for other toys such as puppets that disappear then reappear. Hide toys in cloth bags in front of babies and notice whether they try to find them.

Start looking out for pop-up books, although choose sturdy ones.

0-11 months

One more!

Most children in this age group are beginning to enjoy feeding themselves. Meal times provide many great opportunities to help babies and toddlers learn about calculating.

Choose a meal where a child will be eating finger foods such as slices of bananas, bread or mandarins. Instead of putting all the food onto their plate, give the child just one piece at a time. Each time the child has eaten the individual piece of food, ask if he or she would like 'one more'.

Observation

Does the child begin to understand the game and respond to the words 'one more'?

Does the child enjoy eating finger foods?

Planning

Keep repeating this game over a number of days so that the language can be absorbed. Encourage the child to take 'one more' from the bowl or dish that you are holding.

Put finger foods into trays that have subdivisions or put out three small bowls at the same time with finger foods inside them.

8-20 months

Calculating

What do I need to do?

- Look for everyday opportunities for toddlers to group and sort objects.

- Sing counting songs and rhymes and sometimes use props.

- Play games whereby you pass objects to toddlers one by one so they can see a growing number.

- Draw toddlers' attention to quantity by talking about less and more.

- Use everyday routines such as meal times to help toddlers learn about quantities reducing.

Frequently Asked Questions

At what point should we be doing sums with children?

The EYFS is a play-based curriculum, so even when children are in Reception class, mathematics will be looked at through practical activities. With toddlers, the focus needs to be on drawing their attention to reducing and increasing numbers of items or measures of things such as fluid. The other focus is to build toddlers' language at the same time so they can start to understand what is meant by 'more' and 'less'.

How many times a day should we be doing mathematical activities?

While you can plan some mathematical activities, such as those that are described on the following page, you should really be looking for naturally occurring opportunities each day, such as counting the number of buttons that need doing up on a coat.

Pegs and saucepans

16–26 months

Many children of this age enjoy putting things in and out of containers. This is a mathematical experience that you can build on later.

Put out a saucepan, a wooden spoon and a bag or container of clothes pegs. If the child needs a prompt, you can take out a few pegs and put them in the saucepan and give them a stir. Most children will then take over and start to explore the pegs and the sound they make in the metal.

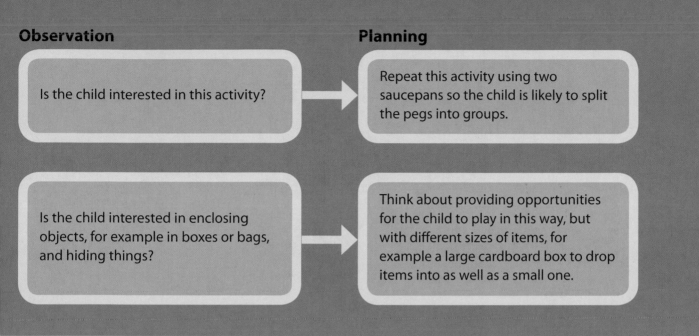

Observation

Is the child interested in this activity?

Is the child interested in enclosing objects, for example in boxes or bags, and hiding things?

Planning

Repeat this activity using two saucepans so the child is likely to split the pegs into groups.

Think about providing opportunities for the child to play in this way, but with different sizes of items, for example a large cardboard box to drop items into as well as a small one.

16-26 months

Five little ducks went swimming one day

22–36 months

Songs and rhymes are a key way in which children can learn the labels of counting. They can also be used to help children learn about addition and subtraction.

Fill up a baby bath with water and put out five rubber ducks. It is essential that time is allowed for the child to play with the ducks before singing the song and then acting out the rhyme.

Observation

How interested is the child in this activity?

Does the child need a more challenging activity?

Planning

Think about repeating this activity on other days. Look for different ways of bringing other rhymes, such as 'Two little dicky birds', to life.

Put out two water trays so that the child can divide the ducks between them. Count the ducks in front of the child.

22-36 months

Calculating

What do I need to do?

- Create mathematical problems for children to solve, for example 'Teddy wants to share these dough cakes between his three friends.'

- Identify opportunities for children to see subtraction and addition, such as making sandcastles and then knocking them down one by one or two by two.

- Use language to draw children's attention to changes, such as how many less or how many more.

- Play games that encourage children to be active in using their emerging skills, for example roll-a-dice games.

- Use counting songs but accompany these with props.

- Play physical games to encourage children to develop a concept of number, for example hopscotch and 'What's the time Mr Wolf?'

- Provide objects for children to sort and classify. Talk about the size of the different groupings.

Frequently Asked Questions

Should we be working on children's number bonds?

Yes you can, providing that you are sure that children have already developed a sense of quantity in relation to each number. Avoid doing this using 'sums', however, as children need at first to see the way that numbers can be combined. Look out for finger puppets that can help children 'see' combinations; for example, 'How many finger puppets are sleeping (fingers curled) and how many are awake?'

Is there a place for worksheets?

The trend is for children to find their own ways of recording mathematics. For example, they could draw items that they have put together or show through a story how the number of objects have been changed.

Roll a dice sand game

30–50 months

Children love building and knocking down sandcastles. This game builds on an interest that most children will already have developed.

Using trays of damp sand, give each child a tray, a spoon and a beaker. Group children according to their level of recognising numbers and adjust a dice accordingly. This can be done by putting stickers on the faces of the dice and writing in the numerals that the children can already recognise. Get each child in turn to roll the dice and then put the number of spoonfuls shown on the dice into their beaker. When their beaker is full, they can make a sandcastle.

30-50 months

Observation

Planning

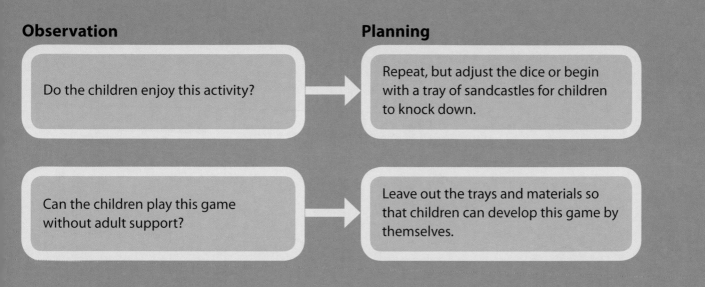

Do the children enjoy this activity? → Repeat, but adjust the dice or begin with a tray of sandcastles for children to knock down.

Can the children play this game without adult support? → Leave out the trays and materials so that children can develop this game by themselves.

Teddy's party

40–60+ months

Most children enjoy birthdays and know about having other children home for tea. This activity builds on children's interest in making dough cakes and food as well as their knowledge of parties.

Tell the children that it is Teddy's birthday and that you are making cakes for his party. See if they can guess how many friends Teddy is having for tea. Ask the children to begin to make cakes. Put each cake in a fairy cake case or a chocolate box tray. Talk to children about 'how many more' are needed. You can also play this game so that Teddy keeps changing his mind about how many friends are coming. This means that some cakes have to be taken away or further cakes are needed.

Observation

Planning

40-60+ months

Do the children enjoy this activity? → Put out the dough, Teddy and a few more chocolate box trays so that children can enjoy using these materials as part of their child-initiated play.

Do the children find this activity easy? → Try using different colour doughs. Explain that Teddy wants one of the cakes to be red, a few to be blue, but most to be yellow. He wants fifteen cakes overall.

Shape, Space and Measures

What do I need to do?

- Make sure that babies have opportunities to experience a range of spaces, such as outdoors, being held at different heights, being put on the floor.

- Create on the floor a range of different textures so that babies are stimulated.

- Create some small enclosed spaces where toddlers can hide, for example a large cardboard box on its side.

- Provide opportunities for babies and toddlers to experience a range of different sensory materials such as rice and oats.

- Provide boxes and other containers for toddlers to explore.

- Think about appropriate wheeled toys as babies become mobile, such as brick trolleys.

- Provide treasure basket and heuristic play for babies and toddlers.

Frequently Asked Questions

Why it is important to take non-mobile babies outside, given that they cannot do much?

The focus on taking babies outside is based on research that shows that babies need to be stimulated. Being outdoors creates a new sensory opportunity as well as helping babies to see wide-open spaces. Ideally, babies should be put outdoors on mats as well as being pushed or carried around.

We have been asked to put out sensory materials for the toddlers. What types of materials can we safely put out?

Look out for materials that are safe if swallowed and that would not be an irritant if a toddler rubbed their eyes. Rice, oats, gloop and tea leaves are often used. Remember to enhance the mathematical experience by putting out scoops, buckets and other containers.

Blowing bubbles

0–11 months

Babies enjoy seeing bubbles. They also need plenty of experiences of being outdoors.

Put the baby in a sling, backpack or stroller. Make sure that you have the baby's attention before blowing some bubbles. Try to have some bubbles within the grasp of the baby, although you should make sure that the bubbles cannot get onto the baby's face. If the baby is in a stroller, you can enhance their experience by holding them up so they can see the bubbles from your eye level. Talk to the baby as the bubbles pop or blow away. Draw attention to the bubbles by pointing at them and talk about where they are going, for example 'Look, that one is going up into the tree!'

Observation

Does the baby follow the bubbles with their eyes?

Are the bubbles of interest to the baby?

Planning

Repeat this activity and notice whether the baby begins to try and 'catch' the bubbles.

Consider whether the baby's eyesight is developing in line with expected development.

Think about other activities that will help the baby to look at objects in space, for example hanging mobiles, baby gyms.

0-11 months

Obstacle course

8–20 months

Babies and toddlers can learn about space and size by climbing and moving over a range of different materials. In the early stages of crawling, this might be just on simple textures such as over a door mat and a woollen rug. Look out for cushions, tunnels and wooden blocks that can be used to create a simple obstacle course both indoors and out. You can assess which objects will work best by observing the babies and toddlers first, to determine their level of mobility.

Observation

Does the baby or toddler enjoy climbing or moving over the objects that you have put out?

Are there any movements, textures or spaces that are of particular interest to the baby or toddler?

Planning

Repeat this activity, but vary the items that you put out. Look for ways of taking this activity outdoors.

How can these be incorporated into other aspects of the baby's or toddler's play?

8-20 months

Shape, Space and Measures

What do I need to do?

- Provide a range of containers of different sizes, for example large cardboard boxes, plastic bottles, beakers and hessian bags, so that toddlers can put things in and out of them.

- Look for ways of creating small enclosed spaces where toddlers can hide such as dens and tents and by placing sheets over tables.

- Provide sand, water and other sensory play where toddlers can use containers and scoops, etc.

- Draw toddlers' attention to objects of different sizes, for example 'Which spoon would you like – the large one or the smaller one?'

- Provide jigsaw puzzles so that toddlers begin to learn about shape and spaces.

Frequently Asked Questions

At what age can jigsaw puzzles be used with toddlers?

Simple four-piece jigsaw puzzles or tray puzzles can be used from eighteen months or so, although you will need to support the toddler at first. Jigsaw puzzles help children with logic as well as spatial awareness.

Why do toddlers keep repeating their play, such as putting things in and out of boxes?

This is part of normal development and seems to be important in helping toddlers develop a sense of space and order. Observe what fascinates them and try to plan other activities that build on this fascination.

Suitcases

16–26 months

Many children of this age enjoy putting objects inside of things and then transporting them. You can build on this interest outdoors by finding some small suitcases with wheels that the children can pack. Put out the suitcases along with some items of varying sizes. You may need to show the children how to open a suitcase, but they will then be able to pop some bits and pieces in. You may find that some children enjoy transporting cuddly toys in this way.

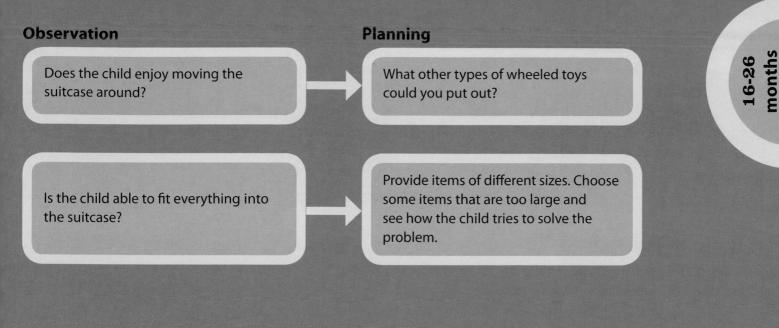

Observation

Does the child enjoy moving the suitcase around?

Is the child able to fit everything into the suitcase?

Planning

What other types of wheeled toys could you put out?

Provide items of different sizes. Choose some items that are too large and see how the child tries to solve the problem.

16-26 months

Jigsaws

22–36 months

Jigsaws are useful toys to promote children's spatial awareness. Look out for some attractive wooden ones as these are particularly sensory and so are more appealing for young children. At first, it is important to choose jigsaw puzzles with only a small number of pieces, for example a four-piece puzzle. Sit with the child to show them what to do. Try and use as much positional vocabulary as possible, such as 'above', 'below' and 'alongside'.

Observation

How much support does the child need?

Does the child enjoy puzzles?

Planning

Vary the types of puzzles to find ones that are challenging, achievable but more importantly enjoyable. Look out for floor puzzles as well so that the child can experience shapes of different sizes.

Take a photograph of the child and laminate it. Use it to create an individual puzzle for the child.

22-36 months

Shape, Space and Measures

What do I need to do?

- Draw children's attention to the names and shapes of objects.

- Provide opportunities for children to measure and compare quantities.

- Look for opportunities to incorporate shapes, measuring and making things into play opportunities, for example making dens with fabric and boxes outdoors.

- Use stories such as Goldilocks that focus on size or quantity, for example large, medium and small.

- Use the language of measurement with children, for example long, longest, small, smallest.

- ωPut out activities such as jigsaws that encourage children to think about shape.

Frequently Asked Questions

How can I get children to recognise shapes?

As with all concepts, children need to see, touch and use shapes in order to remember them. It is also important that adults draw children's attention to shapes by commenting on them or by seeing if children can find them. As with all teaching within the EYFS, activities must be playful for children. Junk modelling is usually an excellent way of helping children to use 3D-shapes and to problem solve.

Do children need to be taught about time?

Most children are not ready to understand the process of telling the time until they are six or seven years old. You can, however, help children learn about ways in which time is measured by, for example, putting egg timers into play or drawing children's attention to the time of day.

Short straw

This activity is based on the traditional game of short straws. It can be carried out indoors or outside.

Hide some straws of different lengths in the sand tray. Leave the ends on show. Ask the children whether they can guess which one will be the shortest straw. The children can then pull out a straw from the sand. Draw children's attention to the idea that you cannot tell which straw is the shortest unless you compare it to some other straws. This is an important concept as measures are always relative. Ask the children to compare their straws with each other. Can they work out whose straw is the smallest? If you feel that recording is necessary, the children can then stick the straws onto a piece of paper in order of size.

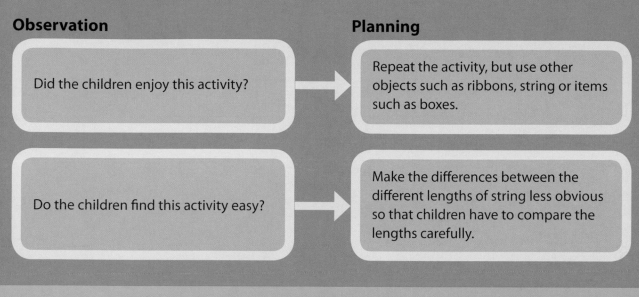

Observation

Did the children enjoy this activity?

Planning

Repeat the activity, but use other objects such as ribbons, string or items such as boxes.

Do the children find this activity easy?

Make the differences between the different lengths of string less obvious so that children have to compare the lengths carefully.

Quatre, quatre cakes

This is a simple, French cake recipe, and children should be able to do most of it by themselves. The key ingredients are an egg, sugar, self-raising flour and soft margarine.

1. Place an egg on balancing scales.
2. Ask a child to put enough sugar on to the scales so that it balances with the weight of the egg.
3. Tip the sugar into a mixing bowl.
4. Repeat steps 2 and 3 with the self-raising flour, and then finally with soft margarine.
5. Break the egg into the mixing bowl and stir the ingredients together until smooth and creamy.
6. Put the mixture into fairy cases or muffin tins. Bake at 180°C/350F/gas mark 4 for 12–15 minutes, or until golden brown.

Observation

Did the children enjoy this activity?

Planning

Look out for other recipes that will encourage children to be responsible for measuring.

Do the children need more practice at measuring?

Play a game using the balancing scales whereby children have to put in objects to the equivalent weight of Teddy.

Knowledge and Understanding of the World

Knowledge and Understanding of the World is about helping children to learn and explore their immediate world and the people within it. Later it will link to early science, ICT, design and technology and the humanities.

This area of Learning and Development includes the following aspects:

- Exploration and Investigation
- Designing and Making
- ICT
- Time
- Place
- Communities

Exploration and Investigation

What do I need to do?

- Recognise that babies and toddlers largely explore using their mouth and hands.

- Provide objects and materials that are sensory and tactile.

- Consider using everyday items made from natural materials such as a wooden spoon.

- Help young babies to explore by holding them and showing them things such as keys.

- Extend for older babies and toddlers by giving them groups of different items.

- Provide sensory materials such as coloured rice and cornflour and water (gloop).

- Make sure that items and materials are regularly varied.

Frequently Asked Questions

Can I use toys?

There is no need to use toys as babies and toddlers will learn as much and possibly more from everyday items, but in theory you could. Avoid plastic toys, though, as they provide minimal sensory feedback.

What about choking?

Choose objects that are too large for a baby or toddler to swallow. Try handling the object yourself to check that pieces cannot come away. Buy a choking tube to check.

How often should I change objects?

Babies and toddlers will become bored if the same objects and materials are always on offer. Vary by swapping around objects so that there are different combinations. Bring in new items from time to time.

Treasure basket play
0–11 months

Treasure basket play can be used with babies until they become mobile. Put out a basket with about fifteen or twenty items in it. The basket should ideally be low and flat-bottomed, so that the baby can reach inside it. Choose items that are different sizes, shapes and textures and that are made of natural materials. Ensure they are clean and not a choking hazard, as they are likely to be mouthed. Examples of suitable items include:

- coconut
- bottle brush (bristle)
- metal mixing bowl.
- small teaspoon
- wooden boxes
- metal saucepan lid
- lemon
- corks
- metal scoop
- silk scarf
- large shells.

Change a few of the items each time the basket is put out so that the babies have something new to explore.

0-11 months

Observation

Watch how the baby or toddler reacts to new objects.

Does the baby or toddler notice them?

Are new objects mouthed immediately or handled first?

Planning

Should this object or similar ones be put out next time?

If objects are no longer being mouthed, can softer or smaller objects be put out?

Coloured rice
8–20 months

Spread out a large sheet. Place approximately 500g of rice into a deep container such as a washing-up bowl. Allow the babies and toddlers to explore the rice with their hands. Expect that rice will be tipped and thrown onto the sheet. After initial exploration, add in scoops and objects.

With older toddlers who are no longer mouthing, you might like to used coloured rice. Add two teaspoons of food colouring to the uncooked rice, put the rice into a bag or container and shake vigorously so that the rice becomes coloured. Spread out the rice onto a tray so that it can dry off. Repeat the process twice with a new batch of rice and a different colour food colouring, then combine the rice so that it becomes multi-coloured.

8-20 months

Observation

Watch how the baby or toddler reacts to the rice.

Do they use one hand or both?

Do they pick out individual grains?

Does the baby or toddler enjoy using scoops?

Does the baby or toddler try to fill containers?

Planning

Could other similar materials be introduced, such as porridge oats or dry pasta?

Could teaspoons and other scoops be added?

Could different sized containers be added?

Exploration and Investigation

What do I need to do?

- Provide play activities that involve discovery and exploration both inside and outdoors.

- Put out tools that can assist exploration such as spoons or scoops.

- Provide objects and items that will be new to children and will encourage them to explore, for example hide shells in the digging area for children to discover.

- Observe the ways that children are playing with items.

Frequently Asked Questions

Do we have to go outside?

It is necessary to go outside for some activities and play because the EYFS puts emphasis on both indoor and outdoor learning. Puddles, cobwebs and even gravel are great starting points for investigation.

What type of objects could I use with these age ranges?

Try trays of buttons, shells, pot-pourri and toys that will stimulate the child to problem solve or investigate, such as a simple jack-in-the-box.

What about safety?

Most children in this age range should no longer be mouthing, but you should carry out observations to be sure of this. If putting out objects that are small, you must check that a child could not choke on them.

Transporting and enclosing

Many toddlers repeat actions during play, and transporting and enclosing are particularly popular. Look out for toddlers who are constantly moving items from place to place (transporting) or are fascinated by putting objects inside each other (enclosing), such as putting pegs into a basket. By repeating the play action with different objects and items, toddlers get the opportunity to explore a thought process. Providing this type of play both inside and outdoors will encourage greater exploration.

Items for transporting:

- sit-and-ride toy with a flap
- shopping basket
- bucket
- brick trolley.

Items for enclosing:

- metal biscuit tin
- cardboard boxes of different sizes
- large cardboard tubes
- purses and handbags.

Items to be enclosed include clothes pegs, shells, cuddly toys, gravel, bark chippings and pom-pom balls.

Observation

Identify the way that new items are used.

Observe the level of physical skill used.

Planning

What other items could be used next time to allow the child to repeat this type of play?

Are easier items required if the child is frustrated?

Dropping objects into water

Children love water. Water trays can be too high for this age group, so fill a large container that can have deep water in it, for example a translucent storage box. Put out a tray of items or, if outdoors, encourage children to find things to drop into the water. Let the children drop things in and hear the splash. Items for dropping might include:

- pine cones
- shells
- large stones
- rubber ducks

- metal spoons
- wooden blocks
- twigs.

Note: do not leave this water activity unattended. Once the activity is finished, the water should be tipped out – perhaps the children could help!

Observation

Are children starting to choose objects rather than pick them up at random?

Are children able to name the items they are dropping in?

Planning

Extend children's choice of items.

Encourage children to guess which items will sink.

Extend children's choice of items and draw attention to what each item is called.

Exploration and Investigation

What do I need to do?

- Draw children's attention to patterns and shapes.

- Encourage children to ask questions about what they are seeing and how things work.

- Look out for new items for children to handle and explore.

- Use the outdoor environment so that children become familiar with nature.

- Provide a balance of child-centred and adult-led opportunities.

- Encourage children to talk about what they have been doing by taking photographs.

Frequently Asked Questions

Our outdoor area is very limited. Any suggestions?

Use planters for growing small things in, such as bulbs or lettuce from seed. Look out for drain covers and brick walls to help children learn about textures by doing rubbings.

What type of items could I use with these age ranges?

Look out for items with moving parts that might encourage children to think and ask questions, for example wind chimes and windmills. Look out for groups of objects that will help children learn about small differences, such as buttons, coins, keys and locks.

What about safety?

Children in this age range should not be mouthing, but be aware of any child who does. Avoid items with sharp edges and those that might break easily and cause a hazard.

Looking at the world around you

Young children love looking at objects using magnifiers. Plastic A4 magnifying sheets are a good investment as they are easy to use and can be taken outdoors. It is essential to build children's language in order that they can talk about what they have seen. This means you should think about ways of drawing their attention to the details, for example 'I like this one, it's stripier than the others.'

Items that could be looked at using a magnifier include:

- leaves (get the children to collect the leaves; make sure that you know their names!)
- outdoor surfaces – tarmac, concrete, brick, metal railings, gravel
- grass and flowers
- ice cubes or 'frost' taken from a freezer; ice and snow outdoors
- hands, knees and toes.

Observation

Does the child know the name of the object?

Can the child talk about the object and describe some features?

Is the child interested in looking at detail?

Planning

Should the activity be repeated so that the child can have more time with an adult?

Could the child be encouraged to take a photograph of the object or to record it?

Windmills

Take some paper windmills outside for children to explore. Encourage them to see how the windmill moves. Ask them to choose places to put their windmills in. Take some windmills indoors. Ask the children to see how quickly the different windmills are moving. See if they can provide an explanation of why some windmills might move. Let the children change the position of their windmills if they wish.

Observation

Can the child understand the link between the wind and the turning of the windmill?

Is the child able to see that some positions are better than others?

Planning

Provide other items that move in the wind.

Can children make a better windmill?

Can children experiment with different positions for their windmills, including different heights?

Designing and Making

What do I need to do?

- Recognise that babies and toddlers largely explore using their mouth and hands.

- Provide objects and materials that are sensory and tactile.

- Look out for objects that make a noise when combined or produce an effect, such as rattles or a spoon and saucepan lid.

- Provide objects that can be stacked, for example large wooden bricks, boxes.

- Look for objects that could be put on top of each other or inside each other, for example stacking beakers, metal tins.

Frequently Asked Questions

Can I use treasure basket and heuristic play to cover this aspect?

Yes, but remember to make sure that you vary the objects that are put out. In these early stages, there is a significant overlap with Exploration and Investigation.

Should babies and toddlers be making things such as cards?

No. At this early stage, the aim is that babies and toddlers realise that they can make things happen such as creating a noise when they drop a wooden brick into a metal tin.

How can I show that babies and toddlers are designing and making?

You can use photographs to show how babies and toddlers are exploring objects. You can also note in your observations when a baby or toddler repeats an action deliberately.

Homemade baby gym

0–11 months

With non-mobile babies, adapt a baby gym by unclipping the toys and instead hanging up a range of new items such as a wooden spoon, a shiny metal scoop and some strips of ribbon. Make sure that items are securely attached and will not fall onto the baby. Think, too, about their shape and weight in case a baby was to hit them with force. With any activity involving new objects, always supervise.

With mobile babies, consider finding a place where objects could be hung vertically, for example from a climbing frame. Again, tie objects securely and check that if they were to swing with force, they would not knock the baby over.

Observation

Watch how the baby or toddler reacts to new objects.

Does the baby or toddler notice them?

→

Planning

Can these items be used again next time?

Can these or similar objects be shown or given to the baby to mouth and handle with the adult supporting the child?

Watch to see if the baby begins to repeat the same actions in order to create a sound or movement.

→

Are there other items that could be used which will help the baby to explore this action further?

0-11 months

Heuristic play

8–20 months

Heuristic play is a development from treasure basket play (see page 159). While treasure basket play uses only natural materials, heuristic play consists of everyday objects which may include plastic.

Look out for objects of different sizes. Examples of suitable items for heuristic play include:

- plastic water bottles
- cardboard tubes
- corks
- metal saucepan lid

- balls of wool
- metal scoop
- cake tins of different sizes
- metal mixing bowl

- wooden pegs
- curtain rings
- ribbons
- cardboard boxes.

Observation

Look out for signs that the baby or toddler is beginning to repeat actions deliberately.

Which materials are engaging him or her?

→

Planning

Think about whether the same materials need to be put out next time along with a few new ones.

Observe the different skills that the baby or toddler is learning.

Have they learnt to put objects inside each other?

Can they make a loud noise with objects?

Can they balance objects on top of each other?

→

Consider whether the materials that are put out are varied enough to allow babies and toddlers to gain a range of early skills.

8-20 months

Designing and Making

What do I need to do?

- Talk to toddlers so they can learn some of the vocabulary associated with building and making things, for example 'Well done! You managed to get that to balance.'

- Provide objects and materials that are sensory and tactile.

- Be ready to offer support if the child appears to want help.

- Avoid telling toddlers what they should do – allow them to explore.

- Use the outdoor area so that children can use more space as well as larger items.

- Observe children's play interests and think about how to build on them.

- Make sure that items and materials are regularly varied.

Frequently Asked Questions

Do I have to provide activities outdoors?

Yes, because toddlers enjoy having the space especially when they are using wheeled toys. As this age group is not likely to be playing cooperatively, it also allows the play to spread out so that each child can explore their own ideas.

Should I put out construction toys?

Yes, you can put out age-appropriate construction toys, but also consider materials such as large cardboard boxes, fabrics and tubing, so that children can explore things on a large scale. Children will need a variety of opportunities to fully explore this aspect of learning, so only using construction toys may be limiting.

How about an art and craft table?

Designing and making using collage and other small materials is likely to be more appropriate for older children. Young children are best building and exploring things with larger, more tactile materials.

Wheeled toys

16–26 months

Most children at this age are mobile and are interested in pushing, pulling and transporting items. Look out for toys or even everyday objects that will support this type of play, for example brick trolleys, pushchairs and sit-and-ride toys, as well as shopping baskets with wheels. Choose toys that are appropriate for the child's level of stability. Provide objects that they can transport if they wish to or that they can use to help them balance items, such as cardboard boxes.

Observation

Watch how the baby or toddler reacts to new objects.
Does the baby or toddler notice them?

Are new objects mouthed immediately or handled first?

How easily are objects handled and manipulated?

Planning

Should this object or similar ones be put out next time?

If objects are no longer being mouthed, can softer or smaller objects be put out?

Should some new objects be put in that are larger or heavier, to provide more challenge?

16-26 months

Stretchy dough

22–36 months

Using self-raising flour and water, which can be dyed with food colouring, encourage children to mix up their own dough. Role model making your own dough, so that children learn how to use tools such as a spoon. Encourage children to handle the dough and to see what they can do with it. Add a teaspoon of baking powder or bicarbonate of soda for extra stretchy dough!

Note: as this dough does not have salt in it, it is not suitable for keeping. You should also supervise children to prevent them from eating the dough, so this activity works best if you are sure that children explore now by using their hands rather than their mouth.

Observation

Does the child enjoy making and exploring the dough?
Can the child manipulate simple tools such as a spoon for stirring?

Is the toddler trying to use the dough to make an object for pretend play, such as a cake?

Planning

Plan other activities involving cooking.

Put out other objects that might support this type of play, for example jar lids that the child could use as plates.

22-36 months

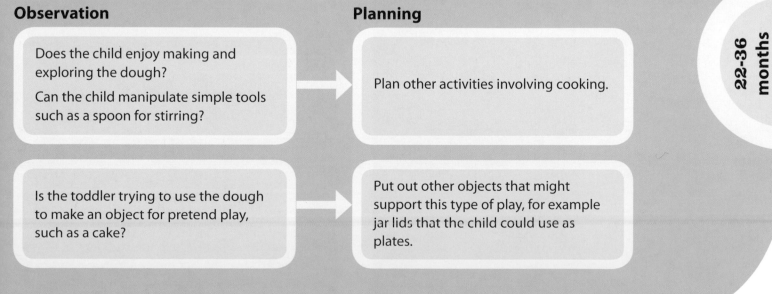

Designing and Making

What do I need to do?

- Provide a range of tools that children can learn to use.

- Show children how to use tools correctly.

- Model language, for example join, fix, glue, snip, support.

- Provide a range of interesting materials of different sizes for children to explore and use.

- Use the space outdoors for children to be involved in large-scale projects.

- Make sure that items and materials are regularly varied.

Frequently Asked Questions

What type of tools should be put out?

The EYFS guidance suggests the following tools: scissors, hole punch, glue spreader, junior hacksaw, rolling pin, cutter and grater. The idea is that children gain experience of a range of tools so they can do different types of design and making.

We do a cooking activity each week. Would this be enough?

Cooking is only one way of helping children to learn about designing and making, so you will need to provide additional materials and activities.

We have a member of staff who tends to 'tell' the children what to do.

Designing and making is about children making their own decisions and following their own ideas. You may have to help this member of staff understand that young children are quite capable of having ideas, although they may need support to achieve them.

Salad making

Most children enjoy cooking. Salads can be made easily and do not require a kitchen.

Put out a range of ingredients for a salad. Encourage the children to choose the items that they would like to use and, if appropriate, wash them. Look out for some ingredients that will encourage the use of tools during their preparation, for example cheese that needs grating or cucumber that needs cutting. Note that you should find out about children's dietary requirements and supervise the use of knives, cutter and graters.

Examples of items to put in a salad include:

- lettuce
- pasta
- apple
- cress
- tomatoes
- Cheddar cheese
- hardboiled egg
- soft cheese
- tuna
- peppers
- cabbage
- cucumber
- pumpkin seeds.

Observation

Is the child confident enough to make choices?

Which tools can the child use easily?

Did the child need any support to use tools?

Planning

Plan more activities where children are given responsibility.

Introduce a wider range of tools.

Could these tools be put out more frequently?

Den making

Children enjoy creating their own structures outdoors. Put out a range of materials which will help them to create their own den. This activity can be enhanced by also putting out role-play props so that children can play inside their den afterwards. Den making will require time if children are to really benefit from it.

Examples of den making materials that children might use include:

- cardboard boxes
- plastic sheeting
- bottle crates
- cardboard tubes
- lengths of fabrics
- pegs.

Observation

What problems did the children encounter and how did they resolve them?

How well were children working together?

Planning

Could the adult help the children to learn a skill that will help them next time?

Could other activities be planned to help children cooperate?

Was the group size appropriate for the task?

169

ICT

What do I need to do?

- Provide a range of safe everyday gadgets for children to explore alongside an adult, for example torches, alarm clocks, mobile phones.

- Talk to children about how things work and how we make them work.

- Look out for toys that have technology embedded, such as an electronic keyboard, books and games.

- Look for opportunities for children to help adults use technology.

Frequently Asked Questions

Should we be encouraging children to use computers?

This is not necessary for this age range. It is better if children explore ICT through practical activities.

Can we carry on using the baby and toddler toys?

Yes, if the children are still interested in them, but try to increase the range of toys so they have sufficient challenge. Look out for toys which make sounds or light up for a purpose, such as a toy torch, so children feel they are 'using' technology rather than just witnessing it.

If children are helping adults, will they be tempted to try things alone?

Children gain a lot of knowledge by trying some everyday gadgets in the company of an adult, such as pressing the start button on a DVD. At other times, however, you must ensure that children are supervised and safety guards are used.

Toy telephones

Look out for some toy telephones or, if this activity is adult-led, an obsolete real telephone. See if the children know how to make a telephone work by pressing the buttons. Play alongside children, pretending to talk into phones and responding to them if they are talking into theirs. Note that children in this age range are unlikely to cooperate with other children so if this activity is carried out with more than one child, make sure that there are enough phones. Expect that children will also attempt to walk with the phones, so make sure that phones are light enough should they be dropped.

Observation

Planning

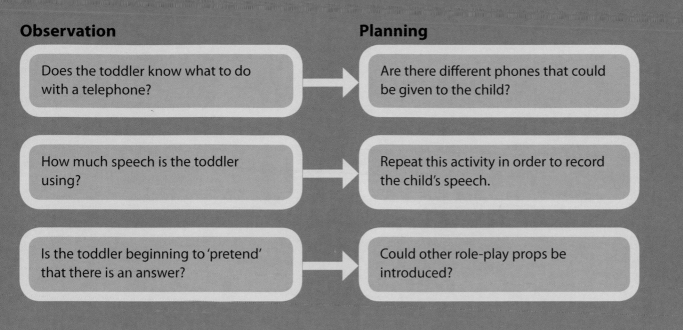

Observation	Planning
Does the toddler know what to do with a telephone?	Are there different phones that could be given to the child?
How much speech is the toddler using?	Repeat this activity in order to record the child's speech.
Is the toddler beginning to 'pretend' that there is an answer?	Could other role-play props be introduced?

16-26 months

Torches

Create an area that can be made gloomy or dark, such as a duvet cover over a table, cardboard box or a tent. Look out for some torches. Make sure that the torches cannot be taken apart by the children easily. See if the children can work out how to make the lights come on. Remind the children not to put the lights into their eyes. Ask the children if they would like to go inside the darkened area with their torches. Let the children play inside, but keep a close eye on their play. See if the children can work out how to turn off the light.

Observation

Planning

Observation	Planning
How easily can the children turn the torches on or off? Are children interested in how the torches work?	Show children the batteries in torches as an adult-led activity.
Did the children enjoy this activity?	Repeat this activity, but put out coloured film such as red cellophane or yellow tissue paper, so that children learn that light can be coloured or diffused.

22-36 months

173

ICT

What do I need to do?

- Provide a range of gadgets that are safe for children to explore and play with independently.

- Provide programmable toys for children to experiment with.

- Look out for software that is age-appropriate which will help children learn about using the computer.

- Look for opportunities for children to help adults use technology.

Frequently Asked Questions

Should we be encouraging children to use computers?

This aspect of learning requires the older age range to perform simple activities using a computer. It is essential to choose suitable software so that the children are actively rather than passively engaged with the computer.

Can we use remote-controlled cars?

Yes. Remote-controlled cars help children learn that their actions and choices have an effect on how the car moves. Once children can use remote-controlled toys, consider using programmable toys, which are more sophisticated.

What is the role of the adult?

Adults need to be mindful of safety and recognise that any toy or gadget using mains electricity has the potential to be a serious hazard. Always maintain good supervision. You should also encourage children to talk about what they are doing and how this is having an effect.

Remote controlled cars   30–50 months

Take children outdoors where there is plenty of space. Give each child a remote-controlled car so they can learn to use it. Model the language of movement and position, such as forwards, left, turn. If children are able to control the car, set them some simple challenges; for example, put a teddy a few metres away and say to the child that Teddy wants the car to come and find him.

This is an example of an adult-led activity since children may need some assistance. Also, children's learning will be enhanced through the questions that the adult asks and comments that the adult makes.

Observation

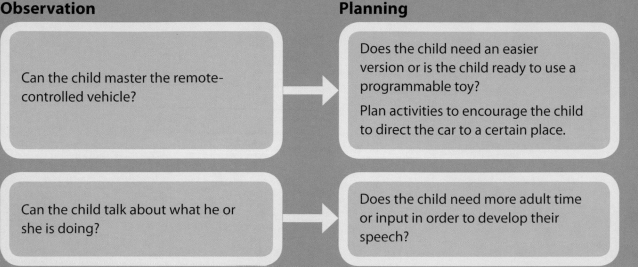

Planning

Can the child master the remote-controlled vehicle?

→ Does the child need an easier version or is the child ready to use a programmable toy?

Plan activities to encourage the child to direct the car to a certain place.

Can the child talk about what he or she is doing?

→ Does the child need more adult time or input in order to develop their speech?

30-50 months

Small everyday gadgets   40–60+ months

Put out a tray of small gadgets that use technology for children to explore. See if they know what the items are used for. Put out some gadgets without batteries. Can the children work out why they are not working? Note that this activity needs to be supervised.

Examples of gadgets that might be used include:

- electronic key ring
- greeting card that makes a sound
- torch
- mobile phone

- key finder
- pocket organiser
- small toy that lights up or makes a sound.

Observation

Are children aware of how the gadgets work?

Can children identify the reasons why some gadgets might not work?

Planning

Plan an activity so that children can insert batteries.

Show children inside a simple device so they can see a circuit board.

Are children able to talk about everyday technology at home and in the outdoor environment?

→ Encourage parents to draw children's attention to everyday technology in the wider environment, for example pressing a button at a pelican crossing or showing them how to programme a microwave.

40-60+ months

175

Time

What do I need to do?

- Make sure that babies hear a running commentary by talking to them about what you are doing.

- Try to reinforce some aspects of a routine by doing things in a certain order, for example putting on a bib before putting the baby in the highchair.

- Use picture books that show objects and scenes that relate to different times of the day, such as a cot or a toddler sitting in a highchair.

Frequently Asked Questions

Should we be encouraging babies and toddlers to look at clocks?

No. Rather, this aspect of learning is about helping babies and toddlers to gain a sense of time by, for example, following routines.

Is it enough just to talk to babies about what we are doing?

Yes. It is actually essential, as this means babies are hearing language and this eventually will help them to communicate. Don't worry if you feel as though you are talking to yourself – the key is for babies to feel part of what is going on around them.

How important are routines in helping babies and toddlers learn about time?

Routines are essential, because an early awareness of time is gained through recognising the patterns of the day. These relate partly to bodily needs, such as hunger, as well as the amount of light.

Routines 0–11 months

Think about how to help a baby recognise the signals that it is time to do something such as eat or have a nappy change. The key is to develop a pattern in the way that you work, so that the baby is able to associate something you do with what will be happening next. There are many ways of doing this:

- singing a certain rhyme during or before an activity such as nappy changing
- putting the baby in the same highchair and in the same place when it is meal time
- putting on the same piece of soothing music when the baby shows signs of being tired
- when putting the baby down for a nap, making sure that you draw curtains, pull up covers or switch on a musical mobile in the same order each time
- creating a routine when handing the baby over to the parents.

Observation	Planning
Do the baby's reactions indicate a recognition of the routine, such as smiling or showing excitement?	Acknowledge the reactions and add more components into the routine.
Does the baby try to show some level of activity in order to be included, for example babbling along with the rhyme or helping to pull the bib on?	Look for ways of allowing the baby to show more independence skills, such as holding a clean nappy at changing time or holding onto the curtain as it is drawn.

0–11 months

'My routines' picture book 8–20 months

Take a series of photographs of the baby or toddler at key events in the day, for example when coming into the setting, during meal time or nap time. Put the photographs onto card or paper and laminate them. Fasten them together by punching holes and tying short lengths of ribbon or string securely.

Show the book to the baby or toddler. Point out the objects that are used, such as beaker and cot, and talk about each event.

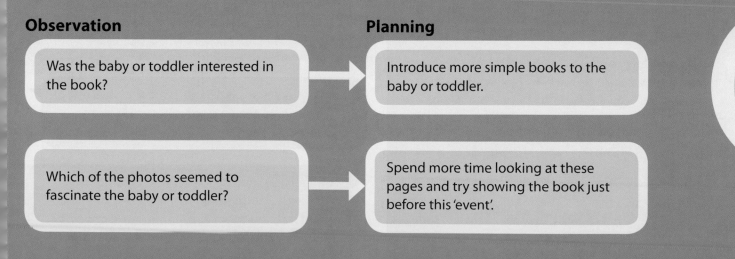

Observation	Planning
Was the baby or toddler interested in the book?	Introduce more simple books to the baby or toddler.
Which of the photos seemed to fascinate the baby or toddler?	Spend more time looking at these pages and try showing the book just before this 'event'.

8-20 months

Time

What do I need to do?

- Provide opportunities for children to talk about what they have been doing.

- Use digital photographs and film clips to help children remember and talk about events.

- Work with parents to help children talk about events outside the setting.

- Plan activities that will help children think about past and present.

- Plan activities that will help children talk about the sequence of events.

Frequently Asked Questions

When should we introduce telling the time?

While some children might be interested in clocks and may even have developed some of the vocabulary of telling the time, it is still too early to formally teach children to tell the time. Children are not normally ready for this until they are six or seven years old.

Should we be talking about days of the week?

Yes, but it is easier for children if there is something that distinguishes each day in a setting, for example Wednesday is the day when there are bananas for snack.

What about outdoor learning?

Take photographs of the same spot at different times of the year and talk to children about what has changed, such as what people are wearing and whether there are leaves on the trees. Help children notice the signs of the seasons changing.

Look what I can do now!

Ask parents if they would supply some baby and toddler photographs of their children. Share the photographs with the children, and ask them to talk about what they can do now which they couldn't do when they were a baby. Bring in bottles, nappies and baby toys to help children realise more about how they have grown up. If possible, show children a baby or young toddler or use a film clip to show a baby being bathed or helped to dress.

Observation

Do the children seem interested in babies?

Are the children able to talk about what they can do now?

Are children using any of the language of time, such as before, now, then?

Planning

Put a doll baby in the home corner and add in some props such as a pram, nappy and baby toys.

Take photographs of the children playing and doing things with the baby, such as dressing it. Make a display of the photographs with the children.

Plan a sequencing activity.

Take photographs of a baby being bathed. See if the children can put them in the right order.

30-50 months

Old and new

Put out a tray of objects that are safe for children to handle. Let the children explore them and talk about them. Tell the children that Teddy wants to play an 'old and new' game and that they have to see if they can sort out the objects. This can be made easier by providing pairs of objects, for example a new book in good condition and an old one.

Objects which can be used in this game include:

* keys
* toys
* boxes
* photographs
* bags
* birthday cards
* books
* watches.

Observation

Do the children know the names of the objects?

Are the children able to make connections between the objects and their own lives?

Are children able to distinguish between the objects?

Can they give reasons for their decisions?

Planning

Repeat the activity, but with more unusual objects.

Ask children to bring in some 'old' and 'new' objects from home to talk about.

Repeat this activity, but using a set of different objects.

Can children choose objects from around the room and say whether they are old or new?

40-60+ months

Place

What do I need to do?

- Take toddlers outdoors so they can explore the environment.

- Point out features such as puddles, a spider's web or a drain cover.

- Organise outings and short walks so that toddlers can see different areas.

- Ask parents to photograph their child's favourite place.

- Read stories about different environments such as the park or the swimming pool.

- Talk to children about what they are doing and seeing. Where possible use precise vocabulary, for example 'That's quite steep.'

Frequently Asked Questions

Do we have to go outdoors with this age range?

Yes. Spending time outdoors is one of the key ways in which to deliver this aspect of learning. You can use stories and show picture books, but it is always better for children to actually touch and see in order to learn.

What about health and safety outdoors?

The benefits from being outdoors mean that you must take a pro-active approach to getting children outside. Carry out a risk assessment, but bear in mind that the staff to child ratio is 1:3, so supervision should not be a problem. It is important for a staff member to check outdoors at the start of the session, to identify any new hazards. Children should be appropriately dressed for the weather and should always wash their hands when coming back inside.

Digging

16–26 months

One way in which children can explore and understand different textures in their environment is by digging. If your setting does not have a digging area, consider collecting some old rubber tyres and filling them with various materials. Put out a range of scoops and buckets and let the children enjoy seeing what they can find. It will be common for children to want to 'transport' materials or to bury things. Note that it can be useful to cover the tyres at the end of a session, to prevent cats from messing in them.

Digging materials can include:

- play sand
- bark chippings
- pebbles
- pea-shaped gravel
- potting compost.

Observation

Look out for play schemas.

Does the child enjoy burying their hands or filling up containers?

Does the child want to move the materials, for example by filling a bucket and taking it for a walk?

Does the child want to throw materials?

Planning

Think about ways in which children can carry on with this type of play indoors, for example by putting out shredded paper and containers, or by putting out wheeled toys such as pushchairs and brick trolleys so that children can move items from area to area.

16-26 months

Small-world sand tray

22–36 months

Children in this age range are starting to take an interest in imaginative play. They can create their own mini-environment for small-world toys in the sand tray. You can either use a large sand tray or provide children with smaller trays of their own. This can be an effective strategy as many children are not yet ready to cooperate or share.

It is useful beforehand to identify small-world play that the child enjoys, such as farm animals, play people or cars. Use these in the sand tray along with some small containers. Let the child explore what they can do and create as they play. Note that the children should be free to play and use the sand tray as they wish – they may, for example, bury their cars or the dinosaurs!

Observation

Is the child interested in other children?

Does the child talk to the small-world toys during play?

Planning

Look for opportunities for the child to play alongside other children.

Consider other ways of providing imaginative play opportunities, for example in the home corner or by using Teddy.

Consider whether the adult could join in with the imaginative play.

22-36 months

Place

What do I need to do?

- Provide opportunities for children to talk about what they have been doing.

- Use digital photographs and film clips to help children remember different environments, such as the playground or local shops.

- Organise walks and visits in the local community.

- Provide opportunities for children to create play maps.

- Use small-world play opportunities to help children create their own environments.

- Provide activities that help children look out for nature, for example planting bulbs, hanging up bird feeders.

- Point out features to children and use precise vocabulary.

Frequently Asked Questions

Should children be able to read maps?

No, not yet. The idea is to introduce maps and to encourage children through drawing and art work to make simple representations of their environment.

What type of trips should we organise?

Small trips into the local community, such as a visit to the local supermarket or post office, will generate a lot of discussion. Use these as a basis for role play later and take plenty of photographs, so that children can talk afterwards about what they did and saw.

We find it hard to take children out of the setting.

Take photographs or film clips of local places that you think the children will recognise. Ask parents if they can take photographs of children's favourite places or where they live. This will not replace a trip, but will at least help you to talk about the local environment.

Where's Teddy? 30–50 months

Take a series of photographs that feature a teddy or similar character, both in and out of your setting. You can laminate the images or put them into a computer or whiteboard. See if the children can talk about where Teddy is and what he is doing. You could also make up a story about Teddy's adventure. Use this as a starting point for early writing and to encourage drawing.

Observation

Do the children seem interested in what Teddy has been doing?

Can the children recognise and accurately name the places where Teddy has been?

Planning

Make a play map with children that shows which place Teddy went to first, then second, etc.

Reinforce knowledge of local places such as the post office and supermarket with additional stories. Ask parents if they can take their child to one of these local places.

30-50 months

Treasure map 40–60+ months

Put out a tray of sand for each child; cat litter trays are ideal for this. Hide a button in the tray. Indicate where the button is hidden by drawing a button in the sand. Tell children that Teddy has buried a button in their tray. Can they find it?

If the children can find the button easily, repeat the activity, but this time put a piece of paper onto the tray. Indicate where the button is hidden on the paper. The children will now have to lift up the paper and use it to work out where the button is buried. This will help them understand that treasure maps show us where something is hidden.

Observation

Are the children able to find Teddy's treasure easily?

Planning

Use a symbol such as a cross to demonstrate where the treasure is.

Put in extra information by, for example, putting out a shell on top of the sand and featuring it on the map.

Can the child now hide something for you and Teddy to find? Can they make a simple map?

40-60+ months

Communities

What do I need to do?

- Recognise that babies and toddlers need to form strong relationships with their key person.

- Provide babies and toddlers with opportunities to play with an adult.

- Sing songs and finger rhymes with babies and toddlers.

- Provide opportunities for babies and toddlers to see older children.

- Provide opportunities for babies and toddlers to play alongside each other, but do not expect them to share or cooperate.

Frequently Asked Questions

Why is the key person system so important?

For babies and toddlers to develop strong social skills, they need to feel emotionally secure. The key person system is designed to give babies and toddlers this emotional security in the temporary absence of their family.

The toddlers become very anxious and clingy for their key person when a new person comes into the room.

This is normal behaviour and is a healthy sign. It shows that the baby or toddler knows who is part of 'their group' and who they should go to if they feel insecure.

Should we be celebrating different festivals?

Yes, but in a low-key way, and at this stage only those festivals that the child's family usually celebrate. Photographs and picture books, however, should reflect the multicultural nature of society.

Peek-a-boo **0–11 months**

This traditional game helps babies to enjoy communicating and making a relationship.

- With very young babies, look into their eyes and smile. See if you can elicit a smile from them. Then slowly move your face and see if the baby turns their face too.
- With older babies, repeat, but cover your face with your hands slowly. Take your hands away so that you reappear. Start saying 'peek-a-boo' or similar.

These games need repeating many times so that the baby learns to predict what is going to happen.

Observation

Watch how the baby reacts. Does the baby anticipate finding you?

→

Try partially covering your head with a cloth. See if the baby can remove it and 'find' you.

Planning

Does the baby pull your hands away from your head?

→

Gently put your hands in front of the baby so that you block their vision. Can the baby push back your hands so that they 'find' you?

0–11 months

Our group **8–20 months**

Photographs hold an immense fascination for babies and particularly toddlers. Take several photographs of babies and toddlers together, for example two toddlers at the lunch table. Do not worry about babies or toddlers smiling for the camera! Laminate these photographs so that they can be handled. Put some on the wall at eye level. Draw babies' and toddlers' attention to their photograph.

Observation

Is the baby fascinated and interested in the photographs? (Do not expect recognition.)

→

Show the baby picture books and other materials that feature photographs and drawings of babies and toddlers.

Planning

Does the toddler seem interested in his or her own photograph? Does the toddler recognise other children in the photograph?

→

Put out a selection of safe mirrors so that toddlers can see their reflection in different ways, for example large mirrors and hand-held mirrors. Make sure that adults use children's names so that toddlers can learn the names of those in the group.

8-20 months

Communities

30–50 months

40–60+ months

What do I need to do?

- Provide opportunities for children to chat to each other and adults.

- Model good listening skills.

- Ask parents if they can tell you about significant events in their family's life, for example a trip to see Granny.

- Read stories about other children, such as *Alfie's World* by Shirley Hughes.

- Make sure that resources in the setting reflect our multicultural society.

- Celebrate special events that have relevance to children in the setting.

- Introduce children to toys, music and clothes from other cultures and countries.

Frequently Asked Questions

Which festivals should we be celebrating?

In the 30–50 months stage, the suggestion is that we should work on special events that are relevant to the children in the setting. It would sensible to continue this approach. So, if a child in the setting talks about preparing a special meal to celebrate Eid, the other children will be able to absorb information about Eid more easily.

Could we use cooking?

Yes, children can learn that other families eat foods that they are not familiar with and that food is a way of making some events special.

How can we get children to listen to each other?

Children are more likely to listen to each other when they are in very small groups and only once they are fairly fluent in their language use. Try encouraging children to talk to each other at meal and snack times.

Language partner activities

Children will often talk to you about what they have been doing and what is important to them when they are relaxed. Creating moments when children are able to come alongside children are essential and often work better than trying to organise a large group activity. Look out for activities where children and adults are engaged in repetitive movements that do not require huge amounts of concentration. Try to imagine that you are a language partner and 'chat' rather than question children.

Examples of language partner activities include:

- sorting buttons
- shelling peas
- washing duplo with a toothbrush
- sorting out books.

Observation

Which children enjoy chatting to adults?

Are there any children who do not seem to talk to adults in the setting?

How fluently do individual children talk?

Planning

Look at routines to ensure that children have regular opportunities for one-to-one talk with their key person.

Take recordings of children's speech to check for language development.

Music from around the world

It is important when introducing children to different cultures that they learn positive messages. Looking for links between what you know children enjoy and finding out about different cultures is important.

Using music is one way in which we can help children find out about differences in an enjoyable way. Visit a record shop and go to the 'World Music' section. Look out for CDs that will be appealing for children. You may also talk to parents about music and songs that they have at home. You could play different CDs as part of the routine, for example when children arrive and at meal times, as well as for children to move and dance to.

Observation

Are there any tracks that children particularly enjoy?

Planning

Use these tracks as starting points for other activities, such as for dance and movement or to put on when children are painting.

Physical Development

Physical Development underpins many other skills that babies and children need in order to fulfil their potential. This area of Learning and Development considers ways in which you might promote babies' and children's physical skills and help them to learn about healthy living.

This area of Learning and Development includes the following aspects:

- Movement and Space
- Health and Bodily Awareness
- Using Equipment and Materials

Movement and Space

What do I need to do?

- Make sure that children have sufficient space to run and move around in.
- Provide a range of equipment that will provide children with different challenges.
- Vary the equipment that is put out to ensure that children develop different skills.
- Look out for ways of providing children with sufficient challenges.
- Create small enclosed spaces, for example using cardboard boxes or a tent.
- Ensure that children spend sufficient time to develop their play.
- Provide opportunities for moving to music indoors and outdoors.
- Encourage children to choose equipment to enhance their play.
- Link other areas of the curriculum to this aspect of learning.
- Make sure that clothing is provided to allow children to be outdoors in damp weather.

Frequently Asked Questions

The boys seem reluctant to do anything other than use the wheeled toys.

While wheeled toys are important for children's development, there are other skills that they need to develop. These include climbing, balancing and learning to move confidently around obstacles. You might like to think about what other things these children would be interested in doing, for example kicking, aiming and throwing, and climbing, and then think about ways to provide these in a fun and enjoyable way.

Some of the children arrive in clothes that are not suitable for playing outdoors.

Make sure that parents know that you have a legal duty for children to play outdoors. You should also think about providing rain ponchos, Wellington boots and other garments which mean that children can play outdoors in the cold and wet.

Going shopping

30–50 months

Imaginative play outdoors can also be used to encourage a range of movements. Create several shops outdoors, for example a shoe shop, a vegetable shop, a clothes shop and a car accessories shop. These can simply be upturned cardboard boxes or crates with items laid out on them. Try to put out some items that are particularly cumbersome or heavy, as well as shopping trolleys, pushchairs and the paraphernalia that goes with shopping such as bags and purses. Chalk out some roads that might lead to the different shops. You could also put out some tricycles or other wheeled toys, so that children have a purpose in using them. Ask adults to staff some of the shops.

Observation

Do children enjoy moving around in the 'High Street'?

Planning

What other shops could be put out?

How could children be involved in decorating and stocking the shops?

What other scenes could be created?

30-50 months

Walk the plank!

40–60+ months

Tyres are a cheap and often free resource that can be used in outdoor environments in a variety of ways. They can be lined with thick polythene and filled with digging materials such as bark chippings or gravel, or they can be used for children to move around and to climb on.

For this activity you will need several tyres and some planks of wood. Simply put out the materials and see if children can find ways of using them to create bridges or gangplanks. Watch out to see which children are particularly confident.

If children do not seem sure of what they need to do, you may need to encourage them so that they 'have permission' to try out new things. It may also mean that more 'loose part' play is required, so that children learn to use things that are lying about in their environment.

Observation

Do the children enjoy this activity?

Planning

Look out for other materials that you can put out for children to create their own structures and obstacle courses.

Put out props so that children can use their structure as part of their role play.

Link this activity to the story of the Three Billy Goats Gruff and provide other props.

See if children can draw a plan of their structure.

40-60+ months

201

Health and Bodily Awareness

What do I need to do?

- Help toddlers learn language relating to their body and their needs, for example head, toes, clean, tired, thirsty.

- Provide opportunities for toddlers to become independent.

- Support toddlers to move away from nappies.

- Meet toddlers' physical needs.

- Provide a wide ranging nutritional diet.

- Support parents by providing information about health issues.

Frequently Asked Questions

At what age should toddlers be toilet trained?

There is no specific age. Most children move out of nappies somewhere between 15 months and 3 years, so it is important instead to focus on signs that a toddler is ready. One indicator that a toddler might have the physical maturity is when they are able to walk up and down stairs using alternate feet.

We have a toddler who is an extremely fussy eater. Any tips?

You will need to work with parents to establish a united approach. First, check that the child is not underweight and is eating a reasonably balanced diet. It may then be easier for adults to become more relaxed, since too much attention can be counterproductive. Look for ways of slipping in foods, perhaps by taking a playful approach. Finally, remember that toddlers' palates are still developing.

Cleaning up mirrors

Many toddlers dislike having their face and hands wiped at the end of meal times. It is useful if you can find ways for them to start to enjoy feeling clean and be motivated to do this for themselves.

Find a mirror that is not glass for the toddler to look into at the end of a meal. Point out that the toddler's mouth and face is dirty. Produce a damp face cloth or baby wipe and pass it to the toddler. Encourage the toddler to clean up while looking in the mirror. Praise the child and sound excited at the way the face is now clean. See if the toddler can also wipe his or her hands as well.

Observation

Does the toddler seem to notice the difference between having a dirty and a clean face?

Planning

Use the mirror at other opportunities to help the toddler notice the difference between clean and dirty.

Praise the toddler when attempts are made at self-cleaning

Take photographs of the toddler with a dirty and then a clean face.

Make a book about clean and dirty.

Finger painting

Learning to use your hands but also keep your hands clean is one way in which toddlers can find out about this aspect of learning. Try organising a finger painting activity by looking out for washable paints and sheets of paper that you can put onto the wall with masking tape.

Pour the paint into a shallow tray. Have a bowl of water close by and some paper towels for cleaning hands. Roll up sleeves and put aprons on the toddlers. You will need to do the same too, as this age group tends to model adults' behaviour. Put your hands in the paint and make some marks on the paper. Encourage the toddler to join in. Afterwards, wash your hands together in the bowl of water before washing them properly in a washbasin. Talk to the toddler about clean and dirty.

Observation

Does the toddler enjoy hand and finger painting?

Planning

Look out for other sensory activities involving the hands, for example those with gloop or shaving foam.

Use language relating to hands, such as fingernails, thumb and palm.

What other opportunities are there for toddlers to wash their hands?

Health and Bodily Awareness

What do I need to do?

- Look for opportunities to help children use language relating to their physical needs, such as tired, thirsty, hungry, rest, sleepy.

- Look for ways of helping children talk about their likes and dislikes.

- Build into the routine times for children to learn self-care skills.

- Provide opportunities for children to learn about cooking and choosing nutritional foods.

- Provide a wide ranging nutritional diet.

- Support parents by providing information about health issues.

Frequently Asked Questions

Many children do not seem to think about taking off jumpers when they are too hot.

Adults can help children learn to regulate their clothing in relation to their temperature by showing them in a mirror the signs that they are hot. Once children have removed a layer of clothing, ask them about the difference it makes.

Some of the children do not seem to drink much during the day.

Try modelling drinking water. This has a surprising effect as once one person starts to drink, others start to feel thirsty. Some children will drink more than others, perhaps because they sweat more, are more active or have more salt in their diet. Remember that fluid in foods also has a hydrating effect, so a child who had porridge for breakfast rather than toast may not feel as thirsty mid-morning.

Making smoothies 30–50 months

Cooking activities are a great way for children to learn about healthy eating, while also learning a range of other skills such as measuring, cutting and using tools. Look out for cooking activities where children can be involved in most of the preparation and can also make choices.

Choose some fruits that children can easily prepare and put out a liquidiser. With individual or small groups of children, show them how to wash, peel and cut up fruits. Talk to children about the names of the fruit and ask them to taste each one. Once the children have selected and put the fruits into the liquidiser, turn it on and then pour out the liquid for the children to taste.

Observation

Which fruits did children enjoy?

Could the children name the fruits that they were using?

Were they able to use the tools?

Planning

Look out for other cooking activities that will help children learn about food and cooking, such as making salads, pizzas or bread.

Talk to parents about the fruit that their children tried.

30-50 months

Packing for Teddy 40–60+ months

Bring out a teddy along with a range of different clothes. Tell children that Teddy needs help deciding what to wear and that his mother says he has to choose clothes that are right for the weather. Tell the children that Teddy is going somewhere where it is going to be very wet and very cold. Can they choose what Teddy should wear?

When children have chosen clothes for Teddy, see if they can tell Teddy why he needs to wear them. Teddy wants to wear one or two very inappropriate items, for example a sunhat and sandals. Can the children explain why they will not be useful?

Observation

Can children choose what is appropriate clothing for different weather?

Can children tell Teddy why he needs to wear certain clothes?

Planning

How can children be given more responsibility for getting ready to go outdoors?

Provide opportunities for children to talk about how hot or cold they are feeling.

Put out a wide range of clothing in the role-play area.

40-60+ months

Using Equipment and Materials

What do I need to do?

- Provide frequent opportunities for treasure basket and heuristic play.

- Provide a range of toys and items that babies can safely handle and explore, for example rattles, balls and cuddly toys.

- Look out for toys that have a cause and effect property, for example turning a button to make a noise.

- Observe how babies' fine motor and hand–eye coordination are developing.

- Provide opportunities for babies to use spoons and beakers as part of the weaning and feeding routine.

Frequently Asked Questions

What types of materials are safe for babies?

The aim is to provide sensory opportunities for babies that stimulate their desire to use their hands, and there are plenty of materials that you might use. Think about dry rice and pasta as well as other food products such as mashed potato. Remember that water and other liquids are also intriguing for babies. Note that you should always make sure that materials are safe for babies to mouth and swallow. You may also need to get permission from parents.

What equipment and materials can we put out for toddlers?

Think about equipment that will encourage them to use their hands such as scoops, pop-up toys, hammers and pegs as well as mark-making materials such as chunky crayons.

Sponges

0–11 months

Sponges are interesting for babies to handle and mouth. They are also good for strengthening babies' hand muscles.

Give a clean sponge, ideally a natural one, to a baby to feel and notice what they are able to do with it. Look to see whether they can focus on it or, later on, if they can pass it from hand to hand. Expect that young babies will often drop items onto the floor. Watch how babies increasingly develop coordination when looking at objects.

Note that babies must always be supervised when given objects, and objects must be risk assessed for choking.

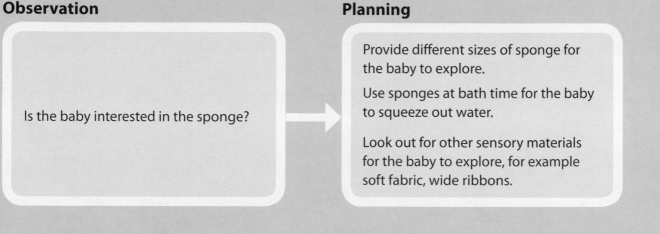

Observation

Is the baby interested in the sponge?

Planning

Provide different sizes of sponge for the baby to explore.

Use sponges at bath time for the baby to squeeze out water.

Look out for other sensory materials for the baby to explore, for example soft fabric, wide ribbons.

0-11 months

Making sounds

8–20 months

Older babies and toddlers enjoy exploring sounds. You can use this appeal to help them use their hands.

Look out for some metal dishes and some spoons. Show an older baby or toddler how to make a sound by banging the beater against the metal. Look to see if they copy your actions.

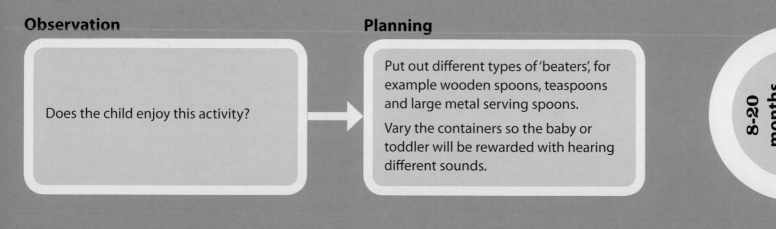

Observation

Does the child enjoy this activity?

Planning

Put out different types of 'beaters', for example wooden spoons, teaspoons and large metal serving spoons.

Vary the containers so the baby or toddler will be rewarded with hearing different sounds.

8-20 months

Using Equipment and Materials

What do I need to do?

- Look out for toys and equipment that will develop fine motor skills and hand–eye coordination, for example scoops, sponges, large brushes and construction bricks.

- Look for everyday opportunities to encourage hand use, such as encouraging a child to find and put on a hat.

- Introduce spoons, forks and other feeding utensils.

- Encourage self-care skills such as tidying up and dressing.

- Look out for materials that will motivate children to use fine motor skills, for example looking at small items, picking out grains of rice.

Frequently Asked Questions

We are worried about putting out small items in case they get swallowed.

Most toddlers should have stopped mouthing by around 18 months, but observation is vital. Use a choking tube to assess whether an item is likely to be a choking hazard. Small pieces are usually fine providing that you supervise children and the items are interesting, for example a collection of buttons. If a bored child finds a single button, they are more likely to put it in their mouth.

We have put out pencils for the toddlers, but they are not interested.

Mark-making is an excellent way of developing fine motor skills, but pencils are hard for toddlers to make a mark with. Try using thick board markers or putting out pencils in a damp sand tray. Toddlers may become more interested if you model mark-making for them.

Brushes and water

Most toddlers love water, so it is a useful material to put out and use regularly with this age group. Fill up a bucket with soapy water and take some large brushes outdoors. Help the toddler into an apron before going outdoors. Pick up a brush and start 'painting' a wall or a window. See if the toddler is interested in doing the same. You may also find that some toddlers will prefer just to stir the water or drop the brushes into it to watch the splash!

Note: you must supervise water play carefully and be sure not to leave children unattended near water.

Observation

Does the toddler enjoy this activity?

What does the toddler want to do with the water?

Planning

Repeat this activity, but base it on what the toddler enjoyed doing.

Extend this activity by putting out clothes so that toddlers could do some washing.

Introduce the toddlers to paint.

Think about lightly colouring the water with food colouring.

16-26 months

Building and knocking down sandcastles

Most toddlers love knocking things down. It seems to make them feel powerful and in control.

Put out some containers of damp sand, some beakers and some teaspoons. Model how to put sand into the beaker and make a sandcastle. Encourage the toddler to knock it down. Make some more sandcastles with the toddler. Make sure that you have a damp cloth nearby to wipe hands and a brush to cope with spills.

Observation

Does the child enjoy this activity?

How easy does the child find this activity?

Planning

Put out other tools for scooping such as tablespoons and different sizes of spoons.

Look out for various containers such as cups and bowls.

Take this activity outdoors so it can be done on a larger scale.

22-36 months

Using Equipment and Materials

What do I need to do?

- Think about putting out equipment and planning activities that will encourage increasing accuracy in fine motor movements, such as putting out very small bottles for children to fill.

- Encourage children to be as independent as possible, for example when dressing, feeding and tidying up.

- Provide a wide range of tools for children to use and be ready to show them how to use them safely.

- Incorporate fine motor skills into all areas of the provision, for example provide mark-making pads alongside wooden blocks or wind-up bells on tricycles.

Frequently Asked Questions

We have a three-year-old who does not seem to have a hand preference. Is this normal?

Most children will have developed a hand preference by around 30 months, but some need more support. Make sure that children have plenty of opportunities to carry out activities requiring two hands. The best activities are those where a child is using one hand to stabilise and the other hand is active, such as peeling a banana.

Is it true that boys have poorer hand–eye coordination than girls?

No, not in my experience. Also, the traditional milestones used by health visitors and paediatricians do not differentiate between boys and girls. One of the most important factors in developing fine motor movement and coordination is providing activities that interest children and encourage them, so observing children's individual interests and planning for these is the best way forward.

Dough
30–50 months

Dough is a popular material for children to use. It is also a great material to help young children learn to use scissors.

Put out some soft dough and some scissors on a table. Sit with children and model how to roll dough into a long sausage shape then use the scissors to snip the dough. Make sure that you have left-handed scissors available and be ready to show children how to hold the scissors.

Observation

Do the children enjoy using dough?

Are children interested in using scissors?

Which children need more support?

Planning

Put out dough alongside other tools such as rollers, cutters and garlic presses.

Think about other ways in which children can use scissors, for example snipping shredded paper or thin cardboard.

Check that scissors are appropriate for the children's needs.

30-50 months

Picnic time
40–60+ months

Most children enjoy cooking, and preparing a picnic is exciting for them. Look out for some simple foods that children can prepare, such as cutting up cheese, cucumbers and tomatoes alongside making sandwiches. Avoid providing junk foods such as crisps as the aim is to help children enjoy foods that are nutritious. See if the children can lay out the foods onto plates and even carry out a tray. This has the potential to be a whole morning's activity, especially if small groups of children also build their picnic tent!

Observation

Did children enjoy this activity?

How did they manage using tools?

Planning

Could this activity be repeated?

What other foods could be prepared for a picnic?

Could you provide other tools for children to use, such as a grater or masher?

How can children be helped to become more independent?

40-60+ months

Creative Development

Creativity is a life skill as well as a means of self-expression. Babies and children have the potential to be creative and this area of Learning and Development looks at how to encourage their budding creativity.

This area of Learning and Development includes the following aspects:

- Being Creative – Responding to Experiences, Expressing and Communicating
- Exploring Media and Materials
- Creating Music and Dance
- Developing Imagination and Imaginative Play

Being Creative

What do I need to do?

- Make sure that your approach to working with children is creative and flexible.

- Show babies and toddlers picture books.

- Sing rhymes and songs to children.

- Take time to talk to babies and toddlers.

- Play peek-a-boo with babies.

- Animate cuddly toys, for example pretend to talk to a teddy.

- Play a range of music and use it to dance with babies and toddlers.

- Regularly provide for treasure basket and heuristic play.

Frequently Asked Questions

This area of learning seems to duplicate the others within the section.

Yes, in some ways it does, but think of it more as an umbrella and a way of linking practice together. The key in this area of learning is to look for ways of helping even very young children express themselves and experience different sensations including sounds, tastes and mark-making. It is also about helping babies and toddlers learn to express themselves through language, facial expression and gestures.

Some of our parents think that their babies and toddlers should be drawing. How can we explain what we are doing?

Talk to parents about the importance of stimulating babies through a wide range of experiences and sensations. Use digital photographs and film to show parents their babies' and toddlers' responses to music, pictures and tastes.

Bouncing and rocking to music
0–11 months

Babies need stimulation which can include physical movements. Put on some music that has a strong rhythm and move the baby in time to the music. Try rocking the baby as well as bouncing the baby up and down on your knee in time to the beat. When holding the baby, make sure that you maintain eye contact as this helps the baby to feel involved in the activity. It is also a way of ensuring that the baby is feeling secure and safe.

Observation

Planning

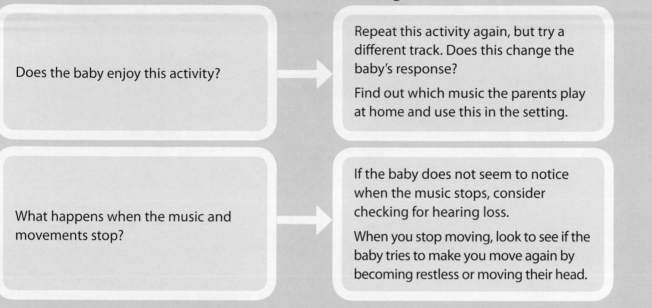

Observation	Planning
Does the baby enjoy this activity?	Repeat this activity again, but try a different track. Does this change the baby's response? Find out which music the parents play at home and use this in the setting.
What happens when the music and movements stop?	If the baby does not seem to notice when the music stops, consider checking for hearing loss. When you stop moving, look to see if the baby tries to make you move again by becoming restless or moving their head.

0–11 months

Scarves and fabrics
8–20 months

Collect together a range of different coloured scarves and pieces of fabrics. Look out for a variety of textures including some fine and coarse materials. Try also to find fabrics and scarves of different lengths, although it is not advisable to put in tiny scraps due to the choking risk.

Place the scarves and fabrics in an attractive basket or low box. When the toddler is not tired or hungry, bring out the box and encourage the toddler to start taking scarves and fabrics out.

Observation

Planning

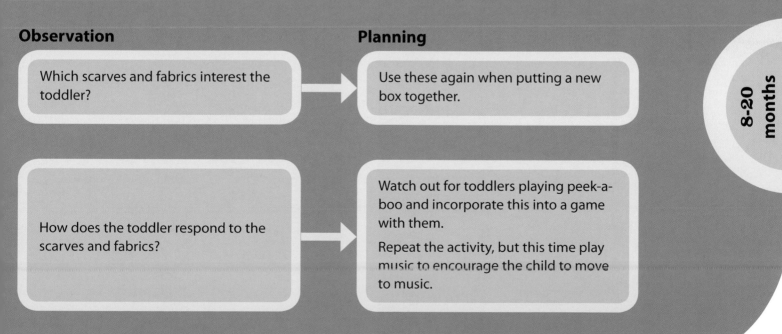

Observation	Planning
Which scarves and fabrics interest the toddler?	Use these again when putting a new box together.
How does the toddler respond to the scarves and fabrics?	Watch out for toddlers playing peek-a-boo and incorporate this into a game with them. Repeat the activity, but this time play music to encourage the child to move to music.

8-20 months

Being Creative

What do I need to do?

- Make sure that your approach to working with children is creative and flexible.

- Look at different images with toddlers including photographs and posters as well as picture books.

- Create a stimulating environment, for example by using displays or mobiles that change frequently, taking trips out of doors and playing outside.

- Put out a range of sensory materials for toddlers to play with.

- Use puppets to help toddlers enjoy animation.

- Provide children with a range of music and ways of making sounds.

- Create opportunities for heuristic and treasure basket play.

Frequently Asked Questions

We have one child who dislikes getting their hands dirty and so will not do any messy activities.

Children's hands are more sensitive than adults and sometimes this can cause some children to perceive sensory activities such as dough, sand or gloop as being unpleasant. It is important to take this fear seriously. Ironically, though, these children need more exposure to sensory activities so their hands can desensitise a little. Start by letting children feel the sensory activities through a barrier such as a clear bag or by wearing see-through gloves. After several times, put out a bowl of water and suggest that the child can wash their hands at any point when they feel uncomfortable. Do not force children to put their hands into something they dislike as the distress can result in a long-term phobia.

Splashing in puddles

The focus of this area of learning for this age group is to elicit responses from children as they are exposed to different sensations. This should take place indoors and outdoors. Splashing in puddles is one of the sensations of childhood that must not be missed.

Go outdoors after it has rained and look for some puddles to splash in with the toddlers. Make sure that they are wearing appropriate footwear. Model walking through the puddle and expect that some toddlers will want to feel the water too.

Note that, as with any water activity, it is essential that children are supervised at all times.

Observation

How do the toddlers respond to finding water?

Planning

Take photographs and show them to the toddlers afterwards.

Use a paddling pool or builders' tray to recreate this experience if you have had a period of dry weather.

Take out objects such as rubber ducks and boats to float on a puddle.

Look out for sticks that toddlers can use to stir the puddle.

16-26 months

Coloured ice cubes in water

Colour three cups of water using food colouring. Choose three different colours – red, yellow and blue are good for this. Use the water to create different coloured ice cubes. Once the ice cubes are frozen, put three of them into the water tray. As they melt they should leave a coloured trail in the water. See if the children notice how the water is changing colour and how the colours are mixing.

Observation

How does the toddler respond to the ice cubes melting?

Planning

Repeat this activity using the other ice cubes.

Let the toddler choose which ice cubes to put inside the water.

Provide sticks, spoons and other implements for the toddler to stir the water.

22-36 months

Being Creative

What do I need to do?

- Make sure that your approach to working with children is creative and flexible.

- Look for ways for children to become independent and have their own ideas.

- Create problem-solving opportunities for children, such as making their own props for a role-play shop.

- Provide opportunities to develop children's language skills so they can take part in role play and express their feelings through words.

- Check that your resources are diverse and offer children varied opportunities, for example musical instruments, collage materials, junk modelling and clay.

- Provide children with sufficient time to complete their play or products.

- Avoid focusing children on the end product.

- Show parents how children's drawings and paintings are linked to development.

- Use ICT as part of this area of learning.

Frequently Asked Questions

We use the 'paint' programme on the computer. Is this appropriate?

Yes, providing that children have other experiences of drawing, painting and expressing themselves. The idea of this area of learning is that children are given a diverse range of opportunities from music and dance through to imaginative play and drawing.

We went on a course and were told not to use templates and colouring sheets. Why?

The aim of this area of learning is that children find their own ways of expressing themselves rather than trying to follow what adults have created for them. Adults can of course support children and teach them skills, but it is important that children have a chance to work through their own representations.

Junk modelling

30–50 months

Junk modelling is popular with children if there are interesting materials on offer. Find out if there is a local scrap project that your setting can join. These take off cuts and surplus materials from local companies and are a real treasure trove.

Put out some materials onto a table. Provide a range of sizes of materials. Do not worry if children do not make anything, but just want to explore what is available. Make sure that you have glue as well as masking tape, staples and other ways of helping children to join items together. You might like also to create your own one off model!

Observation

What items take children's interest?

Do children have an idea of what they wish to represent or are they just happy exploring the materials?

Planning

Look at the materials that are of interest. See if you can provide more or incorporate them into other aspects of play, for example small boxes could be used in role play.

Talk to children about the way that materials have been joined together and what they have produced.

30-50 months

Marking to music

40–60+ months

Put out a large sheet of paper onto a table. Put out a range of tools for marking, such as felt-tip pens, pencils, biros and chalks. Put some music on and ask children if they would like to take their pencil or tool 'for a walk'. You should join in too, as attitudes to marking and drawing are linked to adult participation. Relax and let your pen travel as you want. Talk to children about the marks they have made. Try again with a different piece of music which might change the mood. See if children can see how their marks have changed.

Observation

Do children enjoy this activity?

Are children making representational marks?

Planning

Repeat again with a range of different music.

See if children have a favourite track.

Listen to what children tell you about their marks. Notice whether they make similar marks in other situations, for example when mark-making.

Keep a record of the marks that children make.

40-60+ months

Exploring Media and Materials

What do I need to do?

- Provide different textures, surfaces and items for babies and toddlers to explore.

- Regularly provide for treasure basket and heuristic play.

- Look out for a range of sensory materials for babies and toddlers to explore.

- Encourage babies and toddlers to use their feet as well as hands for touching.

- Talk to babies and toddlers about what they are seeing and doing.

- Provide a wide range of foods for toddlers to taste, touch and see.

Frequently Asked Questions

Treasure basket and heuristic play is recommended as a way of covering several areas of learning. Is this enough?

These types of play help babies and toddlers to explore items, and providing that you vary the type of items that you put in, they will deliver several different aspects of learning. You should look out for other materials for babies and toddlers to explore as well, though.

Toddlers tend to play with food as well as eating it. Should we be encouraging this?

Babies and toddlers are keen to explore textures and tastes and so are likely to play a little with food. For young children, it is worth seeing this as part of their creative development rather than make a big issue out of it. If toddlers enjoy stirring yoghurt, for example, this could help you plan a future activity for them.

Bath time

0–11 months

Bath time is one way in which babies can enjoy new sensations as water seems to provide endless pleasure. Prepare a bath for a baby at a time when they are not tired. Once the baby has been washed and is enjoying the water, pass some objects to the baby, such as sponges and shells. The objects need to have interesting textures while also being safe for the baby to hold and mouth. Watch to see what the baby tries to do with the objects.

Note that activities involving water must be carefully planned and supervised to avoid the risk of drowning.

Observation

How does the baby respond to the objects?

→

Planning

Think about filming the baby's reactions.

Consider other opportunities when you could give these items to the baby.

What other objects could you provide at bath time?

0-11 months

Cold spaghetti

8–20 months

Exploring different materials and textures is the starting point for this area of learning. Babies and toddlers relish this opportunity to explore cold cooked spaghetti with their hands and mouth.

Cook some spaghetti, drain the water and then leave the spaghetti to cool. Sprinkle in a little food colouring (green and blue are good colours as they are not necessarily associated with food) and mix the spaghetti up. Put the spaghetti onto a highchair tray or a large plastic sheet on the ground. Put an apron on the baby or toddler and show them the spaghetti.

Note: this activity is not suitable for children with a wheat allergy, so you should check with parents beforehand.

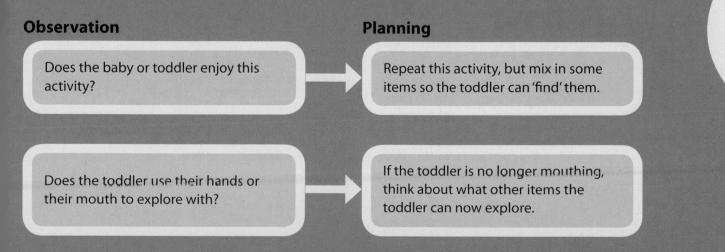

Observation

Does the baby or toddler enjoy this activity?

→

Planning

Repeat this activity, but mix in some items so the toddler can 'find' them.

Does the toddler use their hands or their mouth to explore with?

→

If the toddler is no longer mouthing, think about what other items the toddler can now explore.

8-20 months

223

Exploring Media and Materials

What do I need to do?

- Provide different textures, surfaces and items for toddlers to explore.

- Follow and develop toddlers' interests.

- Create interesting outdoor spaces for toddlers to explore.

- Provide plenty of child-initiated play opportunities.

- Expect that toddlers will want to mix up materials and provide opportunities for this, for example putting handfuls of sand in water.

Frequently Asked Questions

We want to create a digging area outdoors. Would this link to this area of learning?

Definitely, as digging is a way of exploring a material. Digging is also a good example of a child-initiated activity where children can discover textures for themselves. Think about filling rubber tyres with different materials such as sand, gravel, bark chippings and turf. You could use builder's trays indoors if you wish to find a way of creating this opportunity inside.

Can I use cooking activities to deliver this area of Learning and Development?

Yes, providing that children are active in touching and mixing the ingredients. One fun and easy cooking activity is to produce some stretchy dough by mixing self-raising flour and water. Children can shape this into malleable dough using their hands. Note that any cooking activities must take account of children's allergies and dietary preferences.

Dough

16–26 months

Toddlers enjoy dough as one of the first malleable materials they can explore.

Make soft dough which is pliable. Choose a colour such as blue or green to avoid toddlers confusing it with food, and add salt to the dough to discourage toddlers from eating it. Put the dough in the toddler's hands so that they can feel it. Put some dough in your hands too, and act as a role model by squeezing and pinching it.

Observation

How does the toddler respond to the dough?

Planning

Repeat this activity if the child seems to enjoy it.

Consider putting out other items alongside the dough, such as cups and plates.

Try producing different types of dough, for example dough that has sawdust inside it.

16-26 months

Opportunities for stirring

22–36 months

Children enjoy playing outdoors and mixing up materials. Some children will want to include this stirring activity as part of their role play.

Put out a large bucket of water and piles of different materials, such as bark chippings, gravel and sand. Children will need a stick, large wooden spoon or something else that will allow them to stir. Make sure that children are wearing some protective clothes, such as aprons or rain ponchos. Encourage the children to enjoy stirring up some mixtures.

Observation

What materials do children seem to enjoy playing with most?

Do children combine this activity with their role play?

Planning

Make sure that these materials are available at other times.

Look for other materials that children can use as part of their role play, for example dried pasta and dough.

22-36 months

Exploring Media and Materials

What do I need to do?

- Provide as many different items as possible for children to explore, for example feathers, keys and locks, paint, music.

- Link this aspect of Creative Development to Exploration and Investigation in Knowledge and Understanding of the World (see pages 158–63).

- Provide plenty of child-initiated play opportunities.

- Avoid only thinking of art products for this area of learning.

- Make sure that you provide different materials for mark-making, such as paints, pencils, pens and chalks.

Frequently Asked Questions

We want to use loose-part play outdoors. Does this cover this area of learning?

Yes, loose-part play is a good example of how children can explore and respond to different materials. They can be creative in using the materials that they find. Loose-part play is easy to organise outdoors. Look out for objects such as guttering, boxes, fabric and builder's crates, which children can bring together to create their own play opportunities.

How much should adults be involved when children are being creative?

The main role of the adult is to be a facilitator rather than an organiser. Plan to provide materials and opportunities and to encourage children to use them in ways that are of interest to them. The aim is that children become confident in using a range of materials and learn about their properties.

Creating a collage
30–50 months

Collages are one way in which children can explore materials. For collages to work well, it is important that there is a large range of materials available for children to use and that adults act as facilitators rather than demonstrators.

On a table, lay out a range of different materials, including some non-traditional craft items such as bottle tops. Provide different coloured paper and glue. Expect that some children will be more interested in just touching the materials than creating a collage!

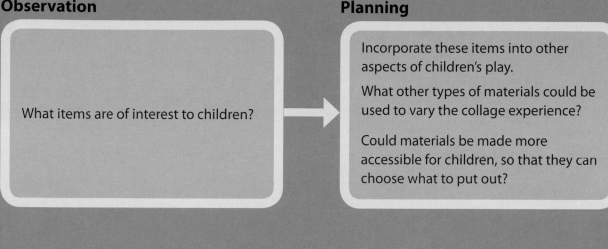

Observation

What items are of interest to children?

Planning

Incorporate these items into other aspects of children's play.

What other types of materials could be used to vary the collage experience?

Could materials be made more accessible for children, so that they can choose what to put out?

30-50 months

Painting wall
40–60+ months

A painting wall is a fantastic way for children to discover an enjoyment of painting. It also helps them to develop their understanding of colour.

Put up polythene sheeting to protect a wall. You can use wide masking tape if you are doing this on brickwork outdoors. On top of the plastic, place paper for painting. Aim to create the largest surface for painting possible. On small trays, put small quantities of the three primary colours plus white. Give children a tray and a brush each. The aim is that children become used to having their own palette of paint rather than being restricted to single colours in pots. You may like to join in with the children, although avoid telling them what they should paint.

Observation

How do children cope with the trays of paint?

Do children enjoy this activity?

Planning

If children are finding it difficult to use the trays as palettes, try using smaller quantities of paint or smaller trays.

Provide this activity regularly.

Change the paints within the tray so that children can learn about colour mixing.

40-60+ months

Creating Music and Dance

What do I need to do?

- Sing songs to babies during everyday activities.
- Put on a variety of music for babies to listen to, including music that reflects the child's home environment.
- Sing nursery rhymes to babies.
- Dance with babies.
- Put babies on your lap and involve them in action rhymes.
- Look out for shakers and other simple instruments that babies can handle and explore.

Frequently Asked Questions

Are we allowed to play pop music to babies?

Babies need to hear a range of music and music styles, so you could play pop music as part of a range of musical experiences.

I cannot sing very well. Would it be better to use a professional recording?

No – babies respond better to hearing music directly from the people they are with. This is more powerful than a recording, so while you can put on recordings from time to time, try not to rely on them.

How can we get babies who are not mobile to dance?

Try putting on some very rhythmic music while babies are lying on their backs. You may find that some babies will wiggle in time to the music, although they may need to hear it several times.

Musical nappy changes

Music needs to be introduced in a variety of ways. Singing to a baby is the best way, but you might also look out for some musical toys which you could use to help the baby associate music with routines, such as nappy changing and bath time. Music can be helpful at these times as it can soothe a baby.

Find a musical toy that you like the sound of, for example a musical mobile. Show the musical toy to the baby before the start of the nappy change and then turn it on. Remember that making eye contact and talking to the baby about whether they are enjoying the music is essential, as babies need interaction.

Observation

How does the baby respond to the music?

Does the baby recognise the music or show that they want to hear it?

Planning

Think about filming the baby's reactions.

Look out for other musical toys that play different tunes.

How could you make other musical toys available for babies to use?

Are there other ways of incorporating music into the baby's routine?

0–11 months

Row, row, row the boat!

Babies and toddlers love to be part of activities that adults are involved in. Action rhymes are a good way of helping babies and toddlers to enjoy music and learn to move their bodies in time with it.

Put on a recording of Row, row, row your boat and sing along with the words. Put the baby or toddler on your lap and involve them in making the actions to accompany the song.

Observation

Does the baby or toddler enjoy this activity?

Does the baby or toddler begin to predict the movements or join in with the sounds?

Planning

Repeat this activity often, so that children become familiar with the action rhyme.

What other action rhymes could be used with babies and toddlers?

What action rhymes do parents use at home?

8-20 months

Creating Music and Dance

What do I need to do?

- Provide opportunities for toddlers to explore different instruments.

- Look out for opportunities to sing rhymes and songs.

- Help toddlers move in time to music, for example by rocking them.

- Put music on and let toddlers see you dancing.

- Look out for props that toddlers can hold when moving to music, such as scarves and ribbons.

- Talk to parents about the types of music that they play at home.

Frequently Asked Questions

Should we be getting toddlers to sit down for rhymes and songs?

No; this age range are not great sitters! You might find it easier to start off by singing and getting out some simple shakers and then expecting the children to come and join you. Sitting down when hearing music is actually quite difficult, as most children naturally want to move their body.

How can we help toddlers follow the beat? At the moment they just shake and make sounds randomly.

Toddlers need to have opportunities to simply explore ways of making sounds, so you will find it hard to 'organise them' at first. Try, instead, to use a shaker yourself and put on music with a strong beat. If you move and shake to the beat, some of the children will start to follow your actions.

Sound box   16–26 months

Put a range of simple musical instruments into a wicker basket or cardboard box for the toddler to explore. Choose instruments that are easy to lift out and use; bells and shakers work well. Make sure that the instruments will produce different sounds. Take time to observe the toddler exploring the instruments. Encourage where necessary, but the focus of this activity is for the toddler to explore sounds independently.

Observation

Planning

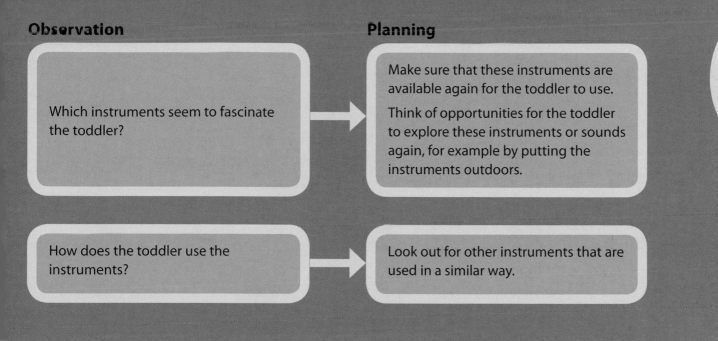

Which instruments seem to fascinate the toddler?

Make sure that these instruments are available again for the toddler to use.

Think of opportunities for the toddler to explore these instruments or sounds again, for example by putting the instruments outdoors.

How does the toddler use the instruments?

Look out for other instruments that are used in a similar way.

16-26 months

Ribbons and scarves   22–36 months

By this age, most toddlers will enjoy moving to music in some way. You can build on this enjoyment by providing them with objects to use in response to music.

Find a piece of music that the toddler seems to respond well to – for example, music that they normally like to dance or bob up and down to. Before playing the toddler's preferred music, put out a pile of different coloured scarves and ribbons. Let the toddler explore these and then put the music on. Pick up a scarf too and start moving the scarf in time to the music. See if the toddler copies you.

Observation

Planning

Does the toddler enjoy this activity?

Does the toddler move in time with the music?

Try putting out different widths, colours or textures of fabrics for toddlers to use.

Model moving to music.

22-36 months

Creating Music and Dance

What do I need to do?

- Provide opportunities for children to explore musical instruments.
- Look out for opportunities to sing rhymes and songs.
- Organise musical experiences for children, for example invite musicians to perform at the setting.
- Make up songs with children.
- Create a sound wall outdoors.
- Provide opportunities for playing music from different parts of the world.
- Help children learn to control the sounds they are making by playing games.
- Provide sufficient space for children to move freely to music.
- Encourage children to choose what type of music they wish to listen to or sing.
- Use language that will help children think about the way they are moving or the sounds they are hearing, for example slow, fast, loud and soft.

Frequently Asked Questions

Is it all right to have groups of children doing music and dance?

Yes, but keep the groups small and be flexible. Music and dance are meant to be enjoyable for children, so forcing them to do something they are not interested in will not work. Make sure that sessions do not become too adult-focused, so that children can explore making their own music or moving in their own ways.

At what age can children be taught to play musical instruments?

This depends on many factors, including the technical difficulty of the instrument and how motivated the child is to learn. Many children can easily use untuned instruments such as shakers, but most children are not physically and cognitively ready for instruments such as the guitar, piano or flute until they are around six or seven years old.

Find the beat
30–50 months

One of the starting points for children when learning about music is to be able to recognise the beat in music and then respond to it.

Look out for some pieces of music that have a strong beat – this may be a drum beat, for example. Begin by seeing if children can clap or tap their feet in time with the beat. Play the music again and put out shakers. Can the children find the beat and move their shakers in time to the beat? The children can then see if they can also move around while making a sound to the beat.

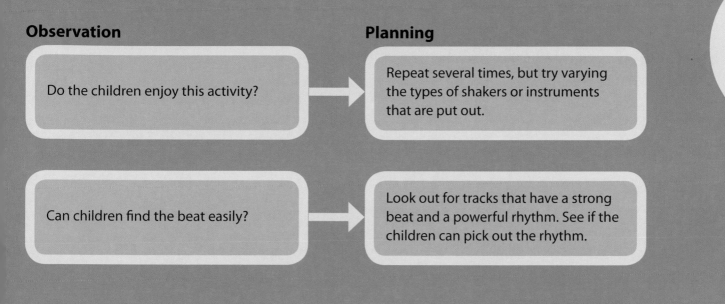

Observation

Do the children enjoy this activity?

Can children find the beat easily?

Planning

Repeat several times, but try varying the types of shakers or instruments that are put out.

Look out for tracks that have a strong beat and a powerful rhythm. See if the children can pick out the rhythm.

30–50 months

Hot and cold
40–60+ months

It is useful if children learn how to control the sounds that they are making with instruments. This is a simple game based on 'Hunt the thimble'.

Put out enough shakers for children to have one each. Choose one child to close their eyes. With the other children watching, hide a shaker. Ask the child to open their eyes and to start looking for the hidden shaker. Tell the children to help this child by making loud sounds if the child is moving in towards the hidden object (getting 'hotter') and quieter sounds if the child is moving away (getting 'colder').

Observation

Do children enjoy this game?

Planning

Repeat this game so that all the children have a turn.

Encourage children to invent other musical games. For example, can they find another way of signalling that the child is near the hidden object?

Think about other musical games that you can play with children, such as going on a bear hunt, musical bumps and musical statues.

40–60+ months

Developing Imagination

What do I need to do?

- Find time for plenty of one-to-one interactions with babies and toddlers.

- Play games such as peek-a-boo with babies.

- Use plenty of facial expressions and smiles with babies and toddlers.

- Have one or two special cuddly toys such as teddies that make regular appearances.

- Look out for books and toys that babies and toddlers have begun to recognise and enjoy.

- Use finger and hand puppets to amuse babies and toddlers.

Frequently Asked Questions

I thought that children showed imaginative play at two years. Why is it included for babies and toddlers?

Yes, you are right. The reason that imaginative play is included for this age range is to show the earliest steps and ways of supporting babies and toddlers. As you have already seen throughout the book, it is often a case of making sure that some of the everyday routines are working well, for example interacting with a baby during a nappy change.

Are we allowed to put cuddly toys into babies' cots?

Safety is always an issue when working with babies. The advice from the Foundation for the Study of Infant Deaths (FSID) is that cuddly toys should not be put in cots with young babies. It is always worth checking the latest advice, though (see, for example, www.sids.org.uk).

Animal frieze
0–11 months

Create a large animal frieze along a wall, for example where you change nappies or near the babies' cots. Make the frieze colourful and interesting – you might like to recruit the help of older children in making it. Consider putting some sticky-back plastic over some or all of the frieze, so that if it is touched by babies it will not tear.

Show the baby the frieze as part of the routine of going for a nap, feeding or having a nappy change. Try and build up a pattern as to what you look at first and then second. Use your finger to point out particular animals.

0-11 months

Observation

Does the baby begin to show signs that he or she recognises the frieze?

Does the baby point to any of the animals?

Planning

Keep on showing the frieze to the baby. Expect that at around six months the baby will show some recognition. If older babies do not seem to recognise or respond, consider whether their sight needs checking.

Provide picture books with animal images.

Make the sounds of some of the animals on the wall.

Thank you!
8–20 months

This is a simple first game that many toddlers will play. It also helps toddlers learn some of the earliest skills that will be needed later in cooperative imaginative play.

Take some items such as pegs and pass them one at a time to the toddler. Say 'thank you' as the toddler takes each item. Then hold out your hand to see if the toddler will give you an item back. Say 'thank you' each time the toddler passes an item to you, even though the toddler may place the item on your palm and swiftly remove it!

8-20 months

Observation

Does the toddler enjoy this game?

Does the toddler sometimes deliberately 'trick' you by pretending to give you something back?

Planning

Repeat this game, but try using other objects.

Try holding out a box of objects and giving the toddler a box to put the objects that are taken in.

Put out a teddy and pretend to give items to it.

See if the toddler will enjoy you 'pretending' to have something in your hand.

Try pretending to eat food or to drink and see how the toddler responds.

Developing Imagination

What do I need to do?

- Provide simple props from real life for children.

- Be ready to join in their play, for example by pretending to drink tea or eat a cake.

- Provide dough and other materials that can be used to make 'food'.

- Have a range of small-world toys available for children.

- Provide 'characters' for children to play with, such as a teddy and other cuddly toys.

- Animate cuddly toys by talking to them in front of children.

- Create small enclosed areas where children can feel that they are playing in private.

Frequently Asked Questions

While most of our three-year-olds cooperate when they are in the home corner, the younger children seem to play alone. Is this normal?

Yes. Playing cooperatively and taking turns and roles in imaginative play is quite demanding in terms of language and cognitive skills. This means that most young children, although interested in playing imaginatively, cannot yet do so with other children. The exception to this is often children who have strong language skills or who are used to playing with older siblings. We can help younger children by being their play partners.

How much small-world play should be out for two-year-olds?

Children seldom need huge quantities of small-world toys, but they do need variety. Aim to have several different types of small-world toys out at a time and think about placing them within some sensory materials (see activity).

Teddy bear's picnic   16–26 months

Toddlers often enjoy playing in enclosed spaces and they love eating picnics. In this age group they are just starting to develop role play and it often begins with them pretending with food and cuddly toys.

Create a little tent for the toddler and put a teddy inside along with a plate with some pieces of food such as slices of banana or raisins on it. Ask the toddler if he or she would like to feed Teddy.

You can do this activity outdoors as well, but you must make sure that the toddler's hands are clean. If you are doing the activity outdoors, you might also like to give Teddy a cup of water!

16-26 months

Observation   ## Planning

Observation	Planning
Is this an enjoyable activity for the toddler?	Repeat this activity again, but put out some different props such as a bowl and spoon for Teddy.
Does the toddler start to 'feed' Teddy? Does the toddler talk to Teddy?	Film or audio record the toddler playing with Teddy. Join in the child's play. Add in other props such as a pushchair.

Farm animals in the field   22–36 months

Children of this age are likely to be interested in small-world play. To make this play more interesting for them, you might like to think about different sensory materials that could be used alongside the toys, for example shredded paper and dinosaurs or sand trays and cars.

One fun idea is to put a square of turf into a plastic tray and then use it for farm animals. You can buy or beg turf from garden centres – quite often they have off-cuts. You will need to water and trim the grass from time to time; the children can have fun helping you do this.

22-36 months

Observation   ## Planning

Observation	Planning
Do children concentrate and play for longer periods?	In what other ways could you provide sensory materials alongside small-world play?
What other small-world toys do children use in the tray?	Look at ways for children to combine small-world play with other areas within the setting, for example digging a race track outdoors for the cars.

Developing Imagination

What do I need to do?

- Make sure that you provide interesting props for role-play areas.

- Create outdoor role-play areas for children.

- Allow sufficient time for child-initiated play.

- Consider taking roles in children's role play.

- Enrich children's role play by telling stories.

- Provide opportunities for small-world play.

- Combine small-world play with sensory materials.

Frequently Asked Questions

Some of the older children seem to take very gender-specific roles. Should we do something about this?

Imaginative play is about exploring differing roles including gender roles, so it is natural that children will want to try out a range of roles as part of their play. If you are concerned that children seem 'fixed' on certain roles, consider taking part in the role play or varying the role-play area to change the type of play.

The children often bury small-world toys outdoors. How do we prevent this?

Children are great mixers of materials so often look for ways of enhancing their play by, for example, moving things from one area to another. It is important that you provide for this. Try putting out small-world play alongside sensory materials or having a box of small-world toys specifically for use outdoors.

Outdoor prop boxes

Role play needs to be on offer outdoors as well as indoors. Creating prop boxes that help to enrich role play is a good starting point when developing imaginative play.

Find some storage containers that can be left outdoors if necessary. Choose props that are taken from real life rather than toys, for example a metal saucepan, shopping bags and belts. In order to choose items, you might like to consider what type of play children are already engaged in. For example, if children pretend to cook, put in a saucepan, while if children are pretending to build, put in a hard hat.

Observation

Which objects are of interest to children?

→

Planning

Do you need to put out more of the same resources?

Can children help to create prop boxes by choosing items that they would like to take outdoors?

Story-based role play

Role play based on stories that you have read to children is popular and a good starting point for imaginative play.

Choose a story that children have enjoyed hearing and follow it up by creating a role-play area. Try hard to involve the children in creating the role-play area by, for example, asking them to consider what items and props are needed – the story *Goldilocks and the Three Bears* might include three bowls, three beds, etc. This could be the start of an excellent activity for children as they help to find the items to go inside and design the area.

Observation

How are children involved in creating the role-play area?

→

Planning

How can you help children become independent in creating their areas?

What other stories might they like to extend into the role-play area?

Are there any children who are not involved in role play?

→

What are these children interested in?

Do you need to help children with their role play by playing alongside them?

Do these children have sufficient language to support role play?

Implementing the Early Years Foundation Stage

How you implement the EYFS education programme will very much depend on the age of children that you are working with as well as the context in which you work. I would argue that there are many paths through the EYFS, which is just as well because while we are all working in the best interests of children, each provider and each type of setting needs to have its own flavour.

Whatever way you choose to go about implementing the EYFS, you should always check that your systems are:

- meeting the individual needs of children and that you can demonstrate this in your planning
- delivering the education programme
- making use of the outdoors as well indoors
- using play as the main tool for children's learning (story time is clearly not play)
- making sure that there is a balance of child-initiated activities and adult-directed activities
- ensuring that adult to child ratios are met in accordance with Appendix 2 of the Statutory Framework (this means that adults should be working directly with children although there are exceptions here for Reception teachers)
- ensuring that children develop a strong relationship with their key person.

Play is pivotal

One of the most important features of the EYFS is its emphasis on play to support children's learning and development.

What is play?

There are many shades of play, going from 'pure play' – the child-initiated variety when children do and use what they want with often little adult input, through to 'playful activities' where adults are heavily involved and

may have planned learning intentions, such as playing picture lotto or setting up an obstacle course. It is important when looking at the balance of activities and the routine in your setting to understand that whole group times such as snack times, lining up and circle times cannot really be put under the heading of 'play'.

'Pure play'

Most adults can recognise the 'pure' end of the spectrum of play. It is where children are busily engaged in 'playland', the place where nothing is impossible and where fantasy and reality can come together. It can sometimes be a messy business as well, and children engaged in pure play may need to mix play materials up in order to fertilise their play a little. This is the type of play when dough is squashed through fences or Lego is served as a main dish! We know that children involved in 'pure play' are more likely to concentrate well, develop problem-solving skills and, once they reach about three years or so, practise their social skills with their peers. In today's environment, this is often the type of play that has become endangered and yet it is vital for children's overall well-being and development. It is therefore essential that this end of the spectrum of play is properly catered for and is the essence of child-initiated activities.

'Playful activities'

This is the type of play when adults might wrap learning intentions into a game, for example sound lotto or hunt the teddy, or even joining in the role play. While this is clearly not the same as 'pure play', it is also of value provided that the adult is effective at creating a playful environment and the activity is right for the age and stage of the children. Some playful activities can be so enjoyable for children that they will go on to incorporate them into their own play. This is a good measure of success.

The 'playful activities' end of the spectrum also provides opportunities for children to develop language skills and to have their thinking skills extended. Babies and toddlers will particularly need plenty of playful activities where adults are involved with them, as they are still learning the skills of both language and play. While older children usually prefer 'pure play', some of the curriculum will need to be delivered through playful activities, such as learning about number and recognising letters.

What type of play is needed?

The focus throughout the EYFS is about recognising children's interests and needs. When it comes to play, it is also worth looking at the overall picture within a child's life. While most children, I would argue, require play activities from both ends of the spectrum, there are some children for whom we need to change the balance. If children outside your setting spend a lot of time carrying out structured activities such as practising writing, going to museums and taking music classes, they may require plenty of time engaged in play that is towards the 'pure play' end of the spectrum. On the other hand, if some children have few opportunities to engage with adults and plenty of time to engage in 'pure play', perhaps the balance needs to be reversed and these children will gain from doing more 'playful activities' such as cooking, playing with musical instruments or guiding a remote-controlled car along a track.

Recognising how play needs change

The play needs of children change as they develop and in relation to their individual circumstances. When working out how best to provide for play, it is therefore important to think about the needs of the children that you are working with.

Babies

Babies need plenty of adult interaction in their first year. This means that, with the exception of treasure basket play and odd times when babies are left to explore toys such as baby gyms and rattles, they will need plenty of play with adults. This often takes the form of repetitive simple games such as peek-a-boo, knocking down stacking beakers and Humpty Dumpty. The role of the adult is to be a partner in babies' play and the best person to be the play partner is someone who has a close relationship with the baby.

Toddlers

Toddlers are often at a half-way house in terms of play. They are starting to play independently but still need the reassurance of an adult to hand. Toddlers also like having their own play partner who, for example, can pretend to eat their delicious cakes or help them create a farm for the animals. As with babies, toddlers tend often to enjoy repeating the same movements, actions and types of play, so it will be common to see a toddler filling a bag with wooden bricks then emptying it out only to fill it again! Interestingly, while frequently interested in other children, toddlers are not team players and often resist attempts by adults to herd them into group activities. This is one reason why the adult to child ratio for the under-threes is set at 1:4.

Onwards from three years

From this point, we start to see that children have definite play preferences and are usually beginning to find play partners in other children rather than in adults. Learning to play with others and to negotiate, solve squabbles and recognise different points of view seems to be vital. Children can only do this well if they are emotionally secure. Recognising which children need more emotional security is therefore essential. For these children, you may need to be more involved with them so they can make the transition to playing with other children.

From around four years onwards, language skills appear to make the difference to how easily children manage to play with others. Children who cannot express themselves may find themselves relegated to perfunctory roles within games or on the sidelines. For these children, it is important that you plan playful activities to develop their language further and find ways of coming alongside them as they are playing.

A key feature in the way that children play as they develop is their need for increasing freedom to try out more complicated and 'deep' play. This usually requires more time to get going. For a group of four-year-olds who are keen to construct a castle and then live in it, fifteen minutes will not be sufficient; an hour and a half is probably the minimum. This means that you need to think about ways to avoid constantly interrupting children's initiated activities. Some clever practitioners do this by sneaking in a learning intention or two, for example asking the children if the royal court would like snacks and if so, could they write down their requests for the Lord Chamberlain!

Where do I start?

Unless you are a brand new provider, you should look at what you are currently doing and think about how it is working before making sweeping changes. You need to be objective when doing this. You will probably have to look at the following areas to check that they are effective in ensuring that children's individual needs and interests are met.

- Routines
- Observations
- Planning

Routines

Routines are often a good starting point because they act as skeletons onto which we build. They can influence the way in which staff are used, the way that a session or day is broken up and the opportunities for children to be outdoors. It is worth noting that a routine that was devised fifteen years ago may have worked well then, but may hamper you in delivering the EYFS now.

Routines for babies and toddlers

Establishing the routine for babies and toddlers is essential. You might find that the routine that you have in place revolves significantly around meeting children's physical and care needs. This is to be expected as a toddler cannot cope with being hungry and tired. It is important, however, to make sure that within your routine, this daily care is seen as a possible source of stimulation.

What does a good routine look like for babies and toddlers?

The ideal routine for babies and toddlers is one in which they have plenty of adult interaction and spend most of their time with their key person. This is 'hands on' stuff and is different from the provision that is needed for older children. This is because emotional security and the development of language go hand in hand.

An ideal routine would also mean that babies and toddlers spend time outdoors so they can experience a change of scenery and all that the outdoors offers. Babies and toddlers also need to be stimulated by going into other rooms and spaces; for example, if you are a childminder, you might take the baby or toddler into a parent and toddler group or to the shops. If you work in a day care setting, you might take your children to visit the older children or, again, out for a walk.

In addition, babies and toddlers need to make relationships with their siblings if they are in the setting. This might mean sharing meal times as well as time for play.

The focus on the EYFS is on meeting individual needs, so in an ideal routine, feeding, nappy changing and sleep will not be done in large groups.

Points to consider

Auditing your routine for babies and toddlers

Note that if you are a childminder, you are automatically the child's key person and so ignore the last two questions.

* How much time is spent out of doors?

* How much individual interaction do babies and toddlers have over the course of a session? (Include feeding, nappy changing and other care activities.)

* How many changes of environment do babies and toddlers experience during the session?

* How are physical care activities used to stimulate children's development?

* Are there opportunities for treasure basket and heuristic play?

* Are there opportunities for children to share books and rhymes with adults, preferably their key person?

* How much time is spent with siblings if they are also in the setting?

* At what times of the session are children the most settled? Why?

* Are there times when children and staff are frazzled? Why?

* Are adult to child ratios maintained at all times?

* How much of children's time is spent with their key person?

What does a good routine look like for children from two years onwards?

What constitutes a good routine for this age group will partly depend on the philosophy and context of your setting. I was recently asked to describe the EYFS approach and came up with the analogy of rearing chickens. In all settings, children should be out and about 'free ranging' and will do this for most of the day – that is, choosing what they would like to do from a range of play opportunities and also creating their own. The role of the adult is then twofold: to extend the learning during the 'free ranging' by working alongside individual or small groups of children, and to supplement the 'diet' with adult-directed activities such as cooking, storytelling, board games or, in a Reception class, unveiling the phonic programme. For this model to work, it is important that the routine allows sufficient time for children to embed themselves into the play opportunities, so timetabling needs to be kept to the minimum otherwise it will feel very fragmented.

The key difference that is generally observed between settings is the way in which the adults go about planning their interventions and activities. This will depend on the approach of the setting as well as the age group of the children. Two-year-olds, for example, will need more opportunities for adults to work alongside them as they play because they are less likely to be involved in cooperative play with other children. They will also find it hard to cope in large adult-directed groups such as a whole group story time.

What we should not see in the EYFS are 'battery hens' who are kept indoors, told what to do and get little chance to learn through genuine play and following their own interests.

Points to consider

Auditing your routine for children from two years onwards

Note that if you are a childminder, you are automatically the child's key person and so ignore the last two questions.

* How much time will children have for 'free ranging' child-initiated play? (Think about adding up the number of minutes or hours.)

* How much of children's time is spent in adult-directed activities, for example specific activities, snack time, tidy-up time and preparing to go outdoors?

* How much time do children spend outdoors on average if free-flow play is not available?

* At what times of the session are children the most settled? Why?

* Are there times when children and staff are frazzled? Why?

* Are adult to child ratios maintained at all times?

* How much of children's time is spent with their key person?

Observing children

Observing children regularly is vital in the Early Years Foundation Stage. The observations should then be linked to your planning, so you will need to look at observation and planning systems together. This makes sense, as before in some settings, good observations were kept but they did not relate to the activities and experiences which were offered to children.

Including parents in the observation process

As part of the Theme of Positive Relationships, you should be sharing information with parents. This includes building up a record of their child's progress. The advantage of getting used to digital methods is that you can share special or significant moments with parents more easily. For some parents who do not often come to the setting, you could consider e-mailing them photos or clips.

As well as sharing information with parents, you also need to find ways of helping them add to the observations. There are many ways of doing this. Some parents may, for example, take photographs of their children engaged in activities at home, or you may ask parents to come and tell you about what their child has been doing. I know that some settings ask parents to look out for certain things related to the Development Matters statements or the early learning goals when their children are at home. This approach has many advantages as it can help some parents feel more involved in their child's education. Some settings also invite parents in to carry out observations of their children in the setting. This requires organisation as parents may need some help in knowing what to look out for. It also requires sensitivity as not all parents find writing easy, so a good starting point can be just to ask parents to use a digital camera or to feedback about their children verbally.

Observation methods

There is a whole range of recording methods that you can use to observe children; some are more practicable than others. Overall, it is worth thinking about using a range and erring towards those that are user-friendly and will help not just you but parents and others later on in transition learn about the child. Below are some of the key ways in which you might choose to observe children; note that this is not a definitive list!

Tick charts and checklists

Many settings use tick charts and checklists, although it is not a good idea to rely totally on these because after reading two or three children's records, it is hard to remember what the child can do. Think about using them as a basis for further observations and to act as an overall audit of how a child is working towards the Development Matters statements and the early learning goals. Tick charts work better if comments are also used to bring them to life or when you link them to other observations that you have done.

Learning stories or journeys

This is a lovely way of both observing children and providing a structure for planning for individual children. This method works well with all age ranges and is popular with parents. The idea is that you carry out a short written observation, take a photograph if possible and then draw some conclusions about what you have seen. You also include some suggestions of what the child's next steps might be and ways in which they might be supported. Note that it is important if you do this to ensure that any activities suggested are then carried out. Some settings rely on this method heavily.

(Many examples of Learning journeys are found on the EYFS CD-ROM. To access these, from the Home page click on 'Enabling Environments', then click again on '3.1 Observation, Assessment and Planning'. When the new page comes up, in the far right-hand column scroll down until you come to 'Resources'. Under this heading you will find Learning journeys for each area

of Learning and Development as well as a Learning journey template.)

In the example learning story below, observations are carried out fortnightly by the children's key person to check that different areas of development are being looked at. Every six weeks, a summative record is produced to check children's progress in each of the six areas of learning based on these observation sheets. At planning meetings, key persons talk about what activities, needs or interests their key children have. These are incorporated into the weekly plans.

Name: Ayse	Date: 12/8/08
Observation	Ayse found her shoes when I said that it was time to go outdoors. She took a moment, but worked out which shoe went on which foot. She managed to fasten the buckles without any support. She was very pleased with herself.
What does it mean?	Ayse can now put on most of her clothes and shoes herself.
What next?	Provide time so that she can get dressed herself. Show her how to use a zip and find dressing up clothes with zips. Look out for role-play clothes that will help her to practise buttons, zips and buckles.
Links to the EYFS	PSE Self-Care (30–50 months). PD Using equipment and materials (30–50 months).
Notes for next observation	CLL Look out for mark-making and also record speech.

Ayse's learning story

Post-it notes

Some settings find it useful to write down notes as and when they see children engaged in play. The notes are named, dated and linked to the EYFS areas of Learning and Development. Some large group settings also create a large grid on a notice board so that as a post-it note is written, it can be popped up alongside the child's name. This is useful because it helps staff to see which children need to be observed. Post-it notes as a method of recording only work if you take the time to collate them.

Digital methods

It is helpful to use some of the digital technology available to make the observation and assessment system easier and also more interesting for parents. I personally think that it is worth setting up a digital folder for children's observations, which can be used alongside some of the 'paper-based' systems. As with paper-based systems, it is essential to think about security; for example, have a memory stick for each child or a password for each digital folder.

You could consider using some of the following digital methods, or better still all of them.

Method	Uses
Digital camera	Ideal for taking photographs of children in 'action' as well as photos of products that children have made. Think about whether children can take some of the photographs, as this links to the ICT aspect of Learning and Development within Knowledge and Understanding of the World.
Film clips	Many digital cameras allow the user to take short videos, or you might invest in a camcorder. Filming children is useful if you find it hard to write down what children are doing or if you want to 'show' parents what their child has been doing. Film clips are especially popular with parents who leave their babies and toddlers in your care.
Sound recordings	You can use MP3 recorders, dictaphones or even mobile phones to get a sound recording. These are very useful to assess children's speech and to monitor progress.
Handheld devices	It is possible to purchase a handheld device which will allow you to take photos and film clips, make sound recordings and also write notes. Some software assessment programmes are also compatible with handheld devices, enabling you to link any recordings straight into the child's records.

Incorporating observations with activity planning

Some settings allow space on their activity plans to make notes about individual children or produce a grid system whereby the names of children who take part in activities are recorded alongside some notes about how they responded and any skills that have been observed. In addition, some settings when planning activities decide ahead of time what they might try to observe during the activity. Working in this way can be helpful when tracking children's progress towards the early learning goals.

Group observations (useful for the over-threes)

One of the anxieties that some practitioners and their managers have is that when children are 'free ranging' they may not be learning or focusing enough on their play. Being able to know what individual children are interested in, how well your provision is working and the levels of engagement that children are showing are therefore useful.

Over a number of years, I have found it helpful to use a group time sample as a way of collecting such information. It works best with children over three years old who are in a group care and education setting and who are busy 'free ranging' while adults are either involved with them or carrying out adult-focused activities. I find that not only can I collect information about individual children in this way, but I can also collect information about how the provision is working.

Steps to producing a group observation

1 Create a simple grid with around nine columns.
2 Use the first column for timings – every five minutes works well.
3 Use the other right-hand columns to record children's activity.
4 At the start of each five-minute slot, look to see where the children are.
5 Use the rest of the minutes to note down any activities that seem interesting and whether children are leaving activities. (It is always interesting to work out why.)

Things to look out for

I tend only to write down anything that I think is of particular note and that I might forget otherwise. I try to use codes rather than words as this is quicker, and have developed my own style. When using a code-based method, I think that developing your own style is essential as otherwise you might spend more time looking at what code you should be using rather than focusing on the action. This is quite an open method of recording so you can decide ahead what you want to look out for, or you can see what comes along at the

Group Observation Sheet

	Amir	Gracie	Elliot	Ollie	Freya	Gaetha	May	Meltem
9.30	Sand C burying cars ↓ ⑤	Painting table ↓	Sand © with cars ↓	Home corner © ↓	~~~ Bricks ②	Dough ↓	Tricycles – outdoors ↓	Digging outdoors ↓
9.35	⑤ ↓	Talking to self ④ ↓	finds lorries ↓	with Jack Dressing up ↓	~~~ Puzzles ②	Sausages © ↓	Siraz © ↓	↓
9.40	cars + spoons Ⓐ ↓	R Handed ⑤ ↓	↓	Fascinated ~ belts ⑤ ↓	~~~ Sand C	Talking++ ↓	Ⓐ ↓	④ ↓
9.45	Argument resolved Ⓐ ↓	⑤ ↓	Argument with Amir Ⓐ ~~~ off to loo	(still with Jack) ↓	Sand ② watching Amir	Making dough food →	Ⓐ → Digging Smiles at May	→
9.50	neglected Ⓐ →wash hands	→wash hands	Jack dominant? Ⓐ	Jack dominant? ↓	story ④ Ⓐ	5 © sharing	5 ©	Playing together 5 5
9.55	Burying hands © 5	~~~ →outdoors	Home corner Ⓐ being changed	Home corner Ⓐ being changed ↓	~~~ outdoors →tricycle	long sausages ↓	↓	~~~ fascinated bucket + spade

Date 20/5/08

Observed by Annie B.

Page 1

Code

Concentration 1=low, 5=High

A = adult present   Ⓐ = adult engaged with child

C = Child/children present   © = Engagement with target child

~~~ = child wandering unfocused

→ = child moves purposefully to new activity

The downward arrows show that many children are staying at activities, although see if you can see a 'wanderer'.

time! For me, there are always a few core things that are worth noting.

Interaction

I am always interested to see whether children are interacting with each other or whether they are playing alongside other children. I use the code 'C' to indicate that there are children alongside the child, and the code Ⓒ to indicate that the child is actively engaging.

Relationship with adults

I also look to see whether any children seem to need to be with adults, either in terms of interacting with them or just need the proximity. (Interestingly, I have often seen that it is the younger children or ones who have just come into the group that seem to need the proximity or attention of adults.) My code for this is 'A' if there is an adult in proximity and Ⓐ if the adult is engaging with the child.

Level of engagement with the activity

I also try to note down the level of engagement that children have with an activity on a sliding scale of 1–5, with 5 indicating that children are so engaged that they are not reacting to other distractions in the environment and are coping with any setbacks in their play.

Summative assessments

Whatever decisions you make about the best way to observe children, you must make sure that you pull together some conclusions about the child. This is known as a 'summative' assessment. There are many ways of doing this, although probably the most common is to look at the child in terms of the areas of Learning and Development. A good summative assessment sheet should also have a 'next steps' box and a 'support' box. These boxes can, if wanted, be transformed into some type of medium-term planning for the child (see below).

You should be carrying out some type of summative assessment every few months, as otherwise you might find that you are not getting an overall picture of the child's needs, interests and level of development. Interestingly, the 'learning story' style of observation does this to some degree, although if you decide to use this as a main method, you should ensure that you are observing all areas of Learning and Development.

It is a good idea to talk to parents before compiling summative assessments, unless parents have been contributors throughout, in which case they should already have a sense of the child's progress.

The Early Years Foundation Stage Profile

The EYFS Profile is effectively a summative assessment for the end of the Reception year. It is not necessary to complete one unless you are in Reception, although you may find that your Early Years and Children's service might produce something for you to use instead. It will therefore be worth accessing any training that is being provided.

Planning

This is one of the biggest anxieties for many practitioners. The official line in the EYFS is that there is no 'correct' way to plan, although some planning is required as part of providing an effective system. It might be an idea first of all to look at what you are currently using and check whether it is showing the following.

Points to consider

Planning checklist

* Are children's individual needs and interests being reflected?

* Can you show how the observations that you have carried out link to the planning?

* Are you showing 'coverage' of the areas of Learning and Development?

* Are you showing how your provision and activities will support progress towards the early learning goals?

* Do your plans reflect the use of the outdoor area including visits?

If you think that overall your planning does show the above, you may not need to do very much apart from trying to do some tweaking. This may mean, for example, putting children's initials into your provision plan if activities have been organised particularly to meet their needs, or adding a comment column to your weekly planner so that any notes of what you have seen the children do can be jotted down. In addition, it is always worth looking around at what other settings in similar circumstances are doing and 'borrowing' and then adjusting their formats.

There is a real need here to emphasise the importance of adjusting planning to meet your needs. Some settings have huge numbers of children and complicated rota systems that require additional planning to help everyone know what they are doing! In other settings, such as childminders and those working with babies, more minimalist planning will suffice, but you may put more focus onto using observations. In the Appendix of this book, I have included some different styles of planning that are currently being used by a range of settings (see pages 265–72).

(The EYFS CD-ROM also has some examples of planning. To access these, from the Home page click on 'Enabling Environments', then click again on '3.1 Observation, Assessment and Planning'. When the new page comes up, in the far right-hand column scroll down until you come to 'Resources'. Under this heading you will find sample planning for different age groups.)

Making planning easier

Planning is easier if you can work on the computer, so learning how to use a computer might have to be your starting point. As with many things, it may seem slower at first, but then once you have cracked it you will soon speed up. If you are not currently confident with a computer, below are my tips.

Essential computer skills

Learn how to:

- 'cut and paste' – this saves typing things out more than once

- 'save as' – this means that you can have several versions of the same plan

- use the 'undo' button – this is fantastic if you press a key by mistake or change your mind

- draw a table – this means that you can create your own charts and tables

- touch type – touch typing changed my life! It was actually easier to learn than I would

have imagined and more fun. I set myself the target of using a typing programme for ten minutes each day. I found it such fun, I tended to stay on for longer and within ten days, my typing was fairly good.

Long-term planning

Long-term plans tend to be used more in group settings where there is a need to plan a long time ahead. If you work in a smaller setting, such as a childminder or with babies and toddlers, you may not feel that you need one.

What do I put in a long-term plan?

Some settings choose some early learning goals, Development Matters statements or the four Themes of the EYFS and use this as the basis of their long-term planning. Others begin with events in the calendar year or even topics that they feel are important. Note that if you use topics, you will need to choose ones that are clearly child-centred and are sufficiently adaptable to allow you to be flexible. Long-term plans can only create the overall brush strokes and you will find it hard to plan for individual children's needs and interests as these may change daily or weekly.

How long is a long-term plan?

The length of long-term planning is variable. With babies and toddlers, I would argue that it is not possible to plan more than a month ahead as their development changes and unfolds in sometimes unpredictable ways. The focus on babies and toddlers should be on planning for their needs and interests on a daily and weekly basis.

On the other hand, if you are working with children in Reception, it is likely that you will need to do a long-term plan which covers the academic year. Long-term plans are rarely detailed and usually no more than a 'statement' of intent!

Medium-term plans

Medium-term plans can be divided into two types – planning for individual children and planning for groups. In many settings it will be important to do both types of planning and I would suggest that producing a medium-term plan for individual children is particularly effective.

Planning for individual children

If you do not currently plan for individual children, you may find that you now need to concentrate on this. Planning for individual children does not need to be wordy or complicated. It is simply a way of collating information that has been collected about the child as a result of talks with parents and observations, and then working out what might be the child's next steps over the coming weeks. Some settings do this by using a play plan, while others use a grid system which shows what the next steps are for children in each of the different areas of Learning and Development. Planning for individual children in this way may be linked closely to the Development Matters statements rather than showing actual activities, for example 'Distinguish between the different marks that they make.'

Planning for groups

Medium-term plans tend to outline the type of adult-focused activities or play themes that are to be looked at in the coming weeks. They are also likely to be tied into the areas of Learning and Development of the EYFS and are one way in which settings can be sure that they are covering these. It is worth completing the plans for individual children first, as this might influence the type of activities or themes that you decide on.

How long is a medium-term plan?

A medium-term plan is likely to last a half term where settings are working using the academic year cycle; otherwise these plans generally last a month. Again, it is hard to be precise and if you are redesigning your planning system, I would always urge you to think about what you actually will find useful and need. It is practical if individual children's planning and the group planning are of similar lengths, although some settings prefer to do a rolling programme of individual plans for children, to spread the workload.

Short-term plans

It is likely that most of your time and efforts need to be spent on short-term planning, and this is essential whether you are a childminder or a Reception teacher. Short-term planning is a key way in which you will be able to build on children's interests and address their needs.

Weekly plans

Many settings find it useful to look at what the adult-focused activities might be over a week. This planning is used by most settings including childminders. In a weekly plan you might include activities such as cooking, outings, games, rhymes and stories. Some settings find it helpful to organise their weekly plans according to the areas of Learning and Development within the EYFS, although this has one drawback in that most activities will be covering more than one area of Learning and Development at the same time.

Daily planners

Some settings use daily planners to show what will be available and at what times. Some daily planners only show the adult-focused activities and are used in conjunction with a provision planner (see below). Other settings use a daily planner to cover both provision and focused activities. A daily planner is essential when working with babies and toddlers and should be considered by childminders.

Activity plans

Activity plans break the adult-focused activities down into more detail. They are useful in group settings where you may need to provide extra detail for staff, parents and volunteers. Activity plans can be broken down to show the specific learning intentions as well as particular children's needs. Some settings also use activity plans to focus on areas for observation.

Activity plans are useful to store on computer so that you can save time in the future when you wish to re-visit an activity but need to adapt it to suit the changing needs of children. Activity plans are also great if you are working with babies and toddlers, as often some of the everyday routines are in themselves 'activities'.

Provision planning

Provision planning is about the type of materials and equipment that will be on offer to the children. This often forms the backdrop for children's child-initiated play or 'free ranging', as I have come to call it. While some settings plan their provision a week ahead, others decide to look at their provision at the end of each session and add things or remove items on the basis of children's play and interests that day. Your provision plan should show what will be available for children both indoors and outdoors.

It is important that provision planning is not so rigid as to prevent a child who, for example, wanted to go and find the dinosaurs from playing with them because only the farm animals had been put out. Some settings also indicate in their provision planning which areas or materials have been put out in order to build on certain children's interests or needs. If you are a childminder, you might not feel that you need a provision plan, although it might be helpful to do it on a small scale to ensure that children experience a wide range of play opportunities.

Sample plans are found in the Appendix on pages 265–72.

Evaluating sessions

It is a good idea to have some mechanism for evaluating what the children have been doing in order to alter plans and find ways of building on what has been successful. Sometimes adult-focused activities need to be left out so that children can build them into their own play, or a particular material may have been an unexpected success with children. I always think it's sad when I hear comments such as 'The children loved the activity – I'll definitely do that again next year.' Next year? – why wait when you have a bestselling activity! Some models of planning and observation incorporate the evaluation of the session and children's particular focuses into the following week's or even day's provision. This system can be seen in the sample planning documents on the EYFS CD-ROM.

Points to consider

Tips for planning

* Remember that a plan is just that – a plan, not a promise!

* Be ready to make promises, drop things that are not working and follow children's interests.

* Look at the way that others in similar settings are planning to gain inspiration.

* Make sure that your planning system does not get out of hand – layers upon layers of planning can drain the life out of you. If you are working in a management position, remember this because tedious planning can result in lazy practice with some practitioners cutting down what they are providing for children so as not to have to think about learning intentions and resources, etc.

Your Questions Answered

We work in a Reception class in a primary school. Our head teacher insists that all the Reception children should attend the school assembly.

The Welfare Requirements apply to the Reception class as well as to nurseries and other provisions. It is important that your head teacher understands that the EYFS directs you to make sure that children are in an 'enjoyable and challenging learning environment that is tailored to meet individual children's needs'. This may mean that assembly is not the right place for all of the children in your class. Some Reception classes attend only some assemblies that are deemed suitable, while in other schools only the children that will benefit attend assemblies, for example children who may enjoy sitting with their siblings. If your head insists that the Reception class must attend assembly, it is important that you balance this 'adult' time with sufficient child-initiated time.

I work as a childminder. I find it difficult to observe children when I am involved with them.

This can be a problem, but I would suggest that you use digital cameras with a film function so that you can 'catch' the odd moments. The advantage of doing this is that you can show parents what children have been doing. You can also make mental notes about what a child has done and when convenient jot them down. A little bit of planning is also useful. Think about which areas of Learning and Development you want to focus on and then consider when you are most likely to be able to 'catch' them.

I am a childminder. How much planning should I produce?

While in theory you could manage without any planning, most childminders I know like to have something down on paper, both to show parents and also Ofsted. I would begin by looking at the overall pattern of the week and linking certain regular events, such as walking to school or snack time, to areas within the EYFS.

For the under-threes (assuming that you are their sole carer in addition to their parents), I would probably suggest that you produce a medium-term individual plan that is based on observations of each child's current stage of development. It should show the type of experiences and activities that will promote their development further.

For children over three years old, you will need to liaise with any other providers of the EYFS in order to get the balance right. For example, if a four-year-old has spent the day in a Reception class, they may be tired and therefore will probably need child-initiated play. For these children, making a list of play opportunities and equipment that is available to them, as well as taking notes of what they have used, will probably be sufficient.

We work in a nursery where there are quite a few children who are learning English as an additional language. When children are taking part in child-initiated play, most of them either do not talk much or talk together in their home language.

Children who come into the Reception class without fluent English will find it harder to break into reading. Equally, we know that children need to maintain and develop their home language in order to gain English more easily. The EYFS is clear that children should be able to play in their home language, so there is no question of trying to stop this from occurring.

Helping children learn English 'from scratch' begins with ensuring that each child has a strong relationship with their key person. While this is a requirement in any case, it is of particular importance when supporting children who need to learn English.

You will need first to look at the routine of your sessions, to check that you are providing sufficient opportunities for individual and very small groups of children to work with adults. This might be through adult-focused and adult-led activities, such as cooking, role play or structured games. The adult-focused activities need to be exciting and interesting, but also carefully planned to maximise the time available for interaction in English. You may also find it useful when planning these focused activities to group children according to their language needs. In addition to adult-focused activities, you will need to play alongside children in English. I would avoid whole group sessions as a way of building English, with the exception of songs and rhymes, as these are unlikely to meet the language needs of some children, who may not be able to follow what is being said.

I work with babies. I am looking at the areas of Learning and Development and cannot see the relevance to our work.

If you work with babies and toddlers, you might be a little nervous about the EYFS, especially if you are not familiar with the areas of Learning and Development. The good news here is that providing you have been following the good practice of the Birth To Three Matters framework, you should have no problem in adapting. One of the main things to do is to think about how some of the everyday events that are part and parcel of working with this age group link to the areas of Learning and Development, and be holistic in this approach.

Overleaf is a chart that I have drawn up which shows just how many Development Matters statements are being worked with during a 'good' nappy change with a baby and the key person. This is followed by another chart that shows how heuristic play, which should be a regular activity for toddlers, will also work within the EYFS.

Development Matters statements that apply during nappy changing with a key person (0–11 months)

Personal, Social and Emotional Development	Communication, Language and Literacy	Problem Solving, Reasoning and Numeracy	Knowledge and Understanding of the World	Physical Development	Creative Development
Dispositions and Attitudes Develop an understanding and awareness of themselves.	*Language for Communication* Make sounds with their voices in social interaction.	*Numbers as Labels and for Counting* Respond to people and objects in their environment. Notice changes in groupings of objects, images or sounds.	*Exploration and Investigation* Use movement and senses to focus on, reach for and handle objects. Learn by observation about actions and their effects.	*Movement and Space* Make movements with arms and legs which gradually become more controlled.	*Being Creative – Responding to Experiences, Expressing and Communicating Ideas* Use movement and sensory exploration to connect with their immediate environment.
Self-confidence and Self-esteem Seek to be looked at and approved of. Find comfort in touch and in the human face.	*Language for Thinking* Are intrigued by novelty and events and actions around them.	*Calculating* Are logical thinkers from birth.	*Designing and Making* Explore objects and materials with hands and mouth.	*Health and Bodily Awareness* Respond to and thrive on warm, sensitive physical contact and care.	*Creating Music and Dance* Respond to a range of familiar sounds, for example, turning to a sound source such as a voice.
Making Relationships Depend on close attachments with a special person within their setting. Learn by interacting with others.	*Linking Sounds and Letters* Listen to, distinguish and respond to intonations and the sounds of voices.	*Shape, Space and Measures* Develop an awareness of shape, form and texture as they encounter people and things in their environment.	*Time* Anticipate repeated sounds, sights and actions.	*Using Equipment and Materials* Watch and explore hands and feet. Reach out for, touch and begin to hold objects.	*Developing Imagination and Imaginative Play* Smile with pleasure at recognisable playthings.
Behaviour and Self-control Begin to adapt to caregiving routines.	*Reading* Listen to familiar sounds, words, or finger plays.		*Place* Explore the space around them through movements of hands and feet and by rolling.		
Self-care Express discomfort, hunger or thirst.	*Writing* Move arms and legs and increasingly use them to reach for, grasp and manipulate things.		*Communities* Concentrate intently on faces and enjoy interaction. Form attachments to special people.	This nappy change assumes that the baby's key person regularly does the nappy changing. It also assumes that the nappy change is not rushed, that the key person talks and engages with the baby, and that toys and objects are given or shown to the baby.	
Sense of Community Respond to differences in their environment, for example, showing excitement or interest. Learn that special people are a source of sustenance, comfort and support.	*Handwriting* Play with own fingers and toes and focus on objects around them.				

Development Matters statements that apply to heuristic play with a group of children aged 16–26 months

Personal, Social and Emotional Development	Communication, Language and Literacy	Problem Solving, Reasoning and Numeracy	Knowledge and Understanding of the World	Physical Development	Creative Development
Dispositions and Attitudes Develop a curiosity about things and processes. Take pleasure in learning new skills.	*Language for Communication* Use single-words and two-word utterances to convey simple and complex messages.	*Numbers as Labels and for Counting* Distinguish between quantities, recognising that a group of objects is more than one.	*Exploration and Investigation* Sometimes focus their enquiries on particular features or processes.	*Movement and Space* Have a biological drive to use their bodies and develop their physical skills.	*Being Creative Responding to Experiences, Expressing and Communicating Ideas* Express themselves through physical action and sound. Explore by repeating patterns of play.
Self-confidence and Self-esteem Make choices that involve challenge, when adults ensure their safety. Develop confidence in own abilities.		*Calculating* Categorise objects according to their properties.	*Designing and Making* Are interested in pushing and pulling things, and begin to build structures.	*Health and Bodily Awareness* Practise and develop what they can do.	*Developing Imagination and Imaginative Play* Pretend that one object represents another, especially when objects have characteristics in common.
Behaviour and Self-control Begin to learn that some things are theirs, some things are shared, and some things belong to other people.		*Shape, Space and Measures* Enjoy filling and emptying containers.	*Place* Are curious about the environment.	*Using Equipment and Materials* Begin to make, and manipulate, objects and tools. Put together a sequence of actions.	
			Communities Like to play alongside other children.		

References and Further Reading

- Bruce, T. (2004) *Cultivating Creativity in Babies, Toddlers and Young Children,* Hodder Arnold

- Duffy, A., Chambers, F., Croughan, S and Stephens, J. (2006) *Working with Babies and Children under Three,* Heinemann

- Featherstone, S. (2001) *The Little Book of Outdoor Play,* Featherstone Education Ltd

- Featherstone, S. (2002) *The Little Book of Sand and Water,* Featherstone Education Ltd

- Featherstone, S. (2002) *The Little Book of Maths Activities,* Featherstone Education Ltd

- Lindon, J. (2005) *Understanding Child Development: Linking Theory and Practice,* Hodder Arnold

- Meggitt, C. and Sutherland, G. (Second edition, 2006) *Child Development: An Illustrated Guide,* Heinemann

- Moyles, J. (1989) Just Playing? *The Role and Status of Play in Early Childhood Education,* Open University Press

- Riddall-Leech, S (2005) *How to Observe Children,* Heinemann

- Tassoni, P. and Hucker, K. (Second edition, 2005) *Planning Play and the Early Years,* Heinemann

- Thornton, S. (2008) *Understanding Human Development – Biological, Social and Psychological Processes from Conception to Adulthood,* Palgrave, Macmillan

- Thwaites, A. (2008) *100 Ideas for Teaching Knowledge and Understanding of the World,* Continuum

- Thwaites, A. (2008) *100 Ideas for Teaching Problem Solving, Reasoning and Numeracy,* Continuum

- Thwaites, J. (2008) *100 Ideas for Teaching Personal, Social and Emotional Development,* Continuum

Appendix

Diseases notifiable (to Local Authority Proper Officers) under the Public Health (Infectious Diseases) Regulations 1988

Acute encephalitis	Meningitis	Mumps	Typhus fever
Acute poliomyelitis	meningococcal	Ophthalmia neonatorum	Viral haemorrhagic fever
Anthrax	pneumococcal	Paratyphoid fever	Viral hepatitis
Cholera	haemophilus influenzae	Plague	Hepatitis A
Diphtheria	viral	Rabies	Hepatitis B
Dysentery	other specified	Relapsing fever	Hepatitis C
Food poisoning	unspecified	Rubella	other
Leptospirosis	Meningococcal	Scarlet fever	Whooping cough
Malaria	septicaemia (without	Smallpox	Yellow fever
Measles	meningitis)	Tetanus	
		Tuberculosis	
		Typhoid fever	

Note: Leprosy is also notifiable, but directly to the HPA, CfI, IM&T Dept

Early Learning Goals

By the end of the EYFS children should be able to do the following.

Personal , Social and Emotional Development	Communication, Language and Literacy
• Continue to be interested, excited and motivated to learn. • Be confident to try new activities, initiate ideas and speak in a familiar group. • Maintain attention, concentrate, and sit quietly when appropriate. • Respond to significant experiences, showing a range of feelings when appropriate. • Have a developing awareness of their own needs, views and feelings, and be sensitive to the needs, views and feelings of others. • Have a developing respect for their own cultures and beliefs and those of other people. • Form good relationships with adults and peers. • Work as part of a group or class, taking turns and sharing fairly, understanding that there needs to be agreed values and codes of behaviour for groups of people, including adults and children, to work together harmoniously. • Understand what is right, what is wrong and why. • Consider the consequences of their words and actions for themselves and others. • Dress and undress independently and manage their own personal hygiene. • Select and use activities and resources independently. • Understand that people have different needs, views, cultures and beliefs, that need to be treated with respect. • Understand that they can expect others to treat their needs, views, cultures and beliefs with respect.	• Interact with others, negotiating plans and activities and taking turns in conversation. • Enjoy listening to and using spoken and written language, and readily turn to it in their play and learning. • Sustain attentive listening, responding to what they have heard with relevant comments, questions or actions. • Listen with enjoyment, and respond to stories, songs and other music, rhymes and poems and make up their own stories, songs, rhymes and poems. • Extend their vocabulary, exploring the meanings and sounds of new words. • Speak clearly and audibly with confidence and control and show awareness of the listener. • Use language to imagine and recreate roles and experiences. • Use talk to organise, sequence and clarify thinking, ideas, feelings and events. • Hear and say sounds in words in the order in which they occur. • Link sounds to letters, naming and sounding the letters of the alphabet. • Use their phonic knowledge to write simple regular words and make phonetically plausible attempts at more complex words. • Explore and experiment with sounds, words and texts. • Retell narratives in the correct sequence, drawing on language patterns of stories. • Read a range of familiar and common words and simple sentences independently. • Know that print carries meaning and, in English, is read from left to right and top to bottom. • Show an understanding of the elements of stories, such as main character, sequence of events and openings, and how information can be found in non-fiction texts to answer questions about where, who, why and how. • Attempt writing for different purposes, using features of different forms such as lists, stories and instructions. • Write their own names and other things such as labels and captions, and begin to form simple sentences, sometimes using punctuation. • Use a pencil and hold it effectively to form recognisable letters, most of which are correctly formed.

Problem solving, Reasoning and Numeracy	Knowledge and Understanding of the World
<ul><li>Say and use number names in order in familiar contexts.</li><li>Count reliably up to ten everyday objects.</li><li>Recognise numerals 1 to 9.</li><li>Use developing mathematical ideas and methods to solve practical problems.</li><li>In practical activities and discussion, begin to use the vocabulary involved in adding and subtracting.</li><li>Use language such as 'more' or 'less' to compare two numbers.</li><li>Find one more or one less than a number from one to ten.</li><li>Begin to relate addition to combining two groups of objects and subtraction to 'taking away'.</li><li>Use language such as 'greater', 'smaller', 'heavier' or 'lighter' to compare quantities.</li><li>Talk about, recognise and recreate simple patterns.</li><li>Use language such as 'circle' or 'bigger' to describe the shape and size of solids and flat shapes.</li><li>Use everyday words to describe position.</li></ul>	<ul><li>Investigate objects and materials by using all of their senses as appropriate.</li><li>Find out about, and identify, some features of living things, objects and events they observe.</li><li>Look closely at similarities, differences, patterns and change.</li><li>Ask questions about why things happen and how things work.</li><li>Build and construct with a wide range of objects, selecting appropriate resources and adapting their work where necessary.</li><li>Select the tools and techniques they need to shape, assemble and join materials they are using.</li><li>Find out about and identify the uses of everyday technology and use information and communication technology and programmable toys to support their learning.</li><li>Find out about past and present events in their own lives, and in those of their families and other people they know.</li><li>Observe, find out about and identify features in the place they live and the natural world.</li><li>Find out about their environment, and talk about those features they like and dislike.</li><li>Begin to know about their own cultures and beliefs and those of other people.</li></ul>
Physical Development	**Creative Development**
<ul><li>Move with confidence, imagination and in safety.</li><li>Move with control and coordination.</li><li>Travel around, under, over and through balancing and climbing equipment.</li><li>Show awareness of space, of themselves and of others.</li><li>Recognise the importance of keeping healthy, and those things which contribute to this.</li><li>Recognise the changes that happen to their bodies when they are active.</li><li>Use a range of small and large equipment.</li><li>Handle tools, objects, construction and malleable materials safely and with increasing control.</li></ul>	<ul><li>Respond in a variety of ways to what they see, hear, smell, touch and feel.</li><li>Express and communicate their ideas, thoughts and feelings by using a widening range of materials, suitable tools, imaginative and role play, movement, designing and making, and a variety of songs and musical instruments.</li><li>Explore colour, texture, shape, form and space in two or three dimensions.</li><li>Recognise and explore how sounds can be changed, sing simple songs from memory, recognise repeated sounds and sound patterns and match movements to music.</li><li>Use their imagination in art and design, music, dance, imaginative and role play and stories.</li></ul>

Dough and the Early Learning Goals

Problem solving, reasoning and numeracy
- use language such as 'greater', 'smaller','heavier' or 'lighter' to compare quantities
- use language such as 'circle' or 'bigger' to describe the shape and size of solids and flat shapes
- use everyday words to describe position

Physical development
- use a range of small and large equipment
- handle tools, objects, construction and malleable materials safely and with increasing control

Knowledge and understanding of the world
- investigate objects and materials by using all of their senses as appropriate
- select tools and techniques they need to shape, assemble and join the materials they are using

DOUGH

Personal, social and emotional development
- be confident to try new activities, initiate ideas and speak in a familiar group
- maintain attention, concentrate and sit quietly when appropriate
- continue to be interested, excited and motivated to learn
- dress and undress independently and manage their own personal hygiene
- select and use activities and resources independently

Communication, language and literacy
- use talk to organise, sequence and clarify thinking, ideas, feelings and events

Creative development
- explore colour, texture, shape, form and space in two or three dimensions
- respond in a variety of ways to what they see, hear, smell, touch and feel
- express and communicate their ideas, thoughts and feelings by using a widening range of materials, suitable tools, imaginative and role play, movement, designing and making, and a variety of songs and musical instruments

Water and the Early Learning Goals

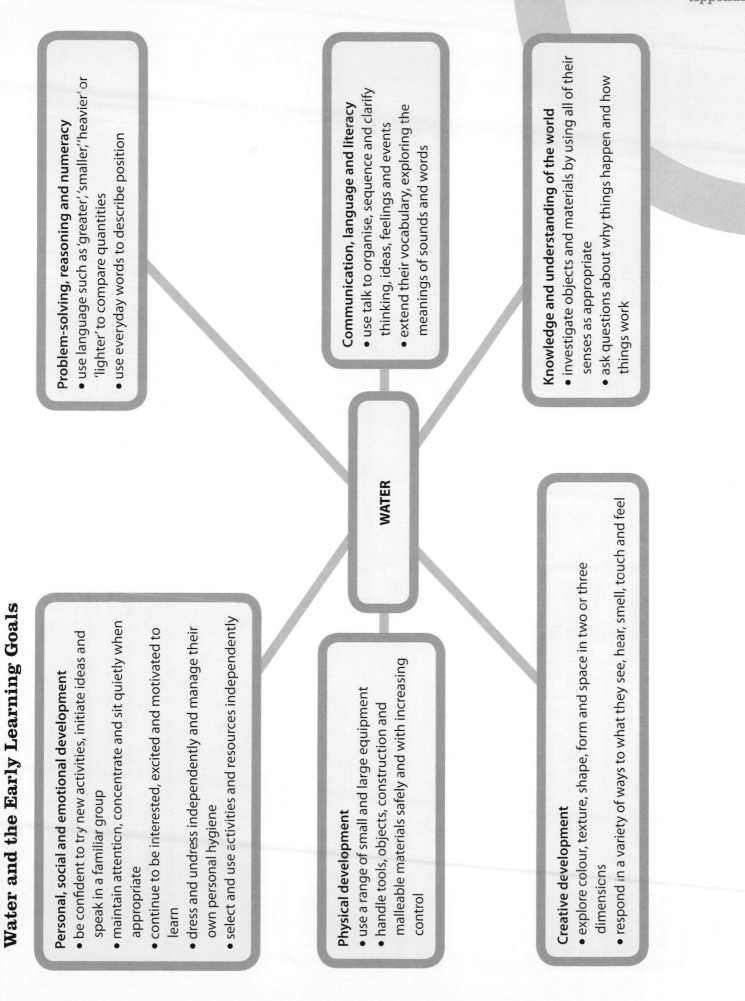

Problem-solving, reasoning and numeracy
- use language such as 'greater', 'smaller', 'heavier' or 'lighter' to compare quantities
- use everyday words to describe position

Communication, language and literacy
- use talk to organise, sequence and clarify thinking, ideas, feelings and events
- extend their vocabulary, exploring the meanings of sounds and words

Knowledge and understanding of the world
- investigate objects and materials by using all of their senses as appropriate
- ask questions about why things happen and how things work

WATER

Personal, social and emotional development
- be confident to try new activities, initiate ideas and speak in a familiar group
- maintain attention, concentrate and sit quietly when appropriate
- continue to be interested, excited and motivated to learn
- dress and undress independently and manage their own personal hygiene
- select and use activities and resources independently

Physical development
- use a range of small and large equipment
- handle tools, objects, construction and malleable materials safely and with increasing control

Creative development
- explore colour, texture, shape, form and space in two or three dimensions
- respond in a variety of ways to what they see, hear, smell, touch and feel

Sand play and the Early Learning Goals

SAND

Problem solving, reasoning and numeracy
- use language such as 'greater', 'smaller', 'heavier' or 'lighter' to compare quantities
- use everyday words to describe position

Communication, language and literacy
- use language to imagine and recreate roles and experiences
- use talk to organise, sequence and clarify thinking, ideas, feelings and events
- interact with others, negotiating plans and activities and taking turns in conversation
- extend their vocabulary, exploring the meanings and sounds of new words

Knowledge and understanding of the world
- investigate objects and materials by using all of their senses as appropriate
- building and constructing with a wide range of objects, selecting appropriate resources and adapting their work where necessary

Personal, social and emotional development
- be confident to try new activities, initiate ideas and speak in a familiar group
- maintain attention, concentrate and sit quietly when appropriate
- continue to be interested, excited and motivated to learn
- form good relationships with adults and peers
- select and use activities and resources independently
- dress and undress independently and manage their own personal hygiene

Physical development
- use a range of small and large equipment
- handle tools, objects, construction and malleable materials safely and with increasing control

Creative development
- explore colour, texture, shape, form and space in two or three dimensions
- respond in a variety of ways to what they see, hear, smell, touch and feel

Painting and the Early Learning Goals

Problem solving, reasoning and numeracy
- talk about, recognise and recreate simple patterns

Communication, language and literacy
- use talk to organise, sequence and clarify thinking, ideas, feelings and events
- extend their vocabulary, exploring the meanings and sounds of new words

Knowledge and understanding of the world
- investigate objects and materials by using all of their senses as appropriate
- look closely at similarities, differences, patterns and change

PAINTING

Personal, social and emotional development
- be confident to try new activities, initiate ideas and speak in a familiar group
- maintain attention, concentrate and sit quietly when appropriate
- continue to be interested, excited and motivated to learn
- respond to significant experiences, showing a range of feelings where appropriate
- dress and undress independently and manage their own personal hygiene
- select and use activities and resources independently

Physical development
- use a range of small and large equipment
- handle tools, objects, construction and malleable materials safely and with increasing control

Creative development
- explore colour, texture, shape, form and space in two or three dimensions
- respond in a variety of ways to what they see, hear, smell, touch and feel
- use their imagination in art and design, music, dance, imaginative and role play, and stories
- express and communicate their ideas, thoughts and feelings by using a widening range of materials, suitable tools, imaginative and role play movement, designing and making, and a variety of songs and musical instruments

Home corner/dressing up and the Early Learning Goals

Problem solving, reasoning and numeracy
- say and use number names in order in familiar contexts
- use everyday words to describe position

Communication, language and literacy
- use language to imagine and recreate roles and experiences
- use talk to organise, sequence and clarify thinking, ideas, feelings and events
- sustain attentive listening, responding to what they have heard by relevant comments, questions or actions
- interact with others, negotiating plans and activities and taking turns in conversation
- extend their vocabulary, exploring the meanings and sounds of words
- speak clearly and audibly with confidence and control and show awareness of the listener, for example, by their use of conventional greetings 'please' and 'thank you'.

Knowledge and understanding of the world
- build and construct with a wide range of objects, selecting appropriate resources and adapting their work where necessary
- look closely at similarities, differences, patterns and change

Personal, social and emotional development
- be confident to try new activities, initiate ideas and speak in a familiar group
- maintain attention, concentrate and sit quietly when appropriate
- continue to be interested, excited and motivated to learn
- have a developing awareness of their own needs, views and feelings, and be sensitive to the needs, views and feelings of others
- respond to significant experiences, showing a range of feelings when appropriate
- form good relationships with adults and peers
- work as part of a group or class, taking turns and sharing fairly, understanding that there needs to be agreed values and codes of behaviour for groups of people, including adults and children, to work together harmoniously
- select and use activities and resources independently
- dress and undress independently and manage their own personal hygiene
- consider the consequences of their words and actions for themselves and others

HOME CORNER/ DRESSING UP

Physical development
- use a range of small and large equipment
- handle tools, objects, construction and malleable materials safely and with increasing control

Creative development
- explore colour, texture, shape, form and space in two or three dimensions
- respond in a variety of ways to what they see, hear, smell, touch and feel
- use their imagination in art and design, music, dance, imaginative and role play, and stories
- express and communicate their ideas, thoughts and feelings by using a widening range of materials, suitable tools, imaginative and role play, movement, designing and making, and a variety of songs and musical instruments

Junk modelling and the Early Learning Goals

Problem solving, reasoning and numeracy
- use language such as 'greater', 'smaller', 'heavier' or 'lighter' to compare quantities
- use everyday words to describe position
- use developing mathematical ideas and methods to solve practical problems

Communication, language and literacy
- use talk to organise, sequence and clarify thinking, ideas, feelings and events
- interact with others, negotiating plans and activities and taking turns in conversation
- extend their vocabulary, exploring the meanings and sounds of words

Knowledge and understanding of the world
- investigate objects and materials by using all of their senses as appropriate
- ask questions about why things happen and how things work
- build and construct with a wide range of objects, selecting appropriate resources and adapting their work where necessary
- select the tools and techniques they need to shape, assemble and join the materials they are using

JUNK MODELLING

Personal, social and emotional development
- be confident to try new activities, initiate ideas and speak in a familiar group
- maintain attention, concentrate and sit quietly when appropriate
- continue to be interested, excited and motivated to learn
- select and use activities and resources independently
- dress and undress independently and manage their own personal hygiene

Physical development
- show awareness of space, of themselves and of others
- use a range of small and large equipment
- handle tools, objects, construction and malleable materials safely and with increasing control

Creative development
- explore colour, texture, shape, form and space in two or three dimensions
- use their imagination in art and design, music, dance, imaginative and role play, and stories
- express and communicate their ideas, thoughts and feelings by using a widening range of materials, suitable tools, imaginative and role play, movement, designing and making, and a variety of songs and musical instruments

Construction toys and the Early Learning Goals

CONSTRUCTION TOYS

Problem solving, reasoning and numeracy
- use language such as 'greater', 'smaller', 'heavier' or 'lighter' to compare quantities
- in practical activities and discussion begin to use the vocabulary involved in adding and subtracting
- use language such as 'circle' or 'bigger' to describe the shape and size of solids and flat shapes
- use everyday words to describe position
- use developing mathematical ideas and methods to solve practical problems

Communication, language and literacy
- use talk to organise, sequence and clarify thinking, ideas, feelings and events
- interact with others, negotiating plans and activities and taking turns in conversation
- extend their vocabulary, exploring the meanings and sounds of words

Knowledge and understanding of the world
- investigate objects and materials by using all of their senses as appropriate
- ask questions about why things happen and how things work
- build and construct with a wide range of objects, selecting appropriate resources and adapting their work where necessary
- select the tools and techniques they need to shape, assemble and join the materials they are using

Personal, social and emotional development
- be confident to try new activities, initiate ideas and speak in a familiar group
- maintain attention, concentrate and sit quietly when appropriate
- continue to be interested, excited and motivated to learn
- form good relationships with adults and peers
- work as part of a group or class, taking turns and sharing fairly, understanding that there needs to be agreed values and codes of behaviour for groups of people, including adults and children, to work together harmoniously
- select and use activities and resources independently

Physical development
- use a range of small and large equipment
- handle tools, objects, construction and malleable materials safely and with increasing control

Creative development
- explore colour, texture, shape, form and space in two or three dimensions
- use their imagination in art and design, music, dance, imaginative and role play, and stories
- express and communicate their ideas, thoughts and feelings by using a widening range of materials, suitable tools, imaginative and role play, movement, designing and making, and a variety of songs and musical instruments

Childminder Planning

The example below is a weekly plan for a childminder who has children of different ages. Some adult-focused activities are planned for each child, while some activities are for all the children attending. Adult focused activities are provisional. Children also have access to toys and equipment at all times. The plan is added to as the childminder observes and responds to children's play interests. The Notes sections are used to record changes, etc. The plan is available for parents to see. In addition to this plan, the childminder observes the children and creates a planning sheet for each child every month – an example plan is shown below.

Childminder's Weekly Plan

Date 18th April

Monday	Tuesday	Wednesday	Thursday	Friday
K first session J's first time Brownies Take photo of Jay in uniform Make stretchy dough Wrap present for T – with A and J Collage card for T	Library group - look also for book on birds Make bird seed cake J an T T's birthday – Birthday games Dough and straws	Make pizza Toddler group Show photo of me in uniform – ask J about Monday. Park with balls – also hunt for birds – take binoculars	Toddler group Buy fruit – also visit pet shop to see birds Make fruit salad – L peel bananas? – Washing up	Builder's trays – soil, spades and other utensils – (link to B. the builder) Singing group Story sack – Owl babies Park – picnic – if fine
Notes	**Notes**	**Notes**	**Notes**	**Notes**
K– fine, but needs blanket. Likes Bob the Builder! L – loved the dough – didn't eat it.	J, A took photos of T using digital camera. Used Internet to find better pictures of birds	J wants to go back to park with camera T absent	L frightened of parrot – peeled banana – love washing up T could use knife to cut apple – loved pets	K really enjoys digging J used camera

Childminder's Monthly Planning and Review Sheet

Name of Child Kai

Date

Observation/ Notes	Development	Next Steps
Has settled in quickly – still needs blanket at the start of the day Loves Bob the Builder story book Joins in with cooking and preparation – can use grater now	PSED Developing relationship with me CLL Enjoys stories. Can recount back stories PD Knows how to use several tools correctly	Build and keep routine going Develop Bob the Builder into activities Use cooking to talk about how changes (KUW) – make pizza
Parent comments		

Reception Planning

The examples of half-termly and weekly planning that follow on pages 267–70 are for a reception class in a school with no nursery provision. The teacher prepares a long-term plan, a medium-term plan (half-termly) and then a weekly plan. These plans show how the adult-focused activities will provide coverage of the areas of development. Activities are differentiated by the teacher, based on her observations of children. The plans also show what the focus for observation and assessment might be. In addition to the adult-focused activities, the children also have access to continual provision both indoors and outdoors. The teacher observes how individual children are playing and uses the information to plan for the next day's provision.

It is worth noting how the teacher provides self-chosen activities to supplement the provision for PRN and CLL.

In addition to the planned adult-focused activities, the children also have access to continuous provision activities such as water, sand and wheeled toys. These are available each day and children's individual preferences and interests are noted and encouraged.

Half-termly Overview

Topic: Growing and changing

Literacy	Numeracy	Knowledge & Understanding	Creative	PHSE	Physical	Music
BB *The Enormous Watermelon* Ww – sounds and phonics games CVC word build – a web of words /seeds inside a fruit to make a word – find the missing sound	Days of the week Numbers to 10+ Use numicon to make teen numbers Seeds in my pot – most/least adding on more – using language of addition	Look at and taste melons – compare and describe similarities and differences Select and preserve seeds to plant Look at and sort seeds – shape, colour, size. Choose some to plant Look at bulbs, observe and describe: what is under the soil?	Observational drawings of different types of melon Taste and compare – do we like it – what does it taste like? Collect seeds and plant	*You'll Soon Grow into Them, Titch* (changes in family and environment) How might Titch feel about the new baby? Getting ready for a new baby *Once There Were Giants* how things and our perceptions change	Movement – ring games/parachute games: cooperation/helping one another Sequencing movements and positions	Soft loud louder, use of percussion for the story and the characters Favourite songs and nursery rhymes
BB *Jessie's Flower* (changes of season in the story) Ff sounds activities High-frequency word flowers BB *Seasons* – non-fiction – how do we find out about seasons – contents page, etc.	Flower maths – make an addition frieze using our giant flowers Revise '+' symbol Lots of counting on and addition games *Fish is Fish* – make a number fishing game	Look closely at flowers – name parts of a flower Look at Van Gogh's sunflower and iris paintings Observe frogspawn, note all changes as they take place + bulbs seeds, etc. Plant sunflower seeds (what is it story) Look at out door environment – changes?	Decorate a plant pot Begin garden centre Observational drawings of flowers Paintings of spring flowers (in the style of Van Gogh)	How have we changed? – Look at pictures of us as babies – can we guess who it is? What has changed about us?	Over/under/around mats and benches – on/off, over/under apparatus Ways of moving around apparatus	The Wide Mouth Frog musical story Spring has sprung
BB *Jack and the Beanstalk* class book High-frequency vocab. – make a climbing beanstalk of words Climb the beanstalk games Vv phonics	Grade size/sequence Comparative lang. of size Measure beanstalks Snails in the pot subtraction Beans maths counting and comparing sets Odd/even numbers	Make a large bean diary Plant beans in different conditions – observe and describe what happens Do big seeds grow into big plants? What happens if you plant half a seed? Will plants grow upside down? Roamer up the beanstalk	Vase of violets, Mother's Day cards Paint our Mummies	What do our Mummies do for us Story *Guess how Much I Love You* Make a pic/card for mummy	Small apparatus skills, beanbag games, travelling – balancing indiv. and paired activities Simple team games	Use percussion to represent giant/Jack Make a musical story I can play you my song –changing tempo/volume/speed
BB *The Hungry Giant* High-frequency words – dialogue – punctuation Phonics Make up dialogue for giant A menu for a giant Size words and descriptive vocabulary	Counting songs and rhymes adding 1 more /1 less Measuring how big is big? Measure our giant Check our height chart – have we grown? Ordering the giant footprints to 20	Look for signs of Spring – what changes have there been in our environment? Collect twigs, etc. Observe our bulbs/beans/frogspawn for signs of growth and change – record what we see Growing frogs story	Make a large giant – add collage/ texture Observational drawings of our twig/bulbs/ tadpoles	What can we do now that we couldn't do as a baby? Visit from a new baby – ask questions what do we know about babies?	Different ways and sequences of movement – partner games – mirror games – follow my leader games Giant steps, tiny movements, enormous jumps, etc.	Bus song Giants dinner song Oats and beans and barley grow 1 potato Spring songs/ weather songs
Jasper's Beanstalk Days of the week Phonics High-frequency vocab. Make a zig-zag book *Meg's Eggs* – lift the flap to see what is inside	Egg maths Addition 2x eggs Estimating how many Days of the week – *Hungry Caterpillar* counting story Give away subtraction games Yuk – those slugs and snails	What may eat our plants? Collect some snails – what do they like to eat? How can we find out? Final observations of our plants (esp. beans) Signs of new life – celebrate by giving eggs, hot cross buns and other traditions	Decorate eggs Make an Easter tree Easter cards Make Easter buns/ biscuits/hats	When I grow up what will I be? – picture/caption Dress up as fireman, police woman, grown-up, etc.	Games using small apparatus Scarves for catching using both hands Make up a game with a friend Bean bags and hoops – balls throwing into – use both hands	When I was 1 Easter songs Eggs are laid by ..... Signs of new life

Weekly Plan for CLL

Communication, Language and Literacy · Week 1 · Theme: Growing and changing

Main Learning Opportunities: To develop high-frequency vocabulary in their emergent writing, reading and play. To hear, recognise and blend phonic sounds. To use storybook characters in role play – to extend their understanding of story language for the youngest pupils.

Ongoing Skills: To develop reading and writing skills via 'sounds play'. To hear and say phonemes to build and segment simple CVC words. Develop awareness of rhyming sounds via oral word play.

Key Questions: How can we use our voice so that we can all hear it? Who are the characters in the story? Can we guess what will happen next in the story? Can we put the events in the right order?

	Carpet Time	Focused Adult-led tasks	Self-chosen activities	Assessment
Monday	BB *The Enormous Watermelon* – looking at characters – story language – clues in picture and text Asking questions (model Qs first)	R/pic /caption T to help Y/TA look at melons compare/describe – cut open – taste, describe B/TA reading/sounds games TA/N sound sort/games Paired reading of big book – use pointer	Role play story – using characters ICT – All day to play phonics/mini-matchers Sand/water Home corner role play Free writing table	Able to listen attentively? (focus on AB, MC and JH) Make comments/ask questions about the story? TA – to observe PF
Tuesday	Ww sound feely bag Make a web of 'w' words Use Max the puppet – can speak like a robot to give us clues to find the items	Cut and stick sound activities B TA jump over the river segmenting game TA/Y sound sheets R/B/T – whiteboard CVC writing R – duplo CVC word build	Whiteboards and pens Wigwam writing patterns – use chalks/wax/felt pens Sand/water Free writing table ICT – mini-matchers/new phonics CD Whiteboard –ABC CD	Word-building skills – can hear 'ch'? (JK, FR and DJ) Hear all sounds/say the sounds – assess via CVC bag/puppet game
Wednesday	The big green bean – make up a class story about a giant vegetable	Nurture group – 5 min sounds play – 'silly soup'		Word wall – what strategies are being used? TA to assess KM and FR
Thursday	Revise sounds for Forgetful Fred – puppet Introduce new V sound – action writing via Big Book Forgetful Fred can't hear the f/v/w sounds – can we help?	T/B use CVC grid to help 'Max' build and write a word (bag of items – whiteboard pens) TA/R magnetic letters CVC word families B/Y – Colour/cut/stick the 'v' pictures onto Vic's van TA – puppet muddles v/w /f – can we help him?	Paired 'say the sounds' game – use box of pics ICT –ABC CD, New phonics CD Sounds floor tiles Free writing/whiteboards Outdoor sounds play – hop skip jump to find the sounds – jump over the river	Identify sounds in written form (use white boards and pens/photocopy)
Friday	*The Enormous Turnip* story – role play using masks and voices (discuss what voice would be like). Encourage children to use voice for character – loud, soft, tiny, etc.	T/B –sequence events in story – add characters – make a story board – to retell story to class R/TA 'pull' a fold-out story sequence TA/Y role play the story/use masks/props – encourage children to use voice	Role play –story bag ICT – 2 simple drawings W/B – ORT – stories Free writing/drawing table White boards/pens Sound sort – sorting hat game Grade the turnips	Can child use voice effectively? Take on a role?

Weekly Plan for PRN

Problem Solving, Reasoning and Numeracy		Week 1	Theme: Growing and changing	
	Group Time	Focused Adult-led activities	Self-chosen activities	Assessment
Monday	Counting rhymes and games / Days of the week song		Number games and puzzles / ICT – Fizzy's first numbers/ All day to play	Do KR and PS join in with counting rhymes?
Tuesday	LI to use lang. of addition / Make a growing spell – use 2x groups to form an addition sum / Write number sentence (revise plus sign)	Melon addition (adding seeds) together (who has the most/least) TA/B / Y/TA How many in the witch's pot – count compare and add together / R/T find my missing number – use simple number sentences – what is missing?	Water/sand / Sort seeds – sizes, shapes, colours / ICT – All day to play/Fizzy's first numbers / Number puzzles / Outdoor number play – bean bags, hoops, skittles	Do B children understand the lang. of addition? Do they count the 2x groups of items together?
Wednesday	LI to use comparative lang. / TV Numbertime – More and less – use vocab. more/most – less/least / Mingledy mangledy rhyme – 2x children hold up fingers – who holds up most /least fingers?	Frog hops – use carpet tiles to create a number line. Y/TA – show a number: how many hops must frog make? / Make 10 – use string-alongs – how many more do we need? – R/TA / T/Y –assess understanding of addition (seeds in my pot game) / TA/N use large 123 dice race frogs to worms	Shopping – fruits and veg – use coins / Feely bag numicon partner games / Washing-line ordering / Number puzzles / Ordering puzzles / ICT games	Do TB and RS understand addition? – joining 2x groups together and counting on?
Thursday	Observe and assess / Counting rhymes and games – guess my number – 1 more than/less than/in between / I'm thinking of a number bigger than ....smaller than..... / Number fans play	Sort the washing – which are the smallest?/ largest? TA/Nurture group		Do CK and MF use language of size? / Understand the biggest number?
Friday	LI to use lang. of size / Grade the sizes of the turnips – use language of size / Learn turnip song for role play – which animal was tiny? Which was the biggest?	Y/TA role play the story – take turns to be the characters – order in size / TA/B outdoor maths – use activity wheel, count the jumps/hops/claps – use more/less than / T/R –use numicon to represent the bigger/smaller number – change to numerals – do children understand the value of numbers?	ICT games / Sand/water / Number puzzles / Weighing and comparing – use the vegetables / Make a number line – use numicon, carpet tiles, lily pads	Understand the value of numbers?

Weekly plan for Adult-focused Activities

Week 1	Adult-focused Activities	Small groups	Theme: Growing and changing

Objectives/skills:

KUW – To observe and describe – how we have changed – by looking at photos of us as babies. To be able to sequence growth in humans. To observe changes in the environment and record what we notice. Develop fine motor skills – planting seeds – patting/digging/sprinkle – tool use – handling seeds, tools. Observational drawings, ICT – learn how to take photographs using digital camera. PHSE – To understand what we need to help us to grow healthy (love, care, etc.).

	Creative	Role Play/PSE	Knowledge and understanding	Physical	Profile/Assessment
Monday	Taste melons. Observational drawings of melon and seeds. Music – growing seed songs and rhymes	Role play watermelon story – use story language – show how character looks/behaves	Look at and taste melons – describe – like/dislike differences? Sort /collect melon seeds – describe and compare – taste /size /smell/seeds/shape/colour/ texture. What other fruits have seeds?	PE – Movement songs and rhymes – growing curling stretching. Fizzy bubble. Large balls practice skills and partner games	Ask questions about what we can do? Talk about self – events – family?
Tuesday	Witch hat – writing patterns. Zig-zag patterns – use a variety of materials, tools and colours (finger paint – use tools)	We need love to help us to grow – who loves us? – how do we know? Story *Guess how much I love you*	*You'll Soon Grow, Alex* – what do we need to help us to grow – what do the children know? Sequence baby to adult in order – photographs and puzzles – sequencing cut/stick sheet	Use of tools, handling seeds – sprinkle/tip/shake – fine motor skills. Use of magnifiers and lenses. Make label for pot	Can sequence events and talk about it?
Wednesday	Observational drawings from our table –bulbs /flowers. Paint some spring flowers. Talk about shapes, colours, patterns on leaf/petal/stem	Role play characters from story land, make up own stories. Story time – *Peepo!*	Look at our photos as babies – how have we changed? Do we still look the same? Poem – When I was a baby. Ask questions: What can we do now that we couldn't do as babies? Use magnifiers to look closely at our flowers bulbs and plants	Bean bag play – make up own game with a partner – positional lang. on/in/ under/between (e.g. knees), balancing	What do children know about planting and growth of plants?
Thursday	TA /B look at our collection of baby things. Discuss size, etc – memories of playing with them/what for, etc. Did you have a ....were you ....?	Getting ready for a new baby – lots of changes – discuss our own families (expecting a new baby – getting ready, etc. too small to help?) Story *You're too small*	*You'll Soon Grow into Them, Titch* – observe and discuss changes in story /environment /family. Look outside for signs of spring – what do we notice – make a record by using our digital camera	PE – Large apparatus move over/under/along/through – remind about jumping and landing safely	Observe children gross motor dev. TA make notes
Friday	Music sound making, growing louder/ softer. *I've grown too big for my boots* song	Role play *The Enormous Turnip* story – use masks/props, encourage to use story lang. and changes in voice, etc.	Plant some seeds – what do we think they will need to help them grow (food/water – and what else? Try out our ideas. Use paper /cotton wool/ soil	PE – hop, skip jump – audio prog.	Listening and responding to instructions

Observation Sheet and Ongoing Planning (0–2 years)

In the example below, observation and planning are brought together for 0–2 year olds. An observation is made each day based on one or more areas of the EYFS. A summative sheet linked to the EYFS is completed each month – see an example on page 272. Key workers share both sheets with parents. Photos and recordings are also used. This format could be used in group care, but also for childminders.

Name of Child Ayse

Completed by Jane   **W/C** 6ᵗʰ October

	Observation	Development	Next steps
Monday	Ayse waved good bye to Mum. Settled down very quickly – no tears today.	Has strong relationship with Mum, but is happy with key person. Is developing gestures and understands 'bye bye'. PSE PD KUW CLL	Build and keep repeating goodbye routine. Use other opportunities to show Ayse other gestures.
Tuesday	Tried to use spoon to feed herself. See photo!	Is beginning to develop hand–eye coordination. Is learning how to use a tool. Is interested in becoming independent. PSE PRN CD PD	Provide spoon at meal times. Put out different sized spoons in heuristic play. Introduce beaker.
Wednesday	Interested in spoons and scoops that we put out for heuristic play. Tried to post them into tins. Surprised at first by sounds, but then fascinated.	Interested in shapes. Enjoys making sounds. Using hand–eye coordination. PSE PRN CD PD	Spoons and cardboard tubes and other containers. Metal objects to bang in heuristic play.
Thursday	Enjoyed being in baby swing. Rocked legs when I stopped pushing her to show that she wanted more.	Communicates for a purpose and makes eye contact. Aware of space and enjoys movement. PSE PD CLL	Will put her in swing again tomorrow. Sing 'see-saw'.
Friday	Pulled self up to look in mirror. Was not sure about other baby!	Still learning about self-image. PSE KUW	Add in tin lids so she can see reflection in heuristic play. Look at photos of babies.

Medium-term Planning and Review Sheet (0–2 years)

Name of Child Ayse

Area of Development	Observed development and interests (home and setting)	Future provision and support
Personal, Social and Emotional Development	Now attached to key person. Enjoys trying to feed herself. Smiles and enjoys watching older cousins.	Introduce a secondary key person. Encourage self-feeding skills including beaker. Take into main room to be with older children.
Communication, Language and Literacy	Babbling well and has some gestures. Understands key words from routine, including 'bye bye' and 'mummy'. Recognises some rhymes – favourite is Humpty Dumpty at home.	Take some recordings to look out for first words. Picture books to encourage pointing and understanding words. Introduce some more rhymes – Row, Row, Row the Boat – Mum to do some at home as well and liaise.
Problem Solving, Reasoning and Numeracy	Understands 'all gone' and 'more'. Has started to look for missing objects.	Play peek-a-boo and hide-and-seek.
Knowledge and Understanding of World	Loves treasure basket play – especially banging objects together. Enjoys books that make sounds.	Continue with heuristic play – adapt to suit current interests. Take outdoors – paddling pool if warm enough.
Physical Development	Trying to stand more. Pulls herself up and can stand alone for a few seconds. Loves being rocked and put in swing. Can move objects from hand to hand and hand-eye is developing.	Provide safe areas for standing and climbing up.
Creative Development	Loves music. Laughs when Dancing Girl is played at home.	Try out sensory mark-making activities, e.g. smearing cornflour.

Response Planning Sheet (2–4 years)

This sheet is used as a way of responding to the observed needs and interests of children aged 2–4 years. The sheet is drawn up at the end of a session, although some of the adult-directed activities have been pre-planned as they link to a monthly plan or individual children's IEPs. During a typical session, there will be response activities available alongside a child-initiated activity, both indoors and outdoors. This sheet could be adapted to suit all settings – and would be perfect for showing how you are responding to children's individual needs and interests.

Date Monday 15ᵗʰ September   **Key person**_____   **Parent**_____

Children	Response/Staff	Location	Comments	Evaluation
Kylie, Joshua	Jo – farm animal memory game to support sequencing and vocab.	Sand tray – indoors – small room	Sheet for Josh needs filling in.	Kylie could match, but found sequence difficult – enjoyed game so can be repeated. Joshua – knew all names and sequenced quickly. Zoo cards? Amir came over and joined in.
Alicia	Emma to bring out Charlie Dog (puppet) – see if Alicia will feel more confident. Take photos if successful.	Indoors – Morning	Strategy to see if she can settle down. Mum's suggestion.	Seemed to work. Alicia interested in photos of herself. Mum much happier. Allun, Sam and Mark also like Charlie Dog – use again tomorrow.
Callum, Bekir and Tom	Provide materials for den making – fabric. Put box of home materials – Greg to observe and support.	Outdoors	Had been playing in bushes – may like challenge of construction.	Great success – Gracie and Hayley also joined in. Callum very engaged. Add in mark-making tomorrow.

Index

Professional Development Series

Inclusion, Equality and Diversity in Working with Children

How to turn good intentions into effective anti-discriminatory practice

- Takes a sensitive, holistic approach to promoting inclusion, equality and diversity when working with children of all ages.

- Practical examples from a wide selection of childcare settings show how to put the principles into practice.

- Written by Sue Griffin, a respected figure with many years of experience in the children's workforce.

978 0 435402 40 2   **Sue Griffin**

How to Observe Children, 2nd edition

The second edition of **How to Observe Children** is fully revised and updated to support the Early Years Foundation Stage

- Retains the popular, practical approach of the first edition, making it ideal for practitioners to dip in and out of for day-to-day guidance and in-depth enough for students learning the theory and skills for the first time.

- Includes updated information relating to the Primary National Strategy to support effective observations in schools.

- Examples of observations throughout enable students and practitioners to relate the theory and techniques to their setting.

978 0 435987 66 4   **Sheila Riddall-Leech**

For more information and details on other titles in the Professional Development Series, visit
www.heinemann.co.uk/childcare

O479